The recipes that punctuate Margie Haack's recollections ... that these stories are from a life truly lived: as tangible as a bite of Swedish pancake with chokeberry syrup. Wrestling with the insolence of memory, Margie tells the story of her childhood and of the discovery of the kindness of God and the meaning of home. As I read the story of young Margie's life, I reflected on my own, and wondered at the goodness in the ordinary—land well-tended, food well-prepared, children sheltered and fed with sweat and tears—and at the unfolding of hope in the midst of hardship and heartbreak.
—Gideon Strauss, academic dean of the Institute for Christian Studies

Gratitude is my primary response to Margie's memoir, gratitude for refusing to be mawkish about childhood and growing up. Margie's early years, rife with earthy mischief, spiritual lucidity, fear and joy are side-splittingly hilarious and heart-rending. She tells these stories with the understanding of a very wise woman, but it's as though the scrape-kneed little girl she was sat beside her and whispered them in her ear.
—Katy Bowser, poet, singer-songwriter, and a co-creator of Rain for Roots

Margie Haack is a great storyteller and this book collects some fabulously entertaining bits from her childhood on a small Minnesota farm—nicely told, sometimes tragic, filled with deep pathos, still with an eye to beauty, but also good humor and a considerable passel of shenanigans (she brought her horse into the kitchen to eat pickles? She caught fish bigger than herself? She used bag balm? Don't ask.) Yet with a sense of God's redemptive purposes played out over a lifetime of rural poverty and a harsh upbrings, these tales form a memoir of note, ruminating on an unusually vivid life in what for some will feel like another world. It is not a cliche to say this book is written with grit and grace.
—Byron Borger, co-founder of Hearts & Minds Bookstore

The most interesting people I've met all seem to have a couple things in common. One, they've all lived very hard, challenging lives. As Garrison Keillor once put it, "It's a shallow life that doesn't give a person a few scars." Well, Margie and her family have had more than their share, but mere scars are easy to come by. It's the second factor that is rare and makes her and her writing so extraordinary: the ability to see and rejoice in God's grace amidst the scars.
—Greg Grooms, director of Hill House, Austin, TX

In her beautiful and honest book, *The Exact Place,* Margie Haack allows us to look over-her-shoulder and through-her-heart, learning the possibility of love in a world that is often very unlovely. Like generations before her, she was

born into the grand land of lakes and woods in northern Minnesota, and that place and its people have formed her, heart and mind, body and soul. Readers of her much-loved essays already know she is a remarkably-gifted writer able to see into the ordinariness of the everyday, and finding unusual grace for all of us. For years we have longed for those tender, truthful windows on life to become a book—and a very good book it is.
—Steven Garber, author of *The Fabric of Faithfulness*

I've spent many good hours around Margie and her husband's open table, but here is a different sort of hospitality, one no less welcoming for being in print: an open life, displayed in stories that are full of sharp wit and graceful intelligence.
—Wesley Hill, assistant professor of Biblical Studies at Trinity School for Ministry

One of the highest compliments you can give an author is to feel a kind of sadness upon reaching the end of their book. This is the way I felt upon coming to the end of Margie Haack's deeply moving, wise, and masterfully told memoir of her childhood, *The Exact Place*. I will read it again. I have long considered Margie to be one of my favorite writers, but after reading this book, she has moved onto my list of most beloved authors. You will see, feel, and think, laugh out loud and want to cry, sometimes all on the same page.
—Andi Ashworth, author of *Real Love for Real Life: The Art and Work of Caring*

I've never lived in a place like the wild remoteness of northern Minnesota. I can't imagine the cold or the isolation, or the swamps. But Margie Haack has invited me to test those waters with a visit to her childhood. In *The Exact Place*, she locates the first memories of her faith, shaped by farm life and a difficult father, and by playful moments of grace, like the time she and her little brother brought horses into the kitchen for pickles. *The Exact Place* is full of surprises.
—Sam Van Eman, Coalition for Christian Outreach

I first read *The Exact Place* alone, and then again with my wife and children. As a family we bonded deeply in the conversations the book sparked off in our living room. If you want a book that can, on the one hand, speak to you personally, and on the other, make for great evening-by-the-fire-conversations, read this book. Like Margie, whose journey has led her to be rooted in God's plan and love, we, too, have come to understand that though we have journeyed many miles from Kenya to Illinois, we are indeed in *The Exact Place* God wants us to be.
—Wainaina Zanjugun, Kenya

# the exact
# PLACE

## A Search
## for Father

BOOK ONE OF
THE *PLACE* TRILOGY

# the exact PLACE

## A Search for Father

BOOK ONE OF
THE *PLACE* TRILOGY

## A Memoir by Margie Haack

FOREWORD BY Jake Meador

**SQUARE HALO BOOKS**

In Christian art, the square halo identified a living person
presumed to be a saint. Square Halo Books is devoted to
publishing works that present contextually sensitive biblical studies,
and practical instruction consistent with the Doctrines of the Reformation.
The goal of Square Halo Books is to provide materials useful
for encouraging and equipping the saints.

Cover painting by Abigail Clark

©2021 Square Halo Books, Inc.
P.O. Box 18954
Baltimore, MD 21206
www.SquareHaloBooks.com

ISBN 978-1-941106-18-1
Library of Congress Control Number: 2021949021

Printed in the United States of America

*for Denis*

He determined the times set for them
and the exact places where they should
live. God did this so that men would
seek him and perhaps reach out for him
and find him thought he is not far
from each one of us
—Acts 17:26–27

# contents

# FOREWORD

The first time I visited Toad Hall, the long-time Rochester home of Margie and Denis Haack where much of the book you're holding in your hands was written, I was a few months away from graduating college. I'd met Denis at a L'Abri lecture years prior and was soon to be moving to the Twin Cities, only an hour and change from the Haacks' home. So, as I passed through the area on my way to apartment shop in the Twin Cities, I was able to stop for a meal and conversation.

There is much I remember—good wine, certainly, and a warm, filling chicken tortilla soup (you can find that recipe in *This Place*, the third book in the trilogy). The conversation was a delight and I was reluctant to leave later that evening when the time came to finish my drive to the Cities.

But the first thing I remember was an amusing skirmish in the living room: The Haacks had recently been gifted a new home stereo system by some friends. Denis had been controlling the stereo for much of the day. He was playing Neutral Milk Hotel's *In The Aeroplane Over The Sea* when I arrived. I arrived as the work day was ending and so, after greeting me, Denis left the living room and went upstairs to take care of one last thing before dinner.

The moment he left the room, Margie dashed in, opened up her own computer, kicked Denis' machine off the speakers, and put on Over the Rhine's *Drunkard's Prayer*. The entire experience of that evening—the receiving of hospitality from the Haacks—was a mixture of warmth and mischief, serious questions and amused laughter. It is the kind of welcome that too few people receive, and I count my receiving it as one of the blessings of my life.

A few years later I read *The Exact Place* for the first time. It was an experience not unlike having the chance to tour the kitchen of a beloved restaurant. You've long enjoyed the fruit of the chef's work; now you get to see where it comes from.

What's surprising about Margie's book is that for someone who has realized a sense of place and rootedness as completely as she and Denis have over their long shared vocation, she was not born into a home of belonging, warmth, and welcome. The gifts she gave at Toad Hall did not come down to her as an inheritance. She was, on the contrary, often treated as an intrusion, even as something unwanted.

There is probably something encouraging in this. We live in a day when it can often feel as if what one is given is one's fate. And so if one is given indifference shading into disdain and even abuse as a child, these things will inevitably haunt you forever. The only way to the good life, it sometimes seems, is to have the fortune of being born into it. We live today on the other side of the Big Sort, where demography is destiny. Margie's book invites you to consider that perhaps that isn't true. Christian theologians talk sometimes of the idea of "providence." It is the notion that God, in his wisdom and power, acts with intention toward human persons in the material circumstances of the world and that he even does this toward creation itself. Nothing, this doctrine tells us, happens apart from God's design.

Now, if one isn't careful, this can come across as something alarming, worrisome. But it needn't. God's providence does not imply indifference to the suffering. God himself exists separately from his creation; the creator is not himself a creature. He is, rather, wholly set apart, belonging only to himself and perfectly at rest within his own being. What this means is that if God does not create you or me or the trees or the stars or animals out of need, he must have created us all for some other reason.

Why then does God create me or the trees or the stars or animals? The answer: he creates out of delight, out of joy. "Love is also a lover of life,"[1] says the English theologian John Webster. And so it is. Our existence itself, even when it comes to us in misshapen, badly-wrapped packages that contain pain and doubt, even then existence itself is a gift. To be alive is a great gift.

This is the conclusion Margie will draw you toward as you read her book. This is not simply a story of one coming to transcend one's difficult childhood in order to find faith and home and love as an adult. It is the story of learning to see even in that unhappy childhood the product of divine action, even divine love. What makes this book remarkable is the bits of joy that Margie is able to embed in what is at times a painful, difficult story. In doing that, she teaches all of us.

Life itself is amongst the greatest of all God's gifts. When confronted with suffering, comedian Stephen Colbert asked, "What punishments of God are not gifts?"[2] Even for those who suffer greatly, indeed especially for them, God's heart is large. And his intention to give them good gifts cannot be doubted, for he has already given them one: life itself. In time those of us who suffer might, perhaps, come to see that even in dark circumstance, God has us in the exact place he means for us to be.

Jake Meador, editor of Mere Orthodoxy and author of *In Search of the Common Good: Christian Fidelity in a Fractured World*

# PROLOGUE

My mother, who was witness to much of this book, read an early draft. I waited anxiously for her to be finished, trying not to hover, and felt tremendous relief when she told me she had laughed and cried. "It is very good," she said. But, there was a "but." There was one thing she disagreed with and I stiffened, waiting, reminding myself that after all, memoir is personal narrative from a particular person's point of view, which is obviously not omniscient. I tell my stories, not the stories of other family members. Referring to the details of a particular event, Mom said, "The military jets that flew over our farm came from the south, not the north." I replied, "That's *it?* They came from the south? From the south?" I fell back to the chair laughing. I'll stick with my version. At the time, Randy and I were outside picking beans, she was inside canning. They came from the north.

One day as I listened to Terry Gross interview a memoirist on NPR's Fresh Air, the author, whose name I don't remember, made an interesting remark: she said a writer should never let the truth get in the way of a good story.[3] I knew I couldn't agree. If I couldn't make a good story out of what actually happened as I remembered it, then I shouldn't be writing. Although it is tempting, I avoid fictionalizing for the sake of cleverness, a humorous moment, or satisfying closure.

In the end, confronting possible disparity between what we each remembered about the years we lived in the shotgun house was a valuable process. I was encouraged and amused when I listened to an interview with Frank McCourt the author of *Angela's Ashes*. He reported that when his brother read his book, he insisted that was not how it happened. McCourt's response was to suggest his brother should write his own damned memoir.

So, these are stories of personal landscapes and spiritual geography. Kathleen Norris describes spiritual geography as "the way a place shapes people's attitudes, beliefs, and myths." She writes, "The spiritual geography of the Plains is complex. But the stark beauty of the land—its strength—also inspires strength in people, in part because it reminds us of human limits."[4] There was a stark, even frightening beauty to the land just north of the Plains where I grew up; it was a constant reminder of the paradox of human strength and its inherent limits. My stories are about place and family, and are firmly rooted in the stark beauty of the northern Minnesota landscape. The people, the animals, and the physical nature of the land shaped my personal landscape. No matter how far I move from them, I cannot shed them. Nor do I want to. They are powerful reminders of my own spiritual geography.

We lived on a small farm in the northernmost part of Minnesota, a place barely reclaimed from the wilderness. A winter blizzard could swallow a herd of cattle. Temperatures that fell below minus forty could freeze a chicken house full of hens. Summer rains could drown fields of hay and in minutes a hailstorm could flatten acres of grain. You never knew. Farming was the practice of faith, the hope that waves of blue flax blooming in June would be golden-brown seedpods in September, that the wet new-born calf would survive to replace her mother, giving gallons of high-fat milk every day, that the hours of spreading manure and plowing straight lines would become your children's and grandchildren's inheritance.

It was remote—remote enough to not have telephone service down our road until 1962, the year before Kennedy was assassinated. Polio was still killing and crippling people in our county; one of our neighbors, a young mother, felt so ill one day, she drove herself to the doctor with her children in the backseat. None

Randy (6), Jan (2), Me (8), Mom holding Dallas (3 mo), Rex (1), Dad. (Mom is expecting Roxanne)

of us went to the doctor for something as minor as an ear infection or the Asian influenza. It had to be major, like when Paul Olson amputated his finger. That day my stepfather and Paul were lassoing calves to brand, dehorn, and castrate as my brother, Randy, and I sat on the rail fence watching. When a particularly large calf hit the end of Paul's rope and flipped in the air, his finger was accidentally caught in the coils that unreeled faster than our eye could see. The force of the calf hitting the rope's limit was enough to take the finger off. Dad rushed him to the doctor with the finger wrapped in a dirty handkerchief.

So, by the time Charlotte drove eighteen miles to the clinic in Baudette, she couldn't get out of the car because she could no longer walk. She never walked again.

We didn't have money for pretty furniture and fancy clothes—or even the plain kind. But we always had food, plenty of the sort that is still lodged in my genes; I can't seem to repress mashed potatoes and fried chicken, even though I can make Thai chicken in lettuce wraps. We were always entertained by life, and even survived to tell about it. Entertainment wasn't just contests of firing rifles at highway signs or climbing the highest tree on the farm. Randy won that contest by climbing so high the swaying tip broke off, and by strange providence, I saved his life by grabbing his shirt as he bounced past. Neighbors were also entertainment; they were endlessly amusing. Some must have had personality disorders. I'm sure they thought the same of us.

It was this place and these people who shaped me. But perhaps my greatest shape-maker was the one Yeats had in mind when he wrote:

> But love has pitched his mansion in
> The place of excrement;
> For nothing can be sole or whole
> That has not been rent[5]

Many times I've considered my life and complained how contrary it is to what I want or think I need, only to find, in the end, that although I've been rent, I've also been loved. No matter how far into the wilderness we wander—no matter how powerful the stench— God can find us. So I follow his trace through this book, not in chronological years, but in themes and stories that wove through my childhood. And I see I was in the exact place I needed to be.

# The Marsh

In May of 1998, John Johnson got lost in the woodland and marsh near his summer home on Lake of the Woods in northern Minnesota. He was looking for logs to build a deck. When he didn't return, a search party was formed. Days went by, he was still missing, and his friends from North Dakota felt the authorities weren't putting enough effort into the search. They organized their own party, rented a bus, and drove to the area where he was last seen. When they got off the coach and saw the tangled impenetrable land of forest and marshes, "Oh," was all they said. That evening they returned to the prairies of North Dakota.

A marsh is an area of soft, wet, low-lying land dominated by grasses and reeds that forms the ecosystem between land and water. Entering a marsh can mean a disorienting loss of direction. Tall grasses loom high, cutting off the horizon. A misstep can plunge you into a waist-deep hole. The tuberous white water lily (*Nymphaea tuberosa*) often grows in the shallow waters next to a marsh. Its large single leaf floats on the water and is called a pad. The blossom, pure white petals with bright yellow stamen, is a cup as large as your hands.

Eight days later Johnson emerged on a gravel road five miles from where he entered. He had survived by sleeping in hollow logs, drinking marsh water, and eating the tubers of twelve white water lily pads.

Not all emerge unscathed from their wanderings, and some never find their way home.

# THE DOGS OF OUR LIVES

The December after my stepfather, Mom, Randy, and I moved to the farm in Lake of the Woods County on the border between Minnesota and Canada, I turned four. That was the winter of my first spiritual awakening. It was Bing's fault.

The day was bitter with millions of frost diamonds glittering in the air, but my mother did not consider twenty below zero an excuse to stay indoors sulking underfoot the entire day, so I was stuffed into a padded snowsuit and sent out to play. Bing, whom I loved almost as much as my mother, was turned out behind me, and we sat on the steps blinking and breathless in the crackling air.

All around us, the snow lay in brilliant waves and deep drifts. The wood stack in the middle of the yard was a round mound with a black cave in the side where my stepfather had dug through to the firewood that heated our house. The fence posts were capped with snow. The farm machinery lined up along the edge of the woods was softened and half buried. Sunken paths led in three directions like an English hedge maze from our back door to the milkhouse, to the outhouse, to the barn.

Bing was the most cheerful and brave of all the dogs we ever owned. He was a white rat terrier with half a brown patch on one ear, a spot on his side, and a tail that curled tightly over his back and wagged to a blur when he was having fun, which was most of the time. Just then he was trying to get up a game of chase. He posed before me, his head on his paws, his rear end wiggling cat-like in the air, ready to pounce. As I rolled awkwardly to my feet he grabbed my hand. Tugging and growling, he pulled off my mitten. He flew through the snow, carrying his prize, disappearing and reappearing like a white dolphin in the surf. I floundered after him, falling down and burying my hands in the drifts. I came out shaking my naked, reddened hand, yelling for him to stop.

"Bring that here!" I wailed. But he ran on, viciously growling and shaking the mitten as if to break its neck. He wouldn't stop, I couldn't catch him, so I screamed every God-will-damn-you curse I could think of. I don't remember my exact words, but Bing's reaction still blazes in my memory: he dropped my mitten and looked at me with horror.

In the bright light, I waded through the snow, picked up my mitten, shook it off, and pulled it on. Bing was not one to give up a thing once he had hold of it. So why did he? My small size, my angry swearing didn't seem reason enough. I had seen my stepfather use his big voice to call Bing away from a hole he was digging. Dad could crush walnuts in his fist, throw calves with one arm, and yet Bing ignored him, a fountain of dirt flying up behind his tail, until he felt Dad's foot coming. Then he dodged, grinning as Dad recovered his balance.

Bing's sudden obedience frightened me. I struggled back to the steps, sat down, sniffled, and began a loud bawling. At that moment, my mother opened the door, the dog raced inside, and she asked me to explain what was going on.

I told her Bing stole my mitten and wouldn't bring it back until I said a lot of very bad words. "Did you swear at God?" she asked. "Yes." And I began a fresh howling. I don't know what my mother really thought. At that time she only had residual spiritual knowledge left over from her own childhood. I had none at all. But she did not find my confession insignificant, nor did she laugh. Kneeling in front of me, her arms about me, and her face in mine, she instructed, "Go into the next room. Get on your knees and ask God to forgive you for swearing and he will." Her confidence relieved me.

Isolated details litter my earliest memories—refusing to resolve into completed pictures. I don't remember what happened after Mom told me to pray. I only know that from that time there was a presence of love that lingered near me. I believed it was God, though I knew nothing about him except that I shouldn't swear using his name no matter how enraged I was.

In the early years on our farm, Dad discovered rats in the broken-down granary. They lodged in the walls and under the foundation and came out at night with their skinny tails and red eyes to eat oats by the bushel. I worried that it was only a matter of time before they took over our farm in seething, squeaking masses.

It was Bing who saved us. He joyfully killed them, refusing to give up on even the biggest, meanest old rat until it was dug out and shaken till its brains fell out. When the job was done, his face and ears were bloodied with rat bites and scratches, and I would sit in the hay stack cradling him on my lap, kissing his head and tracing his scars.

Because he was so brave and loved chasing anything no matter how big, Dad repeatedly warned us not to "sic" Bing on the horses when we were in the pasture.

"Why?" I asked.

"Because they'll kick him!" he replied in a tone reserved for idiots.

It didn't matter that Bing chased the cows and snapped at their heels. Although cows can kick, they aren't athletic like horses. Cows are clumsy and oafish and run with an awkward gait, whereas any old nag of a horse can accurately land a powerful kick while running at a full gallop.

On a spring day four years later when I was eight, I walked to the marsh and through the soggy pasture looking for buttercups for Mom. Bing was with me sniffing out groundhog holes and digging at their burrows. The horses, being curious, snorted and came over to see what I was doing and if I was worth a sugar cube or two. I wasn't. I picked

Wally holding Bing

up a stick and threatened them. They flagged their black and blonde tails and trotted a short way off, and then minced toward me again.

Knowing that Bing only needed the slightest encouragement to chase anything, and loving that power, I knew I could make the horses run away. I weighed the temptation, then pointed to the horses and shouted, "Sic 'em!" Bing happily tore after them, yapping and snapping at their heels.

Some horses love an excuse to panic. They can fake a heart attack over a little piece of white paper on the ground. We had several of that kind. One of them was Duke, a two-year-old bay colt, tall and rangy. With a flying kick, he sent Bing somersaulting through the air until he rested quietly on the floor of the woods among decaying leaves and tiny blue violets. In the distance he looked like a still life, a bouquet of small white flowers pushing through the chilled earth.

My face flushed with heat and my eyes began to burn. I ran toward him and stood a way off hoping it was a dream and I would soon wake up. He didn't move. My throat ached. I called softly, "Bing? Bing?" I couldn't breathe. I knelt on the damp ground among the decaying leaves and saw a tiny marsh of blood forming beside his head.

You can't use me to support the belief that children are born innocent: that if you provide them with the basics—physical protection, intellectual stimulation, and emotional love—they'll do what's right, will listen to their parents and be kind and good. I had what I needed. I had most of what I wanted. Still there was some corruption in me that loved the risk of doing what Dad had forbidden. If I sicced Bing on the horses, no one would ever know.

I stood up and stared at him for a long time. It was the first time I experienced that hopeless desire—the wish to re-call words, to undo an act. At last I turned away, leaving him alone in the dim woods, and stumbled home. My lungs hurt. My stomach churned and I hoped this meant I was going to die too. I made it to the outhouse, where I threw up. Slowly I walked to the house and went to bed where Mom found me a little later. "I think I'm sick," I said. I was sick—with grief and the failure to be a more honorable child.

I decided not to tell anyone what had happened because if I did, I would immediately be turned out of the family. I would be forced to wander and make my own way in the world. Or more likely, the family would keep me, but would hate me and never speak to me again because I had done something so dreadful there was nothing that could ever, ever make up for it. I thought of leaving before anyone found out.

I pushed my face into the pillow, sobbing. As I cried, I became aware of my brother's voice outside. Loud and alarmed. He was yelling for Mom to come quick. Something was wrong with Bing. My heart leaped. Could God actually bring a dog back from the dead? Would he? I peeked out the window and saw him. He was weaving his way across the pasture, dragging himself home, bloodied, and bobbing like a man with a club-foot.

Some deep instinct residing in his heart must have brought him home. It couldn't have been his brain—that was damaged beyond repair. Mom helped Randy and me fix a cardboard box for him, and even though we lined it with our softest, raggedy old towel, he couldn't lie down. We tried to feed him the most treasured of treats, a fried chicken gizzard, but he couldn't eat. Softly whining and leaning against the kitchen stove for support, he stumbled in a path around the stove. All night long his injured brain repeated the circle.

When Dad got home he took one look and declared, "He's been kicked by a horse," and turned his eye on us. "Did any of you sic him on the horses?" We all said no. The next morning Dad gently carried him out, and we never saw him again.

———

A lot of things died on our farm. In fact, death was the fate of most farm animals. At a certain point of growth, fatness, or maturity, they were harvested, butchered, or sold to keep us alive. It was the expected destination for pigs, chickens, steers, old milk cows, and sometimes sheep. We didn't need to learn to live with it. It was simply the way life was.

One of the exceptions to this pattern was dogs. Dogs were purely for pleasure. Our dogs didn't herd, guard, or hunt, as some might expect. They were simply companions for children. They followed us to the pasture, to the woods, to the fields, and to the ditch to play in the water and catch frogs. They ran beside us and playfully pulled at our clothes and wrists. They licked us with their soft tongues and loved us with their fetid breath. However, Dad required them to keep a few rules just like everyone else.

By the time I was nine I had five brothers and sisters and Dad had distilled the laws for children into one basic rule: "Don't do as I do, do as I say." In other words, obey me. There wasn't room for argument or defense when you were confronted. Feed the chickens every day, close the gates so livestock doesn't escape, finish chores before you play, go to bed when you are told—those weren't unreasonable expectations for children. It was the sudden enforcement of a rule and a temper that could melt iron that kept me jumpy, a little afraid and anxious. I was always vigilant, trying to discern unspoken rules conveyed by a look or a sudden movement of his hand. Did he want me to move that chair? Pass the salt?

At the supper table I was especially alert, ducking my head, averting my eyes and making sure I held my fork properly, not using the fingers of my other hand to push food onto my fork. He taught me not to do that by hitting me with the flat blade of a dinner knife. The first time I didn't see it coming, and when it hit, a flaming ball formed in my throat and hot tears dripped to my lap. I quickly placed my hand under the table hiding the red welt, too ashamed to continue eating. It didn't take long to break me of that habit. I watched warily as he ate. He had his own way of hunkering over his plate holding his fork in his palm like one might hold a small scoop shovel while his other forearm rested on the table encircling his plate, a relaxed fist holding it in place. He never had to ask for anything to be passed, he merely stared at it until someone noticed.

The rules for dogs made sense and anyone could see that keeping them would certainly prolong their lives and happiness.

Dog's Rules were:

Stay home.
Don't chase vehicles.
Don't bite humans.
Don't eat chickens or their eggs.
Don't chase deer.

Especially, don't chase deer. That was a crime so felonious, a dog caught chasing deer or even known to have once chased a deer could be shot by anyone on sight. Anyone. That wasn't just Dad's rule, it was upheld by everyone in our county. Deer were loved and protected by all. For despite their shyness and graceful beauty, which were truly appreciated, venison was considered one of the major food groups along with dairy products, vegetables, and dessert. Deer were never resented for crop damage as they daintily stepped through fields of alfalfa and wheat, fattening themselves for the fall hunt.

My husband and a friend from Texas once witnessed this last rule in action, and were astonished by the casual nature of the enforcement. During deer hunting season, they were with my brother, Rex, who stopped his pickup in the middle of the road and got out to talk with Jerry Khrone, who was going the other direction. Jerry had also stopped his pickup in the middle of the road and got out to talk. They stood beside their pickups and spoke of this and that: the effects of weather on the buck rut, some fool who was arrested by the game warden for firing at a deer decoy the night before the season opened. As they visited, Jerry spotted a white dog loping across the far field. He paused a moment: "There's that damn Bjork dog. Been chasin' deer. That's it then." He reached into his pickup, pulled out his rifle, fired once, and the dog flipped into the air and died in the plowed field 250 yards away. Rex and Jerry continued to talk about doe permits as though he had merely paused mid-sentence to hawk one.

There were no rules for dogs about eating horse biscuits, rolling in ripe manure, or chasing skunks. That was expected and left plenty of room for amusement.

We owned a series of dogs, each memorable in his own way, but the death of one still stands out. This dog broke a lot of rules, and we kids worried. Corky was part Dalmatian and part black Lab and was born with the temper of an old crank and the resolve of a terrorist. As soon as he could walk, he had gone to the neighbors' to check out the local females. He also declared war on any vehicle that drove by our farm. He'd lay in wait in the tall grass along the edge of the road, and as a car neared, he would jump out snarling and running after the tires, his teeth bared and his hair standing on end. Any kid within hearing distance would run toward the road, screaming "Corky! Get back here!" Not that he ever paid us any mind. He'd come back with defiance in his eye, tongue hanging out, and his tail up—no remorse at all. He was an addict who couldn't help himself. Dad warned again and again that Corky was going to get himself killed.

This had already happened to one of our dogs—getting herself killed by a car. She was a sweet Dalmatian named Spotty, and we had tried desperately to stop her from chasing cars. We begged and reasoned with her. We beat her. We tied her up, but there was always someone who couldn't bear the sad look on her face and would set her free. Nothing worked. The next thing she'd be hiding in the tall grass along the road and jumping out after anything that dared to drive by. Then one day a fisherman from the Twin Cities whizzed by in a big Buick, and as she chased his tires, he swerved and got her with a dull popping sound. She lifted her head from the gravel, looked at us with sad, apologetic eyes, and tried to drag herself toward us on her front legs.

We ran to her and Randy picked her up, a heavy load for a seven-year-old. He staggered down the drive. Our younger sister, Jan, and I trailed along beside him crying, "Don't die, Spotty, please don't die." As we laid her on the back steps, blood trickled out her nose and ears. She gazed at us with her dark blue eyes that slowly turned a milky gauze. Her body stayed warm and limp for a while, as though she were just napping and could still wake if she chose.

So even though Corky was not going to win any personality prizes, we still didn't want him to die that way. Certainly not that way.

His fatal infraction was the violation of a more serious rule: biting people. He was always short tempered about his food and bones. If you happened near him while he was eating, he would stop and hang over his bowl in a protective stance. His body would rumble, his lips lifting in a snarl.

I guess it was the danger or the challenge that drew my five-year-old brother, Rex, into teasing him. It was like playing roulette in a way. Grab Corky's bone, dangle it in the air above him, and Corky would go ravening, leaping, and snapping for it. The trick was to let go of the bone at just the right moment without making contact with Corky's teeth. One day Rex misjudged and got bit. He went crying to Mom. It was probably the second or third time Corky had bit someone, so Dad made a pronouncement: "I'm telling you, if he bites anybody again, I'm going to shoot him." We hoped he didn't mean it.

Not long after, our uncle, aunt, and four of their children came for supper on a warm summer evening. Our kitchen was too small for everyone, so the children ate in the yard. Supper that night included my mother's fried chicken, the best in the world. Platters of breasts, wings, and legs came out of the cast-iron skillets browned and crisp—especially on the side that touched the bottom of the pan the longest, where it had time to absorb greasy juices and cure to a salty, spicy perfection. We sat in the grass and on the steps with the other children, our plates loaded with the foods that always accompanied fried chicken:

creamy mashed potatoes with milk gravy made from the drippings in the frying pans, biscuits, green beans fresh from the garden, sliced ripe tomatoes, and the contrast of tangy coleslaw.

As we ate, Corky watched, looking grimmer by the second, waiting for someone to give him a chicken leg before he had to take it by force. Rex sucked the last of the meat off his piece and offered it to Corky, who lunged, and Rex lifted his hand, ready to play their game. Infuriated, Corky leaped, grabbing bone and hand in his jaw, he wrenched it away. Rex drew his hand back and this time blood was oozing from three canine puncture wounds. Howling with pain and anger, shaking his hand and squeezing more blood out of the holes, he tried to run to the house, but Randy and I cut him off, yelling, "Aw, c'mon. You asked for it. Corky didn't mean to."

It may have looked like Rex was too young to understand that Dad meant what he said, but I doubt it. He was stubborn. When he was hardly more than a baby, he proved to be so resolute when it came to his own ideas he could have made a mule weep.

He learned how to climb out of his crib when he was barely fifteen months old, and the success of the act was so exquisitely powerful he'd gone out to the kitchen to show Mom and Dad. Since he was the fourth child, and Dallas, the fifth baby, was sleeping in the bassinet beside him, with a sixth on the way, they weren't impressed. They valued what little privacy they could get in the evening after we were all sent to bed at a "decent hour." Mom picked him up, carried him back to the single bedroom where all of us slept, laid him down, kissed him, and said, "Stay there." Her back was barely out of the room before he had his foot over the rail again.

Controlling one's destiny is a heady thing, and he was going to go back to the kitchen. Hoisting himself down, he followed her out. She turned around, surprised, and said, "I thought I told you to stay in bed." He looked at her silently, sucking his thumb as she brought him back. This time she warned him, "If you do this again, you'll get a spanking."

From our beds, we watched him climb out again. "Wow!" we thought, "is he ever stupid." But he wasn't. He was just declaring war. He did get a spanking that time. And he wasn't quiet about crying, even though we were all supposed to be sleeping. He roared and howled. And, while he was still hiccupping and sighing, he climbed out again. We rose on our elbows from the bunk beds and thought we should at least point out that he would get it again. Randy whispered, "Rex, you moron, don't do it!" But he was already on his way to the kitchen. This time Dad brought him back and really let him have it. He lay for a moment, screaming, and then climbed out again and went to the kitchen. I mean, if he wanted to simply get up, why didn't he just sneak into the living room and quietly sit on the couch? But no.

This dedication to autonomy was way beyond us. We begged him to stay in bed. It was the screaming and crying we could no longer tolerate, and we all began to wail. I don't remember how much longer this went on. I don't know how my parents won, but they must have, because it never happened again that I remember.

Perhaps this battle helped prepare him for his own spiritual awakening, which began when he, too, was four years old. It involved nothing unusual, just our family's normal stampede to the table at suppertime. On this particular evening Mom called us in, and Rex was the last to arrive. From the disadvantage of his height, the table looked crowded and full. He'd been forgotten. There was nowhere to sit. With as much withering sarcasm as a four-year-old can muster, he shouted at Mom, "And *where* am I supposed to sit? On your *head*?!" The words were barely out of his mouth, when just like that, our mother whacked him hard on top of his head and sent him to the living room until he could come back and speak properly to her.

Something about that incident melted his heart and caused him to pray and ask God to forgive him. He remembers leaning into the wall and crying with the certain revelation that he was a selfish, impatient boy who had just insulted the best thing in his life. He should have had a faith in his mother built solidly on past experience. Even though he was number four out of six children, not once in all his four years of life had she forgotten to feed him. Not that Rex could have counted them, but that would have been roughly 4,260 times. At least.

But this did not mean he minded risking some flesh in order to have a little fun with Corky.

By this time we were making such a racket over Rex and the dog, Dad came to the top of the steps and boomed his usual inquiry, "WHAT THE SAM HELL IS GOING ON OUT HERE!?" Actually, it wasn't "Sam Hell." It was "Sam Hill," though I didn't learn that until many years later. Still, it amounted to the same thing.

Rex ran up and showed his hand, which had a couple of scarlet drips falling off the ends of his fingers. "Corky bit me," he bawled.

Jan was crying. She was six years old and the most tender-hearted and gentle of all of us. Our cousins were standing a little way off. They had stopped eating. Only Dallas, our youngest brother, sat on the ground contentedly shoveling mashed potatoes into his mouth, oblivious and a little too young for the drama that was shaping up around him. Randy and I stood at the bottom of the steps pleading for Corky, pointing out that Rex had been teasing him.

It was useless. Corky was standing over his chicken bone a few feet away. It was between his front paws; he had cracked the shank and was swallowing the splinters whole. His last memory must have been a pleasant one as Dad shot him point blank between the eyes. He simply dropped.

——

For dessert, Mom had made chocolate cake with chocolate fudge icing. She always spread it just before the cake cooled, which gave it a shiny, satiny skin, a thin, glass-like surface that broke into miniature shards revealing the creamy underside of the icing and the moist cake beneath. Randy and I had no appetite for about ten minutes. We carefully set our plates on the porch and went around to the backside of the haystack and sat on a bale.

Remembering what I had done to Bing, I knew I couldn't stay mad at Rex for getting Corky into trouble. Bing was the dog that began my spiritual journey. He planted an awareness of the transcendent within me—there were realities in life that couldn't be touched by the hand or seen by the eye. This presence, shimmering just beyond our senses, appraised the weight of not only our words, but our actions. For me, Bing was a purveyor of love and grace, and I had killed him. Someone needed to forgive me.

Randy wiped his face with the sleeve of his shirt and said, "They're starting to play ball."

We got up to join the rest of the kids. But first, we ate a piece of chocolate cake.

## Randy's Favorite Chocolate Cake

1 cup boiling water
2 squares unsweetened chocolate
1/2 cup butter
1 tsp vanilla
1 3/4 cup brown sugar
2 eggs
1 3/4 cup flour
1 tsp baking soda
1/4 tsp salt
1/2 cup sour cream

Preheat oven to 325 degrees and grease a 9x13-inch pan. Combine flour, baking soda, and salt. In small bowl, pour boiling water over chocolate. In separate bowl, cream butter and vanilla. Add brown sugar and blend well. Add eggs one at at time and beat. Add dry ingredients; beat until smooth. Stir in sour cream and chocolate. Pour batter into prepared pan and bake for 1 hour 15 minutes, or until a toothpick inserted in the center of the cake comes out clean.

## Chocolate Fudge Icing

1 stick butter
3 tbsp cocoa
6 tbsp milk
1 tsp. vanilla
3-1/2 cups powdered sugar
1/2 cup chopped walnuts (optional)

Melt butter in a saucepan along with cocoa. Add milk and bring to boil. Remove from heat and beat in the powdered sugar and vanilla. Beat until smooth, adding more sugar as needed to make a spreading consistency. Stir in nuts. Spread on cake while slightly warm.

# Balm of Gilead Tree

In areas of Lake of the Woods County where virgin tamaracks and cedars were cut and where fires burned across the land, species of the poplar family grew and spread in their place. Quaking aspen and balsam poplar known as "fire-chasers" tolerated wet ground and grew in groves by the thousands. The balsam poplar, a cottonwood, was locally known by an old name, the balm of Gilead. In spring, the tree blooms with sticky aromatic buds called catkins. My grandfather, Percy Sorenson, gathered them, and using an old Native American recipe, extracted the resin to make a healing ointment. It soothed everything from cuts to poison ivy, but there are times when wounds need a stronger, deeper magic. Jeremiah, an ancient Hebrew prophet, referred to the deep wounds of the soul when he asked, "Is there no balm in Gilead, is there no physician?" (Jeremiah 8:22) Centuries later, in the words of the prophet Isaiah, Jesus answered, "The Lord has anointed me to proclaim good news to the poor, He [God] has sent me to bind up the brokenhearted." (Isiah 61:1)

# CRASH COURSE

I arrived in this world on a cold and snowy day. And I was fatherless besides. My family tree is a series of lost branches and strained grafts—I knew this from the beginning. I knew it like geese fly south, like suckers swim up creeks to spawn. It was my mother, Marjorie Lou Darbyshire Frolander Sorenson Block, who supplied the memories and tried to fill the broken spaces.

On the day I was born, my mother was living in Warroad, Minnesota, with her foster parents, the Frolanders. No one was home when her labor began. Her mother was at a Ladies Aid luncheon. Her father was working at a carpentry job for a local business. Her husband, Keith Sorenson, was gone. Dead four months. My seventeen-year-old mother belted her wool coat over her tight belly, tied a scarf over her auburn hair, pulled on her woolen mittens, and began the mile-long walk to the hospital.

It was the same hospital where she'd been born. In December of 1929, her own mother, Vadna Darbyshire, lay awake in the middle of the night. Vadna's training as a nurse helped her finally make a difficult assessment, one she didn't want to believe. She was suffering from more than a normal pregnancy—she needed to see a doctor because she was seriously ill. Worried she didn't have long to live, her husband, Lester Darbyshire, known simply as Darby, dressed in his parka and boots and trudged through the snow to wake Jake Colson, the only neighbor in the nearby settlement who owned a car. With the temperature far below zero, Darby knew it would be a risky trip across the lake if Jake agreed to drive her into Warroad. Jake did agree; but first he drove across the ice to a nearby island and roused Pete Frolander, another neighbor who could accompany him. Jake and Pete packed the car with blankets and thermoses of hot coffee, and together they drove Vadna across fifty miles of lake ice from Minnesota's Northwest Angle to the hospital in Warroad. Darby stayed behind to care for his two small sons, Steven and Ivan.

———

The Northwest Angle of Minnesota where my mother's parents, the Darbyshires, lived is the northernmost part of the forty-eight states. On the map where Minnesota's northern border bumps up, it looks like a mistake. There is a legend that in the early 1800s the surveyors got lost among the thousands of islands on Lake of the Woods and accidentally gave the US a small piece of Canada. The area was a surveyor's nightmare. Surrounded by Canadian wilderness and lakes on all sides, it was an area so isolated the only access was by boat in summer or across the ice in winter. This was until the early 1970s, when the United States government sought permission from the province of Manitoba to build a gravel road through seventy-five miles of uninhabited cedar swamp up to the Northwest Angle's tiny settlement called Angle Inlet. Living along the shores and on the islands of Lake of the Woods during the 1920s and 30s, the few inhabitants of the area made their living by commercial fishing. Before the populations collapsed, millions of pounds of highly prized game fish—walleye, sauger, and northern pike—were netted and shipped by rail to markets in New York and Chicago.

My mother's parents, Darby and Vadna Darbyshire, had moved from Oklahoma to a small homestead on Lake of the Woods. It was set back a little way from the shore in a small clearing behind the ruins of Fort St. Charles, a sixteenth-century French fort established by fur traders. Here they survived on what Darby earned from fishing in the summer and odd jobs throughout the year. Their two-room log cabin (without electricity or running water) could have fit in a corner of Vadna's childhood home in Enid, Oklahoma. She had been born into a prosperous family and was the oldest of nine children—Mom never knew why they were called prosperous. Maybe the size of that house and the little scraps of detail left with Mom's brothers gave her that impression. While Vadna was in nursing school she met and fell in love with Darby. His parents had emigrated from England and settled near the oil fields of Oklahoma where, as a young man, he found work. That was all Mom knew about her parents' early history, and she often wondered why they left Oklahoma for northern Minnesota after their marriage.

When Jake and Pete arrived in Warroad with Vadna on that cold December night, they took her straight to the hospital where she was kept for several days. The doctor didn't know what was wrong with her, but suggested that since she was in her seventh month of pregnancy she stay in town until the birth of the baby. So Vadna remained with friends until February 12, 1930, the day my mother, Marjorie Lou Darbyshire, was born.

Mom was in perfect health. Vadna, however, continued running a fever with flu-like symptoms and suffered from overwhelming exhaustion. Her gums bled. Her stomach ached. Her arms hurt when she lifted her children. At last the doctor suggested she be taken to the Mayo Clinic to see if they knew what was wrong. So that summer, Darby drove Vadna five hundred miles south to Rochester, Minnesota, where tests pronounced she had leukemia. There was no cure.

A friend advised Darby to take Vadna to California to see the flamboyant preacher and faith healer, Aimee Semple McPherson. Many people reported they had been cured of their diseases when she laid her hands on them and prayed. It was worth a shot. In desperation, Darby left baby Marjorie and her two brothers with neighbors and set out on the long journey to California. Miss McPherson prayed for Vadna and told her she was healed but needed to stay at the Foursquare Gospel Temple in Los Angeles to be certain of the cure. Darby felt that if indeed she was healed, then God could sustain that healing anywhere. He took her home to the Northwest Angle.

For a while she did seem a little better, but gradually her life seeped away. A few days before Vadna died, Zella Frolander made a neighborly visit to the Darbyshires. Zella found Vadna in bed, feverish, her eyes dark and sunken. She was unable to get up even for visitors, and her baby lay beside her crying. Knowing Vadna would never recover, Zella kindly offered to take Margie home to keep until Vadna was well again. Vadna kissed her baby, my mother, good-bye and sank back on the bed.

Several days later Vadna was taken by boat back to the Warroad hospital where she lingered for another ten days and then sank for the last time. An old sepia photo of her sits on my buffet—she is a healthy young woman in her late teens. Her head is demurely bent toward the camera, and she wears the slightest smile, but her eyes are dark and wistful.

My mother was nine months old when Zella took her home. Zella had always wanted a daughter and Pete didn't know he'd wanted one until Mom arrived in their household. Their three school-age boys were amused and delighted to have a little girl in the house.

Darby meant for the arrangement to be temporary, until he got back on his feet, but my mother continued to live with the Frolanders for the next four years until it was natural to call them Mom and Dad and the three boys, her brothers. She made occasional visits to her father's cabin, but the Darbyshire family tree grew more convoluted when Darby took a new wife who was also Marjorie's aunt—Vadna's sister, Beulah. I don't know how they got together unless she made it up to Minnesota to help care for her sister's children and husband. But it didn't take long for the family to grow. Soon after they married, in addition

My mom's mother, Vadna Darbyshire, died from leukemia, 1930.

to Mom's two older brothers, four half-sisters were born into that small log cabin.

When Mom was five years old she began first grade in the one-room schoolhouse on Penasee, the same island on which the Frolanders lived. That fall an incident occurred that cemented the bond to her adoptive family. It happened during one of her short visits to the Darbyshires. She awakened on a chilly school morning to the smell of breakfast cooking on the wood stove. It was a chilly day and Beulah had prepared oatmeal for the children. Darby had already gone out to work. Mom has never been able to eat oatmeal. To her, the word "mush," as they called it then, was entirely descriptive. Who would want to eat something called mush? The sliminess of oatmeal reminded her of an old man who sometimes visited the Frolanders and noisily coughed up large quantities of phlegm and in front of everyone, spit it into an old coffee can, or worse, onto the woodstove where it sizzled and fried. Mom knew her stepmother thought she was spoiled rotten by the Frolanders, but her hatred of oatmeal sent her past caring. With a rising dread she dared to mention she didn't like oatmeal, but was willing to go without breakfast. "You eat that," Beulah responded, "and be thankful for every bite." Mom sat silent and staring, wishing she were home. "Fine," Beulah told her, "you can sit here all day if necessary until you've finished your breakfast." Ivan and Steven were sent off to school without Mom, and her younger half-sisters settled in to watch the outcome of such defiance.

At last Mom held her nose and gulped large spoonfuls as fast as she could. Visions of the old man kept returning to her mind, and she began to gag. Suddenly everything rushed to her throat and erupted in one mighty heave. The mess on the table and floor so infuriated Beulah she grabbed a switch and beat Mom up and down her back, her butt, her thighs. When it was over, Beulah sent her to school. She remembers walking down the long path through the woods, then into the tall brush and reeds near the shore, weeping as she went.

The island where the Darbyshires lived was just north of Penasee, and the two small islands almost touched, being connected by a shallow marsh with a little patch of open water between them. The path from the cabin led down to the edge where an old rowboat was kept for crossing the water, then the path continued on the other side. Mom wondered how she would get to school since the boys would have taken the boat to the other side. However, by the time she arrived at the water's edge the temperature, which had been steadily falling caused a thin sheet of ice to form over the open water. She hesitated, glancing back up the path toward the cabin. She wiped her eyes and nose on the rough sleeves of her coat, and gingerly advanced, step by step across the ice, until she reached the opposite shore.

At noon she went to the Frolanders for lunch since they lived so near the school. When she opened the door that day, the comforting smell of crispy, fried walleye and creamed potatoes drifted from the kitchen. As the family sat down to eat, Zella noticed that Mom's eyes, normally a clear deep blue, were red and swollen. Mom felt she needed to confess: "I didn't want oatmeal for breakfast, so I got a spanking." Pete pulled her gently onto his lap and lifted her dress. Her entire backside was bruised. That evening, Pete and Zella visited Darby and Beulah. Whatever went on between them, all Mom knew was that she didn't see the Darbyshires again for the rest of the school year. Before Pete tucked the blanket under her chin that night, he counted her ribs: "Oooone, twooooo, threeeee, fourfivesixseveneight!"—just to make sure they were all there and until she screamed with laughter and had to be rescued by Zella.

From then on Mom only spent a few weeks each summer with Darby and Beulah. When she was dropped off at the Darbyshires' dock, before she climbed out of the outboard boat with her little canvas bag, Pete always slipped her a pack of Juicy Fruit gum to share with her brothers and half-sisters. Gum was rare for children of the depression so they rationed the sticks to one a day. According to strict guidelines, oldest to youngest, a stick was chewed for several hours and then passed one by one to the next in line.

When Mom arrived she carried her bag up the ladder nailed to the wall and joined the older children who slept in the loft. Beside her cot she took off her shoes and carefully hid them in the bottom of her bag so she could go barefoot like her brothers who had no shoes, and because her canvas sneakers might offend her stepmother, by proving, once again, how the Frolanders indulged her. Darby and Beulah slept on the screened porch until it was too cold in the fall. There was a kitchen/living area and one small bedroom where the younger children slept. Furniture was sparse, the only luxury being an old wooden rocker where Darby sat in the evenings.

Sometimes there was not quite enough to eat at the Darbyshire home. Breakfasts were mostly toast and sweetened tea. Beulah baked fresh bread every day, spread it with lard and sprinkled it with salt for their midday meal. Butter was not affordable—though they had a few cows, the cream had to be sold for the money. At suppertime, Beulah warmed milk, added chunks of bread, and sprinkled it with salt and pepper for the evening meal. But even hungry children must play, so after chores were done, they fished or swam off the dock, dug in the ancient sixteenth-century dump behind the fort and found old apothecary jars, pieces of glass, and brass buttons, and they pretended to be the French explorers who were killed in a bloody massacre by a Dakota war party in 1736.

When Mom became a mother herself there were a few rare mornings when she faced hungry children and wondered what to feed us. I remember her apologizing and telling us she needed to go to town that day and stock up. Those must have been times when our chickens weren't laying or between butcherings so we didn't have salt pork or headcheese on hand. On those mornings she made what became my favorite breakfast: coffee loaded with sugar and cream and a large platter of toasted homemade bread, dripping with butter and cinnamon-sugar. Whatever we had for breakfast, whether it was bacon and eggs or hot cereal, she often called us to the table singing the Cream of Wheat commercial we heard on the radio: "It's Cream of Wheat weather, we repeat, so treat your family to hot Cream of Wheat." Then she laughed at her mimicry and filled our bowls with cereal, sprinkled it with brown sugar, and poured milk and cream across the steaming top. No matter how little there was in the house, we were never forced to eat oatmeal.

When Mom stayed with the Darbyshires her favorite time of the day was dusk, when all the children washed their feet, put on pajamas, and wrapped themselves in blankets against the evening chill. Darby brought out a Bible, lit the kerosene lamp, and read stories while Beulah mended clothes in the soft light. The book fascinated Mom and filled her with questions: where did Adam live? Can we go to the Garden of Eden? Who made God? Who did Adam's children marry? Does Jesus love bad men? But she did not like it when Darby questioned her about her soul. "Do you want to be saved?" he would ask. "Don't you want to go to heaven?" Mom would wiggle and squirm, annoyed at being pressed. She refused to answer her father, but inside she said: "Yes, someday I want to be saved, but I'm going to wait until I am an old woman, because I want to have a lot of fun first."

It's odd how as a child she'd already gained an impression of her father's faith, that if she accepted it as her own, it would mean giving up things that were fun, things that maybe a holy person wouldn't be allowed to do. She wasn't even certain what those things might be. Leather shoes? No lipstick? No dancing? Perhaps her hesitation was a prescient knowledge that turning to God, any god, grants him a claim on your soul, or at least parts of it.

There was no church on the Northwest Angle, but each summer Darby organized travel, room, and board for several young women who came from a mission in central Minnesota to teach a summer Bible School for the children. For my mother, the two most memorable things about this annual event were the chocolate cake Beulah always made for supper when it was her turn to have the women as guests, and the program for parents on the final night. That was when Mom was always asked to sing a solo. It made her nervous, but when she opened her mouth to sing a hymn, she loved the way the room grew quiet, and when she was done, the little pause of wonder just before the people began to applaud.

Then one fall another change occurred that placed Mom permanently in the Frolander family and eventually made them the grandparents I loved best. The one-room school at Penasee only went through eighth grade and the Frolanders' oldest son, Carl, was ready to enter high school; Don and Peter, Jr., weren't far behind. Many people believed that eight grades of education were good enough for anybody, but Pete wanted more for his boys. He decided they should close up their house at Penasee and move into Warroad for the winter so the boys could go to school in town. The boys could finish high school, while he found work as a carpenter.

When Darby heard the Frolanders were moving to Warroad, he sent Mom's brother, Steve, to bring her back in the rowboat. But the Frolanders refused to let her go with him because now she was like their own daughter. A meeting was held and Darby agreed they could be her permanent foster parents, under two conditions: that she keep Darbyshire as her name, and that she be sent to church every Sunday. The Frolanders kept this verbal agreement, and that winter Mom went to school in town, and every Sunday Zella sent her to the Swedish Covenant church just down the block.

As the depression wore on, the Darbyshires began to think that life might be better back in Oklahoma. So in 1940 they moved, leaving Mom for good. She never saw her father again. Three years later she received a letter; Darby had died of stomach cancer. Attending the funeral was out of the question—it was wartime and the buses and trains were filled with soldiers going to and fro. Meanwhile, at school it was complicated to constantly explain her last name. Classmates asked, "How come your name is Darbyshire if the Frolanders are your parents?" At last, she let it go, and her school records began to show her name as Marjorie Frolander. Not many years later, I would have a similar experience. No adoption, nothing official—just little by little Sorenson slipped away, replaced by Block.

Each summer Pete and Zella left Warroad for an island on the Canadian side of Lake of the Woods. With their three sons and Marjorie, they built a resort that became more successful each year. It began with two wooden houseboats, anchored in the shelter of Monument Bay and a few contacts from Kansas—wealthy dentists and doctors looking for the kind of fishing experience found in the wilderness but with good home cooking and comfortable beds.

As the resort grew, so did my mother. Each summer she learned more about helping her foster mother with the cooking, laundry, and cleaning the cabins. Her last full summer at the resort was the year she was sixteen. Late the following summer when it was nearly over, Mom, who was still seventeen years old, wrote asking Pete if he would please come get her. The very next day Grandpa took his launch across the Lake to Warroad, drove thirty-six miles to a farm north of Williams, and brought her back home for three weeks before the season closed.

———

This place, which I came to know as Frolander's Camp, was on a small island shaped like the letter C. The middle was low and narrow, so when a boat pulled up to the main dock in the harbor you could see across the island to the back bay where chains of uninhabited islands stretched shimmering to the horizon and fell off the edge of the world. On both sides, the island rose and thickened in protective arms around a little cove. Tall evergreens flanked by white paper birch grew up the rocky hillsides. Among them Grandpa built log cabins that overlooked the water. They were rich in natural color and filled with the scent of cedar and pine. He plumbed and wired; he even made the furniture—beds, tables, chairs, and chests. The beds were made up with crisp white linens and woolen Hudson's Bay blankets spread tightly across them. If he were alive today, he would laugh to see malls selling replicas of his furniture as Americans try to recapture authentic log cabin style.

He raised a water tower at the top of the hill so each cabin had running water and indoor toilets. He generated electricity for the island by using a gas-powered airplane engine. It was used sparingly, mainly to run the pump that filled the water tower and for Grandma's wringer washing machine. The generator was shut down by ten in the evening when, according to Grandpa, all people everywhere, even the devil, ought to be in bed. Quiet enveloped the island with only the songs of crickets and frogs and an occasional voice echoing across the water. Lemon-yellow squares of light appeared here and there as guests lit kerosene lamps.

Frolander's Camp. My grandparents' resort in Canada.

In the narrow midsection of the island where its arms cupped the harbor, Grandpa built the main log lodge. It included their bedroom, the kitchen, a dining room with pine tables and chairs seating up to thirty guests, and a living room with a massive stone fireplace. The walls were hung with the mounted heads of bear, antlered bucks, moose, and enormous muskies. The hide of a timber wolf was tacked to one wall, and in front of the fireplace a bearskin rug with the head attached stared at me with marble eyes, its teeth bared. I stayed out of that room because I saw him watching me on many occasions. Out of an oak buffet in the dining room Grandpa sold a bit of tackle, colorful lures, preserved salmon eggs and leeches, maps of Lake of the Woods, and best of all, Cadbury chocolate bars. Even as a child, I thought Hershey was no match for this hazelnut-flavored milk chocolate from England.

Grandpa's energy and skill combined with Grandma's cooking and hospitality drew the same guests year after year. It was a strange partnership because in contrast to his good cheer, Grandma was often sad and anxious, humming tunelessly as she went about her work, and her work was hard. Cabins needed to be cleaned. Boatloads of laundry were washed in a wringer-washing machine and hung out to dry. To this day I can't believe the punishing standards she kept for ironing. Everything got pressed, even sheets and dishtowels, with a heavy, hissing, kerosene-fired iron. The more stressed she became the more she hummed. Many

One of Grandpa's log cabins.

things worried her. The weather was unpredictable; a violent storm could blow up without warning and anyone caught out on the lake in a boat could capsize. I could fall off the dock and drown, she warned me again and again. In all the years she lived on the lake she never learned to swim, and she hated the water passionately. She never knew if the young women from the local native tribe who were hired to help her would stay the season. Sometimes they left slipping away to join lovers who made summer camp with the rest of their people somewhere off to the north. Sometimes supplies ran low and it was a challenge to maintain the quality of meals guests expected on that wild island so far from civilization.

Grandma cooked family-style, feeding up to thirty guests and ten guides. (The fishing guides were all young men hired from among the Ojibways who knew the islands and the lake like the back of their hand.) Three times a day, seven days a week, fishermen (and the few wives who accompanied them) filled the tables, expectantly waiting for what came out of her kitchen. I watched guests come to the kitchen door and rave in accents foreign to my ears: "Miz Frolander, ah have nevah tasted fraud walleye this fawn!" "Miz Frolander, that blueberry pah juss about made me think ah died and gone to heaven." They talked strange, like they'd never eaten buttermilk pancakes crisp on the edges, swimming in pats of butter and Karo syrup. Finding meatloaf, mashed potatoes, and great fishing besides, was miraculous to some, I guess. To me, the food was common, everyday stuff. It was what I got at home, because right here was where Grandma had taught Mom to cook when she was a girl.

Every summer when I visited, I slept with her, and Grandpa moved out to the bunkhouse with the fishing guides. I thought nothing of this as a child, but it must not have been ideal for them. I don't remember being a constant nuisance, but I do remember the time I found a chocolate cake cooling on the wide, kitchen window-sill, and I fed it to the orphan fawn that had become a pet that summer. I opened the swing-out screen and Bambi (what else could its name be?) put his delicate nose in my hand nibbling the piece I offered. I dug it out bit by bit and together we ate it all. What was I thinking? I don't know; it seemed the right thing to do for a deer who loved cake. When Grandma saw what I'd done, her hands flew to her mouth and she grabbed the pan. She sent me outside for the rest of the morning and opened canned peaches for lunch dessert.

At night I often heard her crying and whispering in the darkened kitchen just outside the bedroom, and it filled me with dread as I waited for her to come to bed. I didn't know what made her cry. I didn't get the sense that it was me, even though I must have been extra work for her. I was relieved when at last she slipped into bed, and lightly ran her fingers up and down my arm, her softness against my back, until we fell asleep together.

Grandma Frolander resting in a rare moment.

It seems like every morning I rose slowly through the grog of sleep to the thwop, thwop sound of her beating pancake batter and the scrape of the turner as she flipped cakes on the other side of the curtained-off doorway. I'd scooch under the covers trying to stay in that delicious state of semi-consciousness until the smell of bacon and pancakes made my stomach ache so bad, I'd rush into my clothes and out to the porch so I could eat next to Grandpa and the Indian guides.

The back porch of the lodge was where Grandpa and the Indian guides ate their meals around a large pine table with benches. When I visited—which was every summer from the time I was six months old—I sat as close to Grandpa as possible. Although I hoped to marry one of the handsome Indians when I grew up, they made me so nervous and shy, I often choked on my food. They laughed as Grandpa slapped me on the back and shouted above my coughing, "Breathe the air. Drink the milk." Then he would stir his hot coffee and try to lay the spoon on the back of my hand, or he would reach for me under the table grasping my knee. My shrieks would bring Grandma to the porch door crying, "Pete, leave her *alone,* for pity sake." He called me his shadow because I followed him everywhere, but then he never went anywhere without asking me to come. "Motty-oo," he'd call, using my baby-name, "get your shoes on, I'm leaving." Whether it was in Spanky, his fast little outboard, or the big launch on a seventy-mile run to

Kenora and back for supplies, I went with him. He took me blueberry picking on nearby islands, to Penasee to pick up the mail, and to Angle Inlet to visit friends.

Each day the waterfront drew me like a seagull to fish bait. The smells of gasoline, tar, fish, and fresh-sawn lumber hung in the air. The bay echoed with hollow thumps as fishermen stowed gear in the boats. Evinrude and Johnson motors roared to life, pulled away from the docks, and faded into the morning mist. Grandpa's band saw whined as he built another boat. Seagulls circled and screeched overhead. A stone wall ran in a semicircle around the cove and reinforced the shoreline. I could lie down on the wall, and by hanging over the edge, catch minnows with the little dip net and put them in the minnow bucket Grandpa gave me. I moved rocks under the water and grabbed crayfish with my thumb and forefinger as they shot backwards from their hiding places. They splayed their claws when held just behind the head, reaching back, back, trying to pinch what held them.

Along the shore there was a cluster of buildings, the main dock, and five smaller docks that ran out from the stone wall. The fish house held fuel barrels, outboard motors, and boating equipment: cushions, life jackets, and oars hung in neat rows. Next door was the icehouse where, by poking around with a shovel, I could unearth large chunks of ice buried under mountains of sawdust. They had been stored there the previous January when the lake ice was three to four feet thick. Blocks were cut out and packed in wood shavings where they kept all summer long. The guides carried out forty-pound blocks, straining to grip them in the tongs as they dipped them in the lake to rinse off the sawdust, and dropped them into the ice-chipping box at the edge of the stone wall. There, the clear-as-glass ice was pounded into shards. Most of it was used to fill the pine boxes made for shipping fish back home with the tourists, but some of it was carried up to the lodge and placed in the special cooler Grandpa made to refrigerate perishables and to cool our drinks on hot summer days.

There was also the dusty shop where Grandpa moved in a suspension of sunlight and sawdust with a pencil tucked behind his one good ear. The other ear was oddly deformed like someone had folded it over and stapled it to the side of his head. Until I was old enough to pretend physical differences weren't noticed, I often asked about it, "What's wrong with your ear?" He always told a different story. It'd been shot off by a bank robber. It fell off and had to be screwed back on. A dog bit it off. He never told Mom either; she thinks he was born that way. While he sang, drew plans, and planed lumber for a new boat, I randomly pounded a staggering number of nails into scrap lumber. He propped my finished pieces against the wall like they were works of art, just as years later I would tape my children's scribbled drawings to the refrigerator. "Damn! Look at that, would you?" he'd ask.

Grandpa Frolander loved me. I was sure of this. It was like he removed a stick from my spine—a stick that poked it straight and made me alert, always ready to run. Around him an inner-tightness let loose. I didn't need to do anything to delight him, didn't even think about it, I just did. He never sent me away or made fun of me, though I know I amused him. He never told me how smart I was, or how pretty, or how great my cartwheels. He didn't need to. There were two things that really settled the proof of his love.

When I was a child I couldn't have explained the first proof. As an adult it's still not easy because it could be mistaken for a kind of misty-eyed nostalgia. On the surface my proof is

Grandpa Frolander and me.

pretty simple: if someone who is powerful and strong also loves you, they can keep you safe in a storm, even one as terrifying as the one we encountered on a trip back from Kenora, Ontario. It was just an ordinary trip—Grandpa loaded cardboard cartons of canned vegetables and fruit into the boat and other supplies I don't remember. He went to the bank. We stopped at a clothing store and he picked out a pink and gray dress for me. I remember how beautiful it was, and how he had a special knack for picking the perfect colors. Leslie Sandy, one of the Indian guides, met us back at the dock and we started home with the launch weighed down, just the three of us.

Grandpa was watching the sky as we threaded our way through Devil's Gap and past some islands into more open water. I was always glad to be past the rocky cliffs with ancient petroglyphs painted by the Ojibway to curse enemies who passed that way. Clouds were boiling up out of the southwest, it was getting dark, and the water had turned slate gray with curls of white on the mounting waves. When the storm hit, rollers began pounding over the bow of the launch. Each slam flooded the deck with more water as Grandpa tried to make it to the lee of the next island. Above the howling wind and screaming engine I heard Grandpa shout to Leslie, "If we go under you take her, you're a better swimmer than me, and we'll head for that shore over there," then he turned back to the helm whistling a bar tune. I sat calmly on the high swivel seat beside him

Heading to Kenora in the launch.

and thought nothing of what he said. That's how I know he loved me. That I thought nothing. That the possibility of capsizing in a storm with him meant no more than taking a dive off the end of the dock on a sunny day.

The second proof of his love was that he taught me to fish and allowed me to wreck his very best open spinning reel, and he never mentioned it. Grandma did not approve of my learning to fish off the dock. Besides the fact that fishing was a questionable pursuit for a girl, there was the danger of my falling into twelve feet of water and drowning. Or I might put my eye out with a hook, she said. The latter was probably the most realistic of her worries since it took me a long time to get the hang of casting an orange Lazy Ike across the bay. I often forgot to release the line and ended a full-armed swing by slamming the tip of the rod into the water right at my feet. The danger was not so much to myself as to anyone fool enough to come within fifty feet of me. Which is probably why Grandpa always called out instructions from the screened-in porch where he sat drinking a Molson's Canadian on his afternoon break. Only once did I manage to hook my finger on the point of a lure. As for drowning, someone else, perhaps. But not I. I had perfected, not falling, but flying off the dock in the running broad jump and the cannonball. And when I did fall off the dock, it was backwards, and only because I had been fatally shot by an arrow shot off the top of the ridge opposite the dock.

To question the suitability of fishing for a girl seemed absurd. I loved everything about it: the smells of fish and water, the sun glancing off the surface, the lap of waves against the dock, the array of sinkers, leads, and lures in the tackle box. The zing of the line, the whir of the reel, and a distant plop as the lure landed precisely in front of cattails along the far shore. The alchemy of fishing is only partly explained by the setting: islands, shoreline, sand, rock, sky, and water. There are other elements of mystery and danger. What exists beneath the surface and what happens when you intentionally lure it? There is the paradox of wanting to know what this creature is, and yet the fear of what happens if you can't escape once you've caught it because you're stuck in a boat and the possibility of walking away doesn't exist? I now think of Jesus mounting the crests, coming up hills of water, crossing the waves to save his disciples, some of them seasoned fishermen who were scared witless. As a child, I knew that story well. Now I can look back and see that just as our dog, Bing, had led me toward God, fishing awakened another spiritual landscape in me—something about creation that was both heart-break beautiful and frightening, but layering over it was the hope that Jesus could, and perhaps would, come along to control and rescue when needed.

During those first fishing lessons it's a wonder Grandpa didn't despair over my witless, crude technique. If I

Proof. I caught the big one.

did remember to release the line, I often forgot to look down at the reel to make sure the line wasn't knotted before I reeled in. I'd begin winding with the drag on: click, click, click. Solid stop. I cranked hard, my rod bouncing up and down with the effort. Nothing. Only then would I look down and discover an enormous bird's nest of fishing line had grown over my entire wrist and hand.

Then one day I caught a legend. I had made a perfect cast across the bay when something hit my line hard and stopped it cold. At first I thought the shallow-runner had caught on a snag, but suddenly the line began to run out on its own. I couldn't stop the crank from turning. The reel was squealing, and the line kept going out. At last it entered the marrow of my bones, through my artless fingers—I had caught a big one and it was going to get away unless I figured out what to do. I was giving out little sobs as I turned one revolution on the reel only to have it counter with three in the opposite direction. Then, whatever was out there turned and took off across the lake, running away with my orange shallow-runner. Not knowing what else to do, I threw the rod on the dock, began to pull in the line hand over hand screaming for Grandpa. From his post on the porch he had to first run to the fish house for a net, and then down onto the dock, slap, slap, slap as the boards hit the water from his weight. He arrived laughing and hollering, "Don't let 'er go!" My hands stung from the wet line, and my eyes were full of tears from joy and I was hyper-ventilating, but I had finally pulled something up to the dock that was violently pitching and jerking my arms about. When Grandpa knelt down and grabbed it with the net, he landed a northern walleyed pike, or "jack-fish," as he called them. It was a fearful, slimy-looking creature with a jaw full of sharp teeth and a long lean body, but he was so beautiful. I have never since caught his equal, but I was hooked for life by my grandfather's patient love and the magic of fishing. An old photo shows me struggling to hold the fish up to my chin, and still, his tail dragged the ground. Later that day I heard Grandpa telling the tourists and guides who came back from fishing, "Why don't you take a look at what my granddaughter caught off the dock today. It's as big as she is." My catch was lying in state in a pine fish box on a bed of ice chips right on the waterfront. His round eye stilled glared back at anyone who dared peek into his coffin.

There was another paradox I pondered over the years. Grandpa was a man who so despised religion. He would not allow you to mention the word God or Jesus Christ in his presence unless it was a curse. And yet, he was the only man who thoroughly loved me through the summers, birthdays, and Christmases of my childhood. Even when I married, had children of my own, and moved to New Mexico, he and Grandma came to me and loved me. So how was it possible that God could use him to create some deep knowing and a predisposition that this is how God relates to his children? Years after childhood when I understood the connection, it came as a sudden revelation that took out my knees: from my birth, Grandpa prepared and preserved in me an unconscious recognition that this is how God is. Inscrutable and mysterious in his ways, God chooses his own instruments of healing and they aren't always saints. I simply bowed. By the time I understood this link from my grandfather to my early Christian trust in God as Father, it was too late to thank Grandpa. He had died.

The smell of fresh-cut lumber still channels him, and for a moment I think, could he be just around the corner squaring the door of a cabinet and laughing at the crooked nails I hammered into my pine board? The tinkle of ice in a glass of Coke and the tiny hissing sound of bubbles bursting on the surface some-times catches me by surprise—the vivid memory of my grandmother, resting for a moment as we sat on the porch and drank RC Cola in the afternoon sun while Grandpa drank his beer.

The first week of August 1947 was hot and humid. Pregnancy made the heat feel unbearable, so one afternoon Mom went back to the house, took off all her clothes and lay down to cool and rest on the bed. Keith was working in the fields. It's likely that he and his dad were putting up hay at that time of the year. Though it was her first summer away from the resort on the Lake, she had no doubts about being with Keith. She was drifting into sleep when she heard a knock at the door. A friend or a member of her husband's family would have called out to her, so it couldn't be one of them. Their small house couldn't be seen from the road, hidden as it was at the back of a field at the end of a long drive. No stranger

Mom at her HS graduation.

would just happen by. It had to be her husband, Keith, playing another joke on her. "Come in," she yelled. When he didn't enter, she decided to play a trick on him. She threw open the door to surprise him, and the Fuller Brush man took a step back and fell off the steps. Beautiful, teenage women, pregnant, but obviously deranged, were not part of his sales training. He turned and ran down the drive, his brushes and brooms clacking against his case. Mom screamed and slammed the door.

The next day was Sunday, August 3rd, their last morning together; they lay in bed, my father and my mother, his hand resting on her stomach, tracking my movements. Mom had begun to feel flutter kicks across her midsection. With an eerie kind of prescience, Mom told him a dream: Keith had climbed the stairs in his parents' home. He climbed higher and higher until at last he disappeared from sight. Mom stood at the bottom waiting, and then, weeping and calling for him. But he never answered or came back down. Keith also had a dream that night; he had gone to visit some buddies. Oddly, they were all friends who had been killed in the war.

Mom and my father had met the previous fall at a dance club called the Nite Hawk. He was just back from World War II, and Mom was a sixteen-year-old senior in high school determined to have fun even if Grandpa and Grandma didn't approve of what she did. She was singing with a dance band the first time

Keith and Mom's wedding day. (She is 17,
pregnant, and wearing her graduation dress.)

Keith saw her. As he watched her toss her auburn hair over her shoulder and bend toward the microphone, he announced to his friends, "I'm going to marry that girl."

Pictures of their courtship show them sunning on the beach, his head resting on her stomach. Kissing beside an enormous snow bank. Posing on the hood of his car. Her high school graduation picture gives no hint that she is already carrying me. Her figure is slender in a white linen dress. In June their marriage ceremony was quiet and earlier than planned. She wore the same white dress. Their faces still shine from faded wedding photos.

After the honeymoon they returned to make their home in a small house about half a mile from Keith's parents. It was nestled against the woods with a yard full of purple lilacs as tall as trees. Miles of forest stretched out behind, and in front were the fields where Keith and his father raised potatoes, wheat, and alfalfa. Each day after an early breakfast together they went to the Sorenson place, where Keith worked the farm with his father. Mom could have stayed home, but it was lonely spending long days by herself. So she went to her mother-in-law's, where the household was full of extended family and farm help. There was always plenty to be done. There were piles of laundry to fold and ironing to finish. The house always needed cleaning. Her mother-in-law, my Grandma Sorenson, had no interest in arranging her home, but she welcomed my mother's urge to rearrange furniture and rugs in a more pleasing way. My mother's years of experience under her own mother made cooking effortless, and being married gave it a surprising joy and purpose she hadn't known before.

Keith had joined the Army Air Force in 1943 to become a tail gunner of the biggest bombers that flew—the B-29 Flying Superfortress—and he was sent to the Pacific theater where the bombers' mission was to fly to Japan, drop the bombs, and head back to base on the tiny Pacific Island of Tinian.

Tail gunners reached their position in the globe at the end of the tail section by crawling through a long metal tube from the mid-section of the plane. There the gunner sat alone at the gun turret in his glass bubble, scanning the heavens for enemy fighter planes, hoping to shoot them down before they blew him out of the sky. The gunner could not move from his cramped position during the entire eighteen-hour flight to Japan and back. Worse than not moving was the stress of isolation. Radio silence was maintained, so there was no contact, not even with the crew up front, unless absolutely necessary.

Enemy fighters often targeted the tail gunner first, taking him out and attacking directly from behind. If their plane was hit, the tail gunner's chances of survival were slimmer than the rest of the crew—he had to crawl back through the long tube to the plane's mid-section before he could bail out. Years later my father's closest friend in the crew, Kenneth Hamilton, the left wing gunner, told me of one escape. Their B-29 had been attacked by Japanese fighter pilots, who first attacked the the tail gun. One fighter continued to pursue them—a couple hundred yards directly behind them and closing. It was a path that kept the wing gunners of the B-29 from firing at him. My father sat uninjured, amidst shattered glass, his pressurized flight suit keeping him alive at high altitude, his hands on a useless gun, watching the fighter get closer. He radioed the pilot to tell him his gun was out, a Zero was directly behind and closing, what should we do? The pilot yelled, "I don't know! Waggle your gun at him!" Listening to the exchange, Kenneth interrupted the pilot to scream, "Turn two degrees left! Turn! Turn!" The pilot turned and that instantly brought the fighter into Kenneth's gun sights.

Kenneth had to have been in his late seventies when he told me this story; his voice wavered, and I waited for him to say what happened to the fighter. To end it with something like, "And I blew that baby right out of the sky." But there was only a trailing-off sadness and silence as he remembered the scene. All he said was, "We made it back to base."

On each run to Japan at least one bomber didn't make it back. Some were shot down. Some experienced mechanical failure. But most were lost when they ditched in the ocean because they ran short of fuel. It wasn't that they couldn't carry enough to get there and back; it was because no one yet knew about the jet stream. Sometimes the force of flying against it burned up all the fuel reserves and there was nothing left to do but put the "Flying Superfortress" into the sea, hope to survive the landing, and if lucky, get picked up by an American destroyer.

There was a superstition among the men who flew: the more missions you survived the more likely your number was up. Keith's crew had made enough bombing runs to make them think they wouldn't return again. Each time his B-29 left the base, Keith prepared to die. When the atom bombs were dropped on Japan, the war was over for my father. He had survived twenty-four missions.

Still, Army Air Force soldiers faced another nightmare: drug addiction. The bombing runs were eighteen to twenty-four hours long, and just one moment of inattention by any member of the crew could be deadly. So the military issued amphetamines to keep men awake and alert. When the men who flew to Japan and back completed their tour of duty, they could not simply be discharged, given a medal, and told to go home and have a good day. They had to be detoxified. Quietly, the military sent them to recover at Rest Camps in the US. My father was one of the soldiers sent to "rest." It sounds nice. Like a little vacation before hitting civilian life.

As soon as Keith's feet hit solid ground in the United States, he swore he would never fly again. When he was finally released from the Camp, he took the train home. To many of the soldiers who made it safely back from war, being back home was both a miracle and a burden of sadness and guilt for having survived. Keith had come back to his land, his family, to partnership in the farm, and to find what Adam, the first man, called "flesh of my flesh"—my mother. He felt more than lucky. He felt blessed. But all he gave Mom about the war was that old soldier's saying, "There are no atheists in the foxholes."

On that day in August of 1947, Mom and my father dismissed bad dreams and savored a slow Sunday morning. Mom dressed and made them Swedish pancakes from one of Grandma Frolander's recipes. They talked about what to name me if I was a girl. A small plane flew over their clearing and dipped its wings when they ran outside to watch. The pilot circled close enough for them to recognize Stanley Gifford, a friend of Keith's from the war. He landed in a primitive airfield several miles away and a few minutes later, showed up at their door. "I'm heading back to Fargo this morning," he told them, "but I wanted to give Marge a ride first." He was a student pilot doing some solo practicing and not legally allowed to take passengers yet. He invited Mom to go with him because he knew of my father's resolve never to fly again. She was willing, but Keith said, "No. You're not taking her up until I find out what kind of pilot you are."

Together the three of them drove back to the airfield. Keith put on his red baseball cap, turned up the brim, and climbed into the cockpit. "We'll be right back," he yelled. The plane taxied past Mom and roared into the sky. She watched it gradually fade into the distance, a tiny humming insect. And then it was gone.

There was no shelter at the field—just a refueling tank and a storage shed. My mother waited by the car. Then she sat in the grass and looked for four-leaf clovers. Hours went by. She scanned the sky, listening for the engine to return. The sun moved to noon and past. It was getting hotter.

Finally, a car drove down the lane to the airfield and strangers got out. They were talking about an accident. They heard that a plane had crashed and that the pilot was okay, but the passenger was in pretty bad shape. He'd been taken to the hospital in Warroad.

Mom stood nearby, sickened by the rush of adrenaline, wondering what to do. A few moments later, one of Keith's brothers drove up to take her home and give her a message: "There's been an accident. Stanley's plane went down and Keith is on his way to the hospital. Bill Nordine took him in the school bus so they could lay him out flat. Nothing serious. Stanley's okay." Mom felt almost violent. She needed to be with Keith, but back at the house no one would take her to the hospital. It was thirty-six miles away. Everyone wished her to stay home. To wait. To be calm. When she ran outside to drive something, anything to the hospital, someone finally agreed to take her. She doesn't remember who.

My father, Keith Sorenson, 1943.

Witnesses who saw the accident said the plane flew in low over the Fuller farm. Barely above the treetops. There was a hot wind blowing, perhaps a downdraft caught it, they said. They watched a wing hit a guy cable on their hay shed and glance off the roof. The impact tore off a wing and a wheel. The plane continued on about four hundred feet over a small grove of ash trees, where it finally sank into the trees and plowed to the ground. The pilot escaped and began frantically trying to pull my father out. The gas tank above him had ruptured and high-octane fuel was pouring over his body.

My father was still alert and talking when he was laid on the ground nearby. Before he lost consciousness he had begun a journey back in time and was recounting boyhood memories as if they'd just happened.

By the time Mom arrived at the hospital Keith was in a deep coma. He had head and internal injuries. His face was swollen beyond recognition. His hands were limp in hers and he could not respond to her voice. The doctor was unavailable. He had taken the day off with his family—his first in many weeks. The nurse felt sorry about this, but assured her they would try to make her husband comfortable. Mom sat with him, holding his hand, willing him to stay alive. At 7:00 p.m. my father died. He was twenty-two. Mom was seventeen.

The memory of that first night is blacked out. Mom only remembers that someone watched her through the night to keep her safe. The next morning as

Keith's funeral. Mom in the background in same dress.

she walked out of the house, her throat constricted as if squeezed by a choke ring, and she fell on the step. Someone had left Keith's clothes, reeking of gasoline and stained with blood, in a pile beside the back porch.

The local newspaper in Williams, Minnesota, reported:

> Funeral services for Keith Sorenson, who served in the Army Air Force the greater part of the war and who returned unscathed after many missions as a tail gunner on a B-29 Superfortress operating out of Tinian over Japan, will be held at the Williams school auditorium at two o'clock this Thursday afternoon. Keith was, in fact, one of the clean, personable, and outstanding young men of the entire community and his tragic death comes as a great shock and an occasion for mourning by a multitude of friends. The sermon will be read by Rev. Fred Field of Baudette, who only last June 13 officiated at the wedding of Keith and Miss Margie L. Frolander of Warroad.

My mother attended the funeral in the white linen wedding dress with the wide-brimmed hat that shadowed her face. The dress was tight across her middle.

On December 15, 1947, four-and-a-half months later, I was born. The next day, a jeweler and his wife visited my mother at the hospital, bringing with them a tiny gold ring and a heart-shaped locket with a diamond set in the center. They were unable to have children and, knowing about the events of my mother's life, proposed to take me as their own. They offered my mother a chance to begin a new life. She was only seventeen. She had no job and only a high school education. How would she support me, they asked. Who would be my father? They could offer me everything she could not.

Mom looked at me. I was all she had left of her husband. She had already given me a name—her own. It was an unusual thing for a girl to be named after her mother, but my father had made her promise on that last morning they were together: If I was a girl, I, too, would be named Marjorie Lou. I still have that little jewel box—a reminder that though my mother could have left me the day after I was born, she didn't. My mother chose to keep me.

## Balm of Gilead Ointment

1 cup catkins *(the swollen buds of the poplar tree)*
1 cup petroleum jelly

Wear gloves and pick buds in the spring on a cold day. Place catkins and jelly in a large heavy kettle and heat until the mixture begins to foam up. Turn heat down and simmer until it stops foaming and begins to thicken. Strain through cheese cloth and pour into small jars.

# The Yellow Lady Slipper

Lake Agassiz was an ancient glacial lake of the Pleistocene
which covered much of present day Northern Minnesota,
Northeastern North Dakota, and Southern Manitoba. In Lake of
the Woods County it receded, leaving a pristine lake and two million
acres of wilderness, swamps, marshes, and peat bog between the
US and Canada. To some, the land might look uniform—a cold
cauldron of mud and water delivering up seasonal batches of
mosquitoes. Geologists help us define the differences for the
undiscerning eye. A swamp is lowland flooded seasonally and
dominated by trees. A marsh is wetland composed more of grasses.
And a bog supports a peculiar environment of sphagnum moss,
heath, and slowly decaying plant matter called peat,
all of which essentially float on water.

Our farm had fields cleared of timber and brush, pastures
with groves of poplar and birch, and a few acres of swamp filled
with a dense undergrowth of willow, hazel, and bracken. One spring
as I splashed through the brush looking for cowslips, I happened
upon one of North America's rare orchids: the delicate yellow
lady slipper, who is fond of keeping her feet wet. This delicate, slip-
per-shaped blossom is surrounded by variegated burgundy petals and
thrives in a hostile environment. She resists most attempts to
be tamed, so is rarely seen. When found, she causes you to stare:
such an elegant beauty in such an unexpected place.

# COME HOME

As my mother did housework she often sang hymns, her quiet soprano fading in and out as she moved through the three rooms of our house. There was one song I hated: "Softly and Tenderly." Maybe hate is not quite right. Maybe it is more accurate to say it gave me an anxious ache, like when your favorite dog is going to die and not even a veterinarian can save it.

*See on the portals he's waiting and watching. Come home, come ho-o-ome. Ye who are weary, come home. Softly and tenderly Jesus is calling, calling, O sinner, come home.* It works well in three-part harmony, and the "ho-o-ome" part can be bent and slid around until it, too, comes on home. I recently heard it sung in what was, to me, a strange modern context—the wedding ceremony. It was nicely done as a duet accompanied by guitar and cello—not your normal sentimental "There-is-Love" wedding fare. Although I kind of liked it, it still had the power to make me sad. I think this young couple was trying to say that as much as they desire to come home to one another and to their children, if they ever have them, the chances of making a Perfect-Home-That-Never-Fails are pretty slim. But they can't shed their longing for a place where they can lie down naked, unashamed, safe, and loved; we, beneath the protective layers of jaded culture and cynicism, long for it too. They meant, I think, to acknowledge Jesus, who promised that one day those deep longings will be granted in a way we hardly dare dream possible— he really is the Father, the Home-Keeper, who invites us in to stay with a warmth as strong as the scent of our mothers' cinnamon rolls fresh from the oven.

Back then, however, when Mom sang this haunting song as she kneaded bread dough, it made me think she was going to answer Jesus at any minute, and when she mused about having it sung at her funeral it confirmed my alarm. There had already been one parent's funeral and I hoped never to hear of another. She and I, and my little brother, Randy, and my stepfather lived in a shotgun house in Northern Minnesota with more babies on the way. I didn't want know what Jesus was talking about.

Mom inadvertently fed my fears one day when I was seven years old. It was noon, and she was making hot dogs for lunch and had sent me on an errand to the old granary where we kept our freezer. While I was gone she dropped a glass jar full of ketchup. It shattered and spread in a bright puddle across the floor. Looking at the red mess, she suddenly thought, "I can't let this go to waste!" and she lay face down beside it. When I returned all I saw was my mother dead from a head injury.

She sat up faster than I could stop screaming, instantly realizing how reckless her thought had been. Her apology and consolation were also instant, though it took me awhile to get over the terror. I have no reason to condemn her for this, or think I would have been wiser at her age because I played some pretty questionable jokes on my kids, too. Like releasing a garter snake under the bathroom door when my son was inside. Bad, I know. It's inevitable, after being the victim of a prank like that, you feel things you can't understand or voice as a child. I know I felt them—shame for being vulnerable to a trick, and anger because I fell so hard for it. Beneath it was the unbearable thought of losing her, and the apparent tenuous nature of life around me.

Mom had married again when I was eighteen months old, and soon after, my first brother, Randy, was born. Wally Block, her husband, had worked in the gold mines of Lead, South Dakota, for two years, saving for a down payment on the 160 acres of land where we now lived. It was close to where he grew up, and included a barn that could keep eight dairy cows, an old granary, a tiny milkhouse built over the well, a single-seat outhouse, and a three-room house. This was where our family grew from four to eight in less than six years. It was where Mom reconsidered her childhood decision to "have a lot of fun" before she took a serious look at the Christian faith.

The years of her late teens and twenties weren't full of the amusement and pleasure she'd dreamed of; rather, they'd become a crucible of suffering. Desiring forgiveness for her mistakes real or imagined, in need of comfort, and utterly spent in body and heart, she answered Jesus' call to the weary. The melody and words of "Softly and Tenderly" captured a reality she knew well, and she came home to Jesus, who understands how you can be so tired from your life you can't imagine taking another step, and can't think how to rectify things gone wrong. She found a deeper reason for hope, but that didn't mean she was taking off for the next life quite yet, but at the time I wasn't so sure.

My spiritual journey in the direction of home was not like my mother's. Hers was a sudden turning and more about being extruded into belief by her circumstances. Mine began when I was four years old—the age I first remember becoming aware of God. I loved him even then, and my answering has been a long walk in his direction, unfolding gradually through the years. That journey took me through a paradox that clung to my childhood home. How could it have held such happiness and yet filled me with dis-ease? How could I be both proud of it and ashamed? I couldn't wait to grow up and leave—but when I left, I missed something so desperately, I often went back looking for it. When I visited my family as an adult during college and the early years of marriage, Mom was overjoyed to see me, but Dad met me with familiar cold stares and snide comments.

Things can get twisted in your head—all the stuff children are hardwired to want in a father: strength, love, acceptance, protection. It's confusing when they're absent, like maybe you misread the cues and maybe they're there but you, you wretch, simply didn't deserve them and got passed over. There's no doubt Wally was a big, strong man who genuinely loved his wife and other children, which made it more confusing. I couldn't believe I was left out of the circle. I wanted to believe he was a gruff, tough farmer, yes, but also someone who deep-down loved me, and later, my husband and three children. It had to be my mistake, my misperception if he seemed cruel.

The truth is that the ground shifted when I was near him, and I became unsure of myself, tightening up, feeling little surges of adrenaline, and asking, Do I need to be running or fighting here? I couldn't have sorted this out alone, and I have others to thank for chipping away my pretense: my mother, my husband, and even my eight-year-old daughter, who once delivered such an insightful observation about how Dad treated us, it first made me angry, and then I cried. We were in the car on the eight-hour drive home to Rochester when she leaned over the back seat and asked, "How come Grandpa doesn't like us?" My immediate response was to defend him, "Oh, he does. It's just his way with kids. You know he's kind of crotchety." Everyone was silent. Then Denis said, gently, "No. He pushes our kids away, and they stand aside as he pulls the other grandchildren onto his lap to hold and kiss. Our kids stand nearby watching."

Now, years later, I see more clearly how—the farm, the geography, my family, neighbors, even my stepfather—gave both gifts and wounds. They led me to a richer, stronger love for all of life and to the confidence that I am cherished by a God who is, of all things, a faithful and loving Father to his children.

This may smell of rank cheese to those of us who are even a little jaundiced. I get it, because I was obviously tricked even by my own perceptions. Cynicism protects a person, keeps them safe from stupid desires that can't be fulfilled anyway. But here's another paradox I've accepted: although I'm suspicious of the happy ending, I'm also secretly very attracted to it. I want Spider-Man to rescue the girl tied to the tracks before the train kills her, I want Harry Potter to defeat Voldemort, and I want Gandalf to rise from the flaming pit, gorgeously alive again. I actually believe that in a most resplendent and cosmic sense—there is a story about real life that is true, that Jesus is at the vortex, that one day, as St. Julian of Norwich, the twelfth-century mystic, puts it: "All things will be well, and all manner of thing will be well."[1]

At the same time, I'd be a liar if I pretended the way home was either quick or easy.

———

It was a shotgun house. I heard Mom and my stepdad call it that when they described it to friends. When I asked what that meant, Wally said, "You call it a shotgun house because you can stand at the back door with a rifle and shoot straight south and out the front door without hitting a thing inside. Get it? The rooms are all in a row." I never quite understood. Had someone done this? Had someone *needed* to fire a gun through our house?

The house was old. Between the faded cedar shingles on the outside and the wallboard on the inside were hand-hewn virgin, tamarack logs. If our old log house had been the site of a pioneer gun battle, I reasoned, there might be guns hidden in the walls. Or buried in the cellar. Or quite possibly the attic. I told my brother this as we lay on the living room floor staring up at the square door-hole in the ceiling.

The three rooms of the house were all the same size. The back door opened into the kitchen, directly from the outside. No entry hall. No mudroom. In the corner by the door our boots, hats, and mittens were mounded into a cardboard box. Hooks on the wall held our coats. The east wall of the kitchen had a counter with open shelves above and below. Mom made curtains to hang in front of them. I remember the cotton fabric with dancing fruit and vegetables: long bananas and fat tomatoes with smiling faces and twiggy legs spun across the colorful fabric. These were post-WWII years when food was more abundant then it had been during the Great Depression and designers reminded consumers of this with dancing food on everything from cookie jars to dress fabric. Against the opposite wall, our bright yellow, Formica and chrome table was folded into a small rectangle. For every meal it was pushed to the middle of the room and opened up so we could squeeze the matching chairs around it. This was the only hint that we lived in the 1950s; the rest of the kitchen offered no evidence of modernity. The five-gallon Red Wing crock of drinking water on the counter with its tin dipper hanging on the lip, the enormous wood cookstove with upper warming ovens, and the slop bucket for kitchen scraps and bathroom emergencies made you think of a much earlier time. Or of poverty, which it was, in our case.

Shotgun House 1963. We moved here the spring of 1954.

If you walked seven normal steps straight from the back door and through the kitchen you arrived at the doorway to the living room. The wood stove that heated the house dominated that room from where it sat along the inside wall. A few pieces of worn furniture crowded the remaining walls. Conversation with company was not possible here. If you sat on the couch, you couldn't see the person sitting in the rocking chair opposite unless you leaned to one side or the other to look around the stove—which was why Mom invited most visitors to sit at the kitchen table where she could serve coffee and offer them whatever confection she pulled out of the oven that day. She baked cakes, pies, sweet rolls, and cookies as easily as one could lay down money at a bakery. At the kitchen table, everyone could look at one another without neck strain, and Dad could keep an eye on the yard to make sure we kids weren't breaking hay bales in the stack, draining the gas out of the tractor, or strolling about the pasture in a new pair of slippers, which may be why I only ever had that one pair.

The living room also had the only closet in the house. Uncle Peter, a carpenter, built this as a gift for Mom because she was desperate for storage. It jutted into the room, taking up more precious space, but it hid hanging clothes and Sunday shoes for eight people. The closet was a place I knew well since cleaning it was my chore from about as far back as I could remember. In Mom's ongoing battle against chaos and dirt, every Saturday I was assigned to scramble in under the clothing to re-hang anything that had fallen, pick up dirty clothes, sweep out the floor with a whisk broom, and rearrange the shoes. I hated the job, but once in a while it yielded an unexpected advantage. There were few hiding places in our house, but here behind the curtained doorway, in the dark, I sometimes found things hidden or forgotten: a roll of unexploded pistol caps for Randy's gun. A Rudolph the Red-Nosed Reindeer coloring book. A tiny plastic purse with pennies inside. Once, I reached behind Dad's

Wellingtons and found a dead bat.

If you continued walking through our house, seven more normal steps took you through the living room to the bedroom doorway. This room had the most windows, facing south, east, and west. Mom liked it when the sun streamed into the bedroom during all seasons of the year. There was little need for curtains on the windows; privacy from the outside wasn't an issue; hardly anyone drove by our house at night. Privacy inside was another matter. It didn't exist. Nevertheless, when Grandma Frolander redecorated her own bedroom in town, she gave Mom her old white-lace curtains and swags. They lent an elegant, airy look to our bedroom with their ruffles and criss-crossy lines. Mom and Dad's bed never changed position throughout the years, but in a maelstrom around it, she pushed a series of cribs, bunkbeds, bassinets, and the three-quarter bed, ever searching for a more pleasant arrangement. She never gave it a rest, even though fitting eight people into this tiny space was quixotic. Even so, I loved the surprise of coming home to find the bed I shared with one or two siblings in a different spot. I'm certain her love for changing a room was passed down to me—that small joy that comes of regularly shifting furniture and thinking it grants new perspective on life.

Another set of seven steps brought you across the bedroom to the front door, which was rarely used, and then right onto the cement blocks that stepped down to the yard.

The reason I know it was "seven normal steps" is because I babysat whenever Mom and Dad went out visiting in the evening, which was several evenings a week from the time I was … I've tried to reconstruct how old I must have been when I began taking care of the children alone. I remember changing Rex and Dallas' dirty diapers when Mom was gone—they were eleven months apart—and how much I hated it. Roxanne was my youngest sibling and I'm only nine and a half years older than she is. So if they were babies, then, I was between the ages of seven and eight when I started. Anyway, the reason I know about the "seven steps" is because one of the games we played was "Captain, May I," and that's how many steps it took to cross a room. We started at the back door with one of us playing The Captain, who granted step requests. It took three giant steps, twenty baby steps, or one major sneak, to make it from one doorway to the next. As we got older and more of us participated, this game included a lot of yelling and some battles when congestion built up in the doorways. The Captain stood on the couch to keep an eye on cheaters and to have the advantage of height when hurling herself upon those who refused to go back to the beginning when caught.

Perhaps the most alarming thing about the house was the trap door in the middle of the kitchen floor. The door hid a hole that dropped into a dirt cellar that held all the bounty of sunshine and summer—enough food to keep us through fall and winter. But it also held enough darkness to spook a traveling evangelist.

The trap door blended in with the linoleum floor, and you wouldn't have noticed except for the black iron ring in one end that allowed you to lift it out and set it aside when you needed to go down. That required you to lie on your stomach and scoot backwards as you offered your soul to God, then dangle your legs into darkness and swing your feet forward feeling for the shelf-edge below. With one foot on the shelf, you then lowered yourself until you could place the other foot on the dirt floor. Mom considered this a simple enough chore for any child over three feet ten inches. As long as she was cooking supper right above me waiting for her order to be handed up, I could get safely down there and back up again in about twenty seconds.

As well as a place to store food, this hole in the ground beneath our house served as a spot for the foundation jack that sat on a wooden block and kept our house from sinking into the swampy ground. The shelves were crude, just two-by-twelve planks laid out on dirt ledges and several boards on the floor to keep you from losing a shoe in the mud. It had a dank, earthy smell and the darkness was hardly penetrated by the dim light that filtered through the hole above. Every spring when the snow melted and the groundwater rose to the surface of the land, our cellar filled to the bottom of the kitchen floor.

In the fall, when Mom was done canning and everything was preserved, there were rows and rows of quart Mason jars filled with the harvest of the garden and woods: blueberries, apricots, raspberries, tomatoes, corn, green beans, peas, pumpkin, strawberry jam, sweet pickles, dill pickles, bread and butter pickles, sauerkraut, choke cherry jelly, and canned venison. Carrots and potatoes were stored in gunnysacks. Squash and onions filled the baskets.

By March, the carrots were gone, the onions were shriveled, and the potatoes were enough to startle the dullest imagination. They grew long, pale, white suckers that curled through the gunnysacks and advanced along the floor toward the trap door, hungry for sunlight and unwary children.

In April and May, when the water came up, whatever remained of my mother's bounty floated past the hole in the floor and on into the darkness. Then we lay on our stomachs with a broom handle, stabbing the black water, and trying to grab whatever jars drifted by. I was pretty certain that the bottom dropped out of the cellar when the water rose, and what we saw under our kitchen was a bottomless pit: an ancient graveyard where previous owners had buried their dead, or drowned their victims. During the day I always walked around the trap door, and at night I sometimes lay in bed and worried about the black hole beneath us.

The spring of 1951, the year we moved in, was one of the wettest on record. Day after day it rained, and the water table, which was naturally high anyway, rose to the surface of the earth to blend with snowmelt and rain, until parts of the county looked like a vast inland sea. My world was limited to looking out the window at the yard between the house and barn. I watched the cows splash through pools of water on their way to the stock tank, and I saw Bing getting his white coat filthy every time he went out for hole-digging and other doggy business. On warm, sunny days Randy and I were allowed to run a race course on the loose flax-straw banking that had been piled high against the foundation of the house to serve as insulation through the winter. Joyously we ran round and round like gerbils chasing one another; occasionally we slipped off and sank to our ankles in water and icy mud.

Over the years, most arable land in the county had been cleared, drained, and reclaimed from the swamp. When the weather was dry, farmers tended to forget this. They came to expect that each year they would be able to get into their fields to plant and harvest. During wet years, like 1951, fields sat like giant reflecting ponds. Some impatient farmers mired their machines so deep in mud a few of the farmers simply walked away never to return, while migrating ducks on their way to nests in northern Canada happily changed their minds and stayed to raise families.

The original settlers to this part of northern Minnesota arrived in the early 1900s during times of terrible drought in the West. They migrated from the south and the west, escaping the hot prairies where year after year of parched, locust-eaten land had finally defeated them. Northern Minnesota was also having a drought, but the deceit of nature had turned it to a temporary paradise. It was no longer two million acres of swamp and bog land, but fertile green meadows stretching between virgin forests of tamarack and cedar. Situated on the border between Canada and the US, it also contained one of the world's largest freshwater lakes—Lake of the Woods. The Ojibwa word "Minnesota" means "Land of the Sky Blue Waters," and this lake was the template for the state's ten thousand other lakes. Sixty miles wide and seventy miles long, it is dotted with more than fourteen thousand islands. It brimmed with wildlife and teemed with fish: walleyed pike, perch, sauger, and sturgeon. And for those who'd rather swim than fish, it had, some said, the finest white sand beaches in the state.

The year we arrived, nature simply did what it had randomly done for centuries: revert the land to swamp. Regrettably for us, our house and barn were built on the lowest point in all the 160 acres. When our eight black and white

Holstein dairy cows stepped out the door and off the barn's cement foundation, they sank to their bellies in mud and water. Twice a day, after the morning and evening milking, they dragged themselves and their enormous udders through the muck from the barn to the pasture where they searched for a blade of dry grass. It looked as if our barnyard and fields were trying to become another of Minnesota's ten thousand lakes. Even more distressing to me, it seemed as though all the excess water that drained across our farm, our county, and perhaps the world was flowing into the cellar under our house and, loosed from its moorings, we were about to float like a Noah's ark.

You might think that with all the standing water cows wouldn't need to drink from the stock tank, but that's not true. So, because of the flooding, the cows' path to the tank was re-routed through the yard, and I failed my first lesson in farm life: pay attention to the details or you'll get hurt. Dad temporarily strung one strand of barbed wire from the front door of the barn across our backyard to the stock tank, which sat just outside the milkhouse. It passed within a few feet of the house.

One fine morning in April, Mom surprised me by bringing out a new Easter dress to try on. It was a rare and exciting occasion, and after she tied the big pink bow in the back, she suggested I run out to the barn to show Dad how pretty I looked. I pulled on rubber boots and ran toward the barn, carefully looking down, trying to avoid puddles and holes. Forgetting about the new fence—which was exactly the height of my nose—I ran smack into it. I went right back to the house crying. Mom comforted me, dabbed at the scratch on my face, and sent me out again with a warning to be more careful, and I ran into it again. The third time I cautiously approached the fence, ducked under, and was so proud of remembering, I ran back to tell Mom. That time I hit it hard enough to leave a scar that now lies hidden in a crease on my face. The next time I finally got it right, but I could see my mother was amused that it had taken three hits. It was Dad who recounted the story to each neighbor who stopped by, laughing uproariously each time.

When I heard him tell it, I ducked into the corner, ashamed of being so dull-witted.

Karl Jung, the psychoanalyst, liked to rightly point out we learn nothing from our successes and everything from our mistakes. So the lesson wasn't wasted; I began to pay attention. I became a watchful and determined child; I'd win this man's praise with work. It was already a tormenting little seed in me, my desire to please whatever it cost. All it needed was a little watering to grow—something like the potato plant whose leaves are poisonous to eat, but at the end of the season, in the dark earth beneath, you find that all along it was busy making food for whoever was wise enough to dig it up.

From the earliest years of life when memory is just beginning to function and your brain slowly gathers a few files until, faster and faster, more and more, the numbers rise like a graph at a 45-degree angle. At first there were only fragments of barn and cows, the penetrating scent of manure and hanging around Dad as he did the evening chores. I was fascinated by cows even though they could hurt children, mostly by accident. Cows can purposely switch their tails in your eye. They kick at flies. They step heavily on your toes, which is excruciating, and they are not moved by your cries of pain or your efforts to push them off. On the other hand, cows have attractive eyes with long lashes. They magically make milk. Their calves are gangly, and cry maaa-maaa like a baby. Their sticky tongues lick hair round and round leaving it in circles just like Randy's cowlick that Mom oiled down with Brylcreem before we went to town. They are more intelligent than you might think; when they were let into the barn each one went without being told to her own place—a stanchion where she was latched in. They never made a mistake, and they didn't run into fences, either.

They had names and individual personalities. Betty was long-legged and nervous. Eddie was a good mother, easy-going, and always led the rest to and from the pasture. Red was a shorthorn mix, small and round, who always broke out of the fence when she was going to calve, and headed for the woods on the north end of the farm. Most of them were named after Dad's old girlfriends, which made Mom laugh. She was never a jealous person, but it's possible having a cow named after you wasn't much of a compliment anyway. In the summertime the cows were turned out between milkings to feed in the pasture, but in the winter they were kept inside where they ate hay and ground oats, chewed their cuds, and stayed warm.

I carefully observed as Dad washed their udders and inspected their teats. This was important especially when the mix of mud and manure was one to two feet deep in the barnyard. Tender spots and sores were gently rubbed with Bag Balm. This salve was not limited to cows; Bag Balm was the farm family's secret remedy for everything from infected cuts to chapped lips. As a teenager I was embarrassed to admit I knew what it was, but some people still swear by it.

Although we had dairy cows, we couldn't sell the milk. That required being classified as a "Grade A" dairy by the US Department of Agriculture, which would have taken many more cows and an array of stainless steel holding tanks, coolers, and other equipment Dad couldn't afford.

Until the late 1960s small dairy farmers had another option: a farmer didn't need to be "Grade A" to sell the cream—every small town in rural America had a creamery where butter was made locally. Farmers separated the milk from the cream and hauled it to town in five or ten-gallon stainless steel cans to receive cash. (The folksy, painted cream cans with padded lids I occasionally see at garage sales actually had a practical use at one time.) So, when milking was over the buckets of warm milk were carried to the milkhouse where Mom or Dad poured the milk through a filter into a stainless steel basin on top of the cream separator. As it drained, the milk was spun through a centrifuge with a series of cone-shaped discs that separated the milk from the cream. The liquid came out two spouts: one stream was skim milk, the other poured a current of pure, thick cream.

Sweet cream brought a higher price and made the best butter, so Mom was careful to keep the cans clean and the cream as cool as possible to prevent it from souring. The concrete floors and cold water from the well kept our milkhouse cool even on the hottest days of summer, but controlling the bacteria that soured milk was still a constant battle, which meant scrubbing the milking machine, pails, and cream separator every day of the year.

Twice a week, Mom made the trip to town, the trunk of the car weighed down with cans of cream. At peak production, eight cows could give as much as fifteen gallons of cream a week. A five-gallon can of cream was worth seven or eight dollars, which was money to buy groceries.

From the enormous quantities of milk the cows gave, we kept what we needed to drink. We didn't like store-bought pasteurized milk from bottles and cartons. Unlike our fresh, raw milk, it tasted strange—like processed cardboard and chemicals. The rest of the milk was fed back to the calves, who loved it so much they would thrust their noses deep into a bucket of frothy milk and drink with great, heaving gulps.

We also kept some of the cream for our own use. Mixed with brown sugar, it topped our hot cereal at breakfast, imparting a rich, glorious taste. It was whipped and mounded on top of angel food cakes, chocolate puddings, and berry pies. It stuffed cream puffs and éclairs, spilling out the edges and holes, and it gave coffee a rich, buff color. The recipe for chocolate fudge, perfected by Mom and passed down to each of us, requires one cup of thick sweet cream. Even as children, any one of us, boys included, could boil up a batch of fudge in a cast-iron skillet, cool it in the snow, and then beat it to perfection at a moment's notice. We poured it on a buttered platter just before it set, then cut it into generous squares. The fudge was always gone by bedtime.

I relentlessly pestered Dad to let me help him with the chores, and by the time I was six, I was opening barn doors, turning the pump on to fill the stock tank, and pushing hay bales through the haymow door. I was a perfect eldest child, fitting the stereotype: serious about responsibilities, obedient, and eager to please.

I enjoyed all the little things I did and fancied they were important, but there was a more obscure reason behind my eagerness to help: I wanted my stepdad to fall in love with me. In the end, I didn't win him, and the roots of this rejection penetrated my heart. Whether I thought consciously about it or not, it was going to affect the way I related to anyone important, but most especially God.

While courting my stepfather, an unexpected grace grew in my heart: I was the one who fell, headlong, for the world around me. The land and its wildlife, the long summer days, the cold winters with glittering nights, the shaggy cows and horses, the frozen lake where some years we could skate for miles on ice so smooth and clear we could see the bottom many feet below, the sing-songy accents of Minnesota speech—all became a part of what I loved, who I was, who I am. Work that made sweat and hard muscles, even work that had to be done over and over again, like stacking the woodpile and cutting weeds along the fence line, had a sweetness to it. I loved the daily ritual of feeding a crowd of chickens who waited eagerly for you to dump their oats and mash into the feeders, of gathering eggs so fresh they were still warm in your cupped hand, of throwing slabs of hay over the fence to the horses who nickered to you as they watched. If you take care of animals day after day, see to their well-being, they will change you. You think you are beginning to love them, but in reality they are teaching you to love yourself and your place in the world.

Over the years our farm didn't make enough money to support us, so Dad took on seasonal work. In the winter, he worked in the woods cutting pulp to sell to the paper mill in International Falls. Day after day in sub-zero temperatures, he and a partner cut down trees with a chain saw, skidded the logs through deep snow, and, by hand, stacked cord after cord of pulp wood on the back of a truck, to be hauled to a flat-bed train car parked on a siding in the little town of Williams.

That was when I first learned to love coffee. When Dad came home in the late afternoon he would return the metal lunch box Mom packed for him every day. Randy and I would scavenge it like crows to see if he'd left half a venison and mustard sandwich or some peanut butter cookie crumbs. Then we unsnapped the thermos from the inner lid and drained the last of the coffee into the little red cup that screwed on the top. Those last swallows of lukewarm liquid, heavily laced with cream and sugar, began my lifelong addiction.

In summer Dad often worked on a road-building crew. There were always road projects somewhere in the county or surrounding area. He worked huge draglines, Caterpillars, and dump trucks with the same ease he had worked horses as a boy. His natural ability to organize and oversee a project often led to a foreman's position with a little higher pay. One year he accepted a foreman's job on a project that took him too far away to come home at night. He worked five days and stayed in a motel each night. This lasted for one week. He came home Friday night and the following Monday morning he quit. I don't think he missed us kids much, but he couldn't stand being away from Mom. He said to her, "I'd rather be poor and with you than away from you and rich." For a long time I didn't know we were poor; I thought only the exceptionally rich had indoor plumbing and separate bedrooms for children.

As we grew older, chores were not voluntary; they were a requirement for all of us kids. In summer the garden was weeded and harvested. The lawn needed to be mowed. Wood was split and carried from the woodpile to the house. The kitchen slop bucket needed to be carried across the road and dumped in the ditch. That was the worst chore because it stank, and the heavy weight of it banged and sloshed against your legs as you labored up the driveway. We had to haul water in from the well and collect eggs from the chicken house. The barn was cleaned every day in the winter. In the evening, Dad was not always home in time to begin the barn chores, so when Randy and I were ages seven and nine, we started them and Mom or Dad finished up.

Since the temperatures never rose above freezing during the winter months, the first thing we had to do in the late afternoon was start a fire in the wood-burning heater, which was inserted into the stock tank every fall. Each day the fire melted the ice long enough for new water to be pumped in for the livestock to drink. Randy was inspired by fire starting, since it involved throwing kerosene on the wood in the heater, and, if done right, it created a muffled ka-boom and shot flames out the chimney. While he did that, I went to the barn to let the cows out for exercise and a drink of water, and began pitching manure from the gutter into the wheelbarrow.

Cows produce milk and shit in about equal quantities, although we never called it that around our parents. No matter how far I've moved from the pungent aroma of cow pies and bullshit, the smallest whiff that randomly wafts through the car's air conditioner on a summer's day as we pass a farm can remind me of where I came from. Randy and I sang a little rhyme about it as we worked in the barn—after all, singing has always lightened the load for laborers and this little ditty made us laugh because we understood the punchline:

> Shave and a haircut, six bits.
> Water off a duck's back, quack-quack.
> Shit in a barnyard, knee deep.

In the winter, the frozen pasture made it a little easier to push a wheelbarrow of steaming manure out the back door and across to the pile. Manure couldn't just be hauled out and dumped anywhere, it had to be piled neatly—not to be tidy, but to save it. Manure was an asset. Ours sat in a huge mound for a year or so as it decomposed and cured, but it lost none of its earthy attraction. Every dog we owned, even Duffy, our elegant collie, found it impossible to resist and ecstatically rolled in it about once a week. In the spring it was hauled out to the fields and scattered as fertilizer.

On wet days, getting to the manure pile with the wheelbarrow required a civil engineering degree, which none of us had. A path made of planks laid end to end across the mud served as a causeway. My method was to start off at a good clip, keeping that single wheel precisely centered on the board, roll over the bumps, and still have enough momentum on the last little rise to capsize the load onto the pile in a final heave-ho.

Some things naturally worked against this, like the planks, which were often slick with a kind of greenish-brown algae. A tiny misstep was fatal. Stepping off the side to keep my balance might keep me from falling, but it almost certainly meant the muck would suck my boot off as I lunged for the next solid purchase on the board. Trying to reinsert my stocking foot into a buried boot was very nearly impossible. Hopping on the board with one foot, balancing the wheelbarrow with one hand, and grabbing my boot with the other was even more demanding than ducking under a barbed-wire fence. You had to know which piece to sacrifice, and I was never good at chess.

Worse than losing a boot was running the whole load off the planks and getting the wheelbarrow stuck in the mire. The barrow would be too heavy to drag out, and stepping off the planks to heave it back meant I would be leaving both boots behind, dancing on the board with sopping socks. These were moments when I had no such lofty notions of working to please anyone, and I hated every doe-eyed animal, and every forkful of piss-filled, liquefied straw they created. I was poor, dear Cinderella forced to work on this farm, thinking bloody anarchy and vengeance. Let the Soviets come. This was the real Cold War. Blowing up the whole damn farm with an A-bomb would be too good for it.

However, there was one gratifying thing that sprang from the muck in the barnyard. It was our moment of sweet revenge on kids who grew up privileged, ignorant, and in town. It had to do with the haymow, which is that soaring second story of the barn where a farmer stores as much of the first cutting of hay as can possibly be hauled up there.

The haymow was a favorite place to play. To get there from inside the barn, we climbed up the ladder rungs nailed to studs in the wall. They took us up to and through a hole in the floor of the haymow. Dad often yelled up at us to "STAY OFF THE HAY BALES, YOU'LL BUST 'EM UP." Right. He rarely climbed the ladder to actually see what was going on. Depending on how we arranged the bales, the haymow was our playhouse, our fort, our jail, or our castle. We corralled the kittens hidden under loose hay and pretended they were our babies. We ate picnic lunches in fancy restaurants as if we had ever been to one. As pioneers we slept there in covered wagons. We flipped off the highest stack and landed in a soft pile of broken bales just like Tarzan.

Once my brother misjudged a landing. He did a fancy somersault that sent him through the door-hole into the barn below where he landed on a cement manger and had the breath knocked out of him and a near-death experience— at least that's what he said. I didn't feel sorry for him, thinking a person gets what he deserves when he's showing off. When the same thing happened to me, it was different. I was developing an important skill and could have been fatally injured when I landed on a pitchfork that went through my tennis shoe and into my foot. The handle flew up and hit me in the head besides. I'd only understand how lucky I was years later when we visited the Mayo Medical museum to view real-life models of actual farm accidents treated at the clinic. The one that evoked the loudest cries and caused viewers to clutch their butts was the one of a farmer who'd jumped down from a hay wagon and landed on a pitchfork handle that was driven up his rectum. You see what I mean.

High above the ground there were two large doors that opened to the outside at either end of the haymow. You could stand with your toes on the edge and get so dizzy looking down from such great height you might just accidentally fall. Barns were designed so that loaded hay wagons could pull up from the yard-side, and Dad, and whoever was helping could place the hay bales on a convey-or belt that lifted them up through the haymow door where they were neatly stacked and stored for winter. What didn't fit into the haymow was stacked out-side, and the top of the haystack was covered with loose hay to protect the bales from the weather. At the other end of the haymow, the door opened out onto the pasture side. From there, as needed, hay could be thrown down to the ground in the winter and eaten by the outdoor livestock—steers that were sold to a lo-cal locker plant for butchering, young heifers that might replace an aging milk cow or be sold at market, and whatever horses we might own. At feeding time, without fail, they gathered in a circle below, faces upturned, expectant, hungry.

Day after day, leftover hay accumulated in soft mounds on top of snow, cow pies, and frozen mud. When temperatures rose in the spring, a knee-deep, pun-gent soup brewed beneath the surface hay. Looking out the door from above you'd never guess what was a hidden under that layer.

Since jumping from high places was a passion for Randy and me, we learned to jump out the yard side of the haymow onto a giant pile of loose hay. No prob-lem. It was the closest thing to flying. When friends or city cousins who didn't know better came to visit, we would take them there for a jumping demonstra-tion. I must have been about ten years old when we first thought of this: in order to tempt them into making a scary, exhilarating, 12-foot jump, we would soar out the yard-side door, models of such courage and fun. When they hesitated, we would take them to the other end of the haymow—to the pasture side. There, as we looked down together on the loose hay, we convinced them that this was the softer side: the safer side. The place for beginners. Randy and I would have liked to help them take this leap of faith, but we never actually touched them, so we could honestly say it was their choice to jump.

The splat of their landing was so spectacular and hilarious, we were temporarily unable to breathe. The kiss of death for the unfortunate kid was when he not only sank to his knees, but bent at the waist in order to cushion the fall with his arms. This deception had one disadvantage: it strained their willingness to play with us for the rest of the day.

Once the gutters in the barn were cleaned, the worst was over, and I pretended we were preparing for guests—bright yellow straw was spread over the floor making fresh beds, ground oats were doled out in individual servings, and the mangers filled with slabs of sweet alfalfa hay. When Randy and I opened the back barn door and called "ka-boss, ka-boss," the cows eagerly came, heading straight for their own stanchions, and we hooked them in. They ate with enthusiasm, licking up the tiniest bits of grain before starting on the hay. Tugging 60-pound hay bales, dragging the sack of feed from the granary, and even cleaning the gutters was worth it. A small thing, I thought, not big-important like being president or captain of the hockey team, but their contentment gave me a sense of pleasure. I had done something good. I'd made cows happy, and I might make Dad happy, too. The cows were now ready to milk.

Often, he arrived at the barn crabby—he must have been tired at the end of the day. But there I'd be, waiting expectantly for him to see that we'd spread the straw properly under the cows and fed each of them the right amount of ground feed. What I mostly remember is the disappointment of having failed, having forgotten to hang up the bale twine after opening the bales or having left the pump running so the tank was overflowing, and of him yelling we were meatheads and numbskulls.

When the evening milking was done, the cows would lie down on their beds of clean straw, chewing their cuds, eyes at half-mast. Our barn cats took advantage of these placid creatures. On nights when it was thirty-below outside, we would find the calicos napping on top of a cow's belly, gently rising and falling with the rhythm of her breathing.

Sometimes the winter moon was so bright it cast sharp shadows across the snow banks. Before we went in for supper, we'd say, "C'mon, Dad, play us a little hockey. Please." And with old brooms and broken hockey sticks we found at school, he would join us to play a little hockey on the ice rink we made behind the milkhouse. Us against him, pushing, shoving, and laughing, until we heard Mom calling us to supper through the darkness, "It's time to eat! Come and get it before I throw it out!"

It was almost enough to answer her call. Her love was almost enough to cover the chronic anxiety and doubts I had about Dad. She made me feel right with the world—appreciated, acceptable. I worked hard for her, too, but for an altogether different reason. When I cleaned the house, washed diapers, weeded the garden it was because I wanted to lift a corner of the load she carried. Sometimes when she was sick or her back was so painful she couldn't get up, I feared she might die if someone didn't help her.

I thought the richness of the experience—growing up where I did, when I did, with my mother—could compensate for Dad's cynical scrutiny and harsh discipline. I grew up, married, had children of my own, and established a home that welcomed other wanderers, and I still returned expecting a welcome from him. *This time, it'll be better; this time you'll find a father who's been there all along, you were just too blind to see it*—so I told myself.

Not too many years ago I saw a delightfully quirky movie with a great soundtrack called *Garden State*. It's still one of my favorites, maybe because Zach Braff, who wrote and directed it, and also starred as "Large," the main character), posed the questions I should have been facing when I was his age. With poignancy and ironic wit he asks Sam, the girl he's falling in love with, if there was a moment when she realized the place where she grew up was no longer home, which would make her wonder if it ever really was home. He says, "you get homesick for a place that never really existed, and then you create your own idea of home. Maybe family is a group of people who miss the same imaginary place."

I was astonished to see, passing before my eyes in surround sound and huge cinematic frames, the big question that I had taken so long to face. I was a young mother in my thirties before I finally began to admit that my longing for home to be the place where both a mother and a father welcomed me as their own was only that. Wishful thinking.

## Chocolate Cream Fudge

2 cups sugar
6 tbsp cocoa
1 cup thick sweet cream
1 tsp vanilla

Mix sugar and cocoa in a 10-inch cast-iron skillet. Stir in cream. Stir over medium heat until sugar is dissolved and it comes to a boil. Gently boil without stirring until it reaches the soft ball* stage. Remove from heat and set outside in the snow for ten minutes. Beat with a wooden spoon until it is smooth and silky. When it begins to thicken and set, pour onto a buttered platter. Cut in squares.

*Soft ball stage is when a half teaspoon of the boiling mixture forms a soft ball between your finger and thumb when dropped into a glass of ice water.

# Wild Chokecherries

In northern Minnesota wild chokecherry bushes grow along the edges of fields and among the brushes of woodland openings. They commonly reach a height of twelve to fifteen feet with the main trunk rarely more than four inches in diameter. The fruit itself is no larger than the tip of my thumb and its pit takes up most of the inside. In midsummer they become bright crimson clusters hanging from branches you can bend toward the ground. Every year I ate a chokecherry at this immature stage. It was a mystery why something so attractive should taste so unpleasant. When fully ripe they were a dusky purple, almost black, and didn't taste much better. Still, I could not resist them. Their astringent flavor flooded my mouth to the back of my throat, shriveling my tongue, and puckering my taste buds. Their bitterness made my teeth squeak and I clawed at my tongue. Anything that touched chokecherries—fingers, lips, clothing—was stained a deep violet. In August, Mom and I picked them, popping chokecherries off into buckets, pulling clusters, stripping branches bare. At home we sorted them just enough to remove leaves and twigs. Then Mom boiled them in a large pot, strained the juice through old dish-towels, added sugar and fruit pectin, and boiled it down to a sweet, jewel-toned pancake syrup or thickened it for jelly. It was by far our favorite topping for toast and Swedish pancakes.

# LIKE A GOOD NEIGHBOR

"If you don't like it here you can pack your bags and get on down the road to the Beckers. See how you like living with them."

When Dad said that it sobered us right up. I left the kitchen angry, but was careful not to slam the screen door. I had no doubt our neighbors, Billy and Lorraine Becker, would take us in. They were just that way and they probably wouldn't even notice the addition to their family, but that wasn't even a remote temptation.

A spanking from Dad—for such things as starting up the Minneapolis Moline tractor when Randy was five and I was seven, throwing hens up on the chicken house roof to see if they could fly, or back-talk—made us feel particularly persecuted. When he said, "Go get the belt," we never dared say, "Go get it yourself!" Obediently, we brought him the razor strop that was kept in the magazine rack in the living room and handed it to him. "Turn around!" he commanded. Then, grasping us by the shoulder in one hand, he would strike us with the other. Arching your back and hopping in a circle only made him more determined to teach you a lesson.

At one time the strop had belonged to a barber who used it to keep the edge keen on the blades of his straight razors. It was a pair of wide leather straps about two feet long, four inches wide, and bound together at one end. In its new life as an instrument of discipline, having two straps was better than one. When Dad hit us they also hit each other, doubling the sound with a resounding crack. Because we were sent to get the belt and needed to return to wherever Dad was waiting, which could be anywhere on our 160 acres depending on where the infraction was discovered—it gave us time to consider. Not repentance, but how to lessen the pain of punishment and whether now would be a good time to run away. My usual strategy was to "take it like a man" and cry only enough to let Dad know how badly it hurt. If you didn't cry a little he didn't think the message was getting through and waled harder. I admired Randy, who once dared to stick a copy of *Successful Farming* in the seat of his pants. We thought it could work, but right away Dad noticed the outline when the first whack gave an odd crackling sound. Randy got it worse than usual. And since I'd helped him get it in place, I got a licking also.

The boys really caught it hard from Dad. I can't remember exactly all they did to deserve it. I think it was being lazy, fighting, neglecting chores—things like that. He would beat them with the belt and kick them with his boot if they fell down, though Mom pointed out it was never with the point of his toe. When it was happening you just wanted to melt away, and if your eyes filled with tears of sympathy he yelled, "Do you want me to give you something to cry about, too?" I don't know what Mom thought about his displays of anger; she never interfered, and it wasn't like any of us didn't believe in spanking children. He was easier on us girls. Jan was always his favorite, Roxanne was the baby, and I was always trying hard to be the good girl. I think I was eleven when I got my last spanking—I remember it well because of what we were doing to actually deserve discipline. It was bedtime and I think Mom and Dad were in bed reading. Randy and I were peeking around the stove in the living room, watching Jan get ready for bed so we could snatch her pajamas when she was naked. As soon as she had taken off all her clothes, we grabbed them and ran to the kitchen with her chasing. We tossed them back and forth between us while she screamed and tried to catch them. The ruckus would have drawn any parent and when Dad came out to investigate he put a stop to it by spanking both of us, but not very hard, and I could tell he wasn't really that upset. It was barely over and Randy and I were snickering behind his back.

When I seriously thought of running away, I couldn't think of where it would be, unless to my Frolander grandparents or into the worlds of my storybooks. There wasn't anything about the neighbors that made me want to live with them, no matter how harsh Dad's discipline. They were fascinating, even amusing in their ways, but I'd like to think that exposure to them not only established some appreciation for our own home, flawed as it was, but eventually increased my compassion for marginalized people, who were going to be found in any neighborhood where I lived. I admit a lot of my behavior lacked compassion back then—that's why I say *eventually* taught me a little more. It's also true that one of our neighbors, Carl Grovum, really does beggar my belief in that theory, but for good reason. What I gained through Carl was an unexpected revelation about my stepfather. But I'll get to that later.

The Beckers lived half a mile east of us, and they didn't believe in spanking their children, plus they allowed them to eat as much candy as they liked even though it plainly gave all the younger children black stumps for teeth. Billy and Lorraine did as little as possible to interfere with the natural course of life, which meant they believed that if left alone, kids will naturally learn to eat green beans and not touch themselves in public.

They seemed to practice the same relaxed policy when it came to animal reproduction and this astonished me, for it put their rabbit population into the stratosphere. Their cages were in constant rapturous motion, wall-to-wall thumping, hopping, and vying for positions with females and food. When one of their kids set the rabbits free one day, including the baby bunnies, their numbers rallied for several months. But then between an infectious disease that wiped out a lot of them, and their dogs who ate them dead or alive, nature sorted itself out, I guess.

Most farmers did not trust nature that much when it came to their cows' breeding schedule. That was carefully orchestrated: the bull was turned out to pasture only when the cows were in season. However, the Beckers' bull stayed in the pasture with their cows year-round, never restricting his pleasure, which upset the cow's cycles and surprised them with calves during all seasons of the year. A lot of them died that way because they were born during midwinter storms and deep freezes. Dad always called Northwest Breeders to come out and artificially inseminate cows who were ready, so that they calved in the warmth of the barn in late winter and early spring.

The Beckers' fields were plowed if it wasn't too hot or too cold, and grain got planted if the seeder was repaired. When they baled alfalfa, Billy said a guy could just as well leave it lay on the field and let the cows out to find their own hay rather than going to the extra trouble of hauling it into the barnyard for them. This would have been a better idea if he'd had the giant round hay bales farmers make now, rather than the smaller 60-pound bale that grew moldy in the rain and were regularly buried in the snow by mid-November. Their farm machinery rusted in the yard, old sheds caved in, and the skeletons of new ones stood unfinished for years until they, too, blended with the old.

The four Becker kids enjoyed their parents' laissez-faire attitude: they ate, slept, and played whenever they wanted, but they never fought with each other, which puzzled me. Why were we kids always squabbling? The only mean things on their farm were their snarling dogs. It didn't matter what gentle breed they raised, they were all vicious—even the St. Bernards they had for years. Perhaps the Beckers' special fondness for conspiracy theories seeped into the minds of their dogs. At the height of the Cold War, with our living so close to the Canadian border through which any spy or criminal could sneak, Billy Becker said, "Lord knows who might bust into our farm, kill us, and take everything of value." That's why they were the first of our neighbors to invest in the new mercury vapor yard-lights that automatically went on when the sun went down. Every night of the year from then on, it lit their entire yard and cast a cold, blue light that could be seen for miles. The invention of these lights, which are now standard, set the entire countryside alight. Before then it was black at night; barns and buildings disappeared into the darkness and slept until dawn. All that was left to see were stars and small squares of soft light escaping the windows of a farmhouse here and there.

Occasionally, Mom let us walk down the road to play with the Becker kids on an afternoon, as long as we didn't pester Lorraine and were home by chore time. Their dogs made our approach tricky, but as soon as the Becker kids recognized us, they called the dogs off, and we walked down the driveway to play in the yard.

These visits gave us intimate insights into what their home life was like. We held so many things in common: farming, poverty; they had four kids, we had six. But their lack of discipline and freedom from structure, which was so different from our daily regimen, didn't bring the advantage I imagined it would. I couldn't help staring at the dirty dishes on Lorraine's kitchen table. The same ones were always there. Not just from the previous meal, but from days, perhaps weeks. Lorraine seemed to sense my looking. "Why bother to wash them?" she philosophized. "You only need to get them out for the next meal and do it all over again." They had a real kitchen sink, but it was plugged with a mound of garbage, and the counters were hidden by stacks of crusty pans, magazines, canning jars, and leftovers. "Once," she said with good humor, "I found an entire ham under that pile. I had told Jimmy (her oldest son) to put it in the fridge when he was done eating off it. Of course, by the time I noticed, we had to give it to the dogs." Her stove was spattered with grease and boil-overs. A frying pan with congealed fat and bits of blackened bacon sat on a burner. The smell of rotten cheese hung in the air, and two dogs lay on the floor chewing on something. Lorraine offered us cookies, but I said, "No thank you, I just ate."

At home we didn't have running water or a sink, we had two enamel dishpans sitting on the counter—one for washing the dishes, the other for rinsing, and Mom always made us do them. We couldn't even let them drip dry, we had to dry them with a towel and put them away after every meal. When Jan and I were done with the dishes, and Mom walked through the kitchen, just out of reflex she ran her hand across the table and counter and if she felt the slightest smudge or crumb, we were called back to do a better job. I never appreciated the beauty of a clean kitchen until I was able to observe the disgusting effect of never doing the dishes.

In the summer Lorraine did her laundry in the backyard. She had a new wringer washing machine plugged into the light pole. Her reason for this location was both ingenious and convenient. It was near the well house, and on their way in from the barn, Billy and the boys could stop at the washing machine when their clothes got too dirty, strip right there, and throw them in. The machine was always churning a load, which gave off an industrious air, the impression of work being done. There were usually piles of clothes waiting on the ground, and the chickens didn't mind walking across them, leaving their own deposits. As we passed the lidless machine, I couldn't resist glancing in the tub as the clothes sloshed back and forth to see if I could guess what she was washing. It looked like blue jeans. It was hard to tell with the water so black, but there was the distinct aroma of manure hanging over the agitator.

In contrast, Mom always did our wash on Mondays, except for the years when she had three babies in diapers—then she had to wash every other day. Before breakfast Dad brought in the copper boiler and set it on the stove. He filled it with buckets of water from the well, and when it heated to boiling he carried it back to the milkhouse where our old Maytag wringer-washer was kept, and dumped it in. In every season of the year clothes were dried on the lines outside. In the winter I helped enough to know that temperatures below zero hurt your hands like a hundred needles pricking them and instantly froze the sheets into giant crackers as you wrestled to pin them onto the lines. When the clothes were gathered at dusk, you shook them and a layer of frost flew off like snow, leaving the clothes mostly dry and stiff. In rainy weather, laundry was crowded onto lines strung across the milkhouse and on a wooden rack in the living room. The rest were draped and hung on the backs of chairs and across bed frames.

I actually enjoyed the smell of laundry soap, bleach, and the heaviness of clean, wet clothes. There was a soothing, sacred pleasure in the ordinary task of smoothing rough, dry towels and bending blue jeans into neat stacks. I didn't think the Beckers ever went to bed in crisp cotton sheets that smelled like fresh wind from the north.

While the way they lived doused any desire to run away to them, I did lust after the television set they bought in the late 50s and placed in the new living room Billy added to the back of the house—this was one of a number of additions he built when other rooms became so full, they shut the door and never went back in. This was utterly inconceivable to us, living as we did in three rooms. With a roof-mounted antenna, a set could pick up two stations, one from Winnipeg and one from Grand Forks, depending on the weather. The Beckers watched the snowy black and white screen so late into the night, they finally moved their beds into the living room, forming a semi-circle around it. From there the children could watch TV until they fell asleep in the early morning hours after "O Canada" was played, and the flickering station signed off. When the Beckers got on the school bus in the mornings their eyes were red and watery, and all the way to school they dozed, their heads resting against the frosty windows.

The last time I visited the Beckers' house, Candy, who was a year older than me, invited me inside to show me her birthday present—a diary that came with a little gold lock and key. As we came through the door Lorraine yelled from the kitchen, "Don't step on those newspapers, Jimmy got sick last night and I haven't had time to clean it up yet." I looked down and saw the papers were slick with vomit. Someone had already stepped in it and left footprints across the floor. The air that met us was so foul, I clapped my hand to my mouth and backed out the door. I was embarrassed for Candy. I could see she was embarrassed too. We didn't play together much after that; I was close to being a teenager and increasingly conscious of my image. All of us went to the same school, grades one through twelve, but I wouldn't sit with Candy on the bus because other kids might think our families were alike. My reputation was already seriously impaired by poverty and five younger siblings.

Once, after an especially hard spanking, Randy did walk down to their place to spy on them from the brush in the ditch and to think about running away, but we both knew he would never do it.

———

Mom and Dad were extremely hospitable to our neighbors, and the ones I knew best were the ones whose land adjoined ours or very nearly did. The Beckers were the only exception because Dad didn't respect Billy, but anyone else was welcome anytime, and they often stopped in for coffee or a meal. We children liked to hang around listening to adult conversation because it offered a bit of entertainment. If we were very quiet, Mom and Dad forgot about us and we heard fascinating stories like about the Nelsons, who lived around the corner up towards the Graceton Beach, who were renting the old Burns place, and how they'd gotten so drunk they drove in the ditch late Friday night, and Tom Howard had to pull them out with his tractor. It's strange that, excluding the Beckers, the rest of our closest neighbors were not families, but a peculiar assortment of people living alone, each of them with unique, sometimes-painful stories. This was the odd mirror I held up to our home and family to see whether theirs was a life I envied. The answer was easy.

Simon Roth, a bachelor, who lived a mile west of us, was unintentionally our most entertaining neighbor. He was a small man, but his eyebrows were fantastically large and eloquent. They reached out and over his glasses like the roots of a hairy, white plant, and waggled up and down as he talked. He wore striped bib overalls and a matching train engineer's cap, but most amusing to us was the way he stuttered when he talked. He suffered from what is now known as Tourette syndrome, a neurological disorder that causes severe facial tics and compulsive utterances or sounds. His speech impediment grew worse the older he got, and the odd clicks and sounds exploding from his mouth as his face involuntarily twitched and jerked culminated in a kissing sound as he puckered his lips and smacked them over and over. Conversations were startling combinations of all these things, and Mom and Dad knew when we were about to lose control of stifled laughter. I really hoped he didn't notice our unkindness before they sent us outside with a warning to stay away from his car.

That was another entertaining thing about him—he owned a Model T Ford he'd kept running since the day it rolled off the assembly line (I'm thinking it probably dated to the 1920s), and in our county it was one of the few that still remained road-worthy. It was irresistible: the black leather seats, the hand grips on the doors, and the big bug-eye lights mounted above the fenders. It had pull-down shades for the back windows, and a crank to start the engine. Sometimes Randy dared to gently squeeze the black bulb by the steering wheel. The loud aaa-OOO-ga of the horn brought Dad to the kitchen door with a warning: "You want a licking? Get away from there, then."

The Model T was so light that Randy and I could rock it back and forth, and once we got it rolling, with Rex standing on the running board to steer, we could hide it behind the haystack. Then, we waited for Simon to come out of the house, spluttering and woo-hooing, his eyebrows flickering up and down. We appreciated his feigned amazement as he pretended to look for his missing car.

When he finally got the engine started and headed out the driveway, we grabbed the rear bumper, and with all our strength braced our heels in the sand. The engine would strain and sputter. His tires would spin, spraying us with gravel, until at last, he would get out to see why his old car couldn't seem to gain any traction. He'd find three or four of us standing behind him grinning with innocence. On his next try, we gave a contrasting boost that sent it flying up the drive to the road. This pleased us so well that for the rest of the day we spontaneously laughed aloud at the thought of Simon Roth and his Model T Ford.

Then one day in his sixtieth year, after all the years of living alone, he shocked everyone by suddenly marrying a widow from Park Rapids who moved into his farmhouse with her china teacups, Persian rugs, and maiden daughter, Bernice.

Not long after they married, Mrs. Roth invited me and Candy Becker to get off the school bus when it passed their house on the way home and spend the night with them. She ushered us into her living room where we sat on Victorian chairs and held a cup and saucer on our laps as we chewed tiny cucumber sandwiches and thumbprint cookies for our after-school snack. I don't remember who arranged this, but I think it must have been an effort to teach us poor country girls an etiquette worthy of our sex, but all I learned was how much I couldn't wait to get out of there to drink water from the tin dipper hanging on our crock and wrestle with the dog. The conversation and meal that followed was so taxing I was able to purge all memories except the acrid smell of mothballs coming from the blankets on the bed where Candy and I spent the night.

At first Simon couldn't believe his good fortune: two women who cooked and kept house, while he worked the farm. But soon, very soon, his ways were no longer charming to them, if they ever were. He was no longer welcome in his own home after a long day in the fields. Eventually, Simon moved into the basement where he felt more at ease and less apt to dirty or break things. This seemed to please his wife, but apparently not enough to keep her, because one day Mrs. Roth and Bernice went away and never came back—again, much to everyone's surprise and secret satisfaction.

———

Nellie Engebrotten was our closest neighbor; she lived between us and Simon Roth. Nellie always seemed old to my child's eye, although she was only in her sixties when I knew her as a girl. She eventually sold her farm and moved seven miles east of us so she could be closer to one of her daughters. Despite her many physical complaints and loss of eyesight, she lived into her late nineties, and my brother, Dallas, who eventually became county sheriff, often stopped by her little cottage, checking on her during his night patrols, knowing this elderly insomniac would be awake, listening to the TV, and delighted to have company.

Nellie's long driveway was west of ours about a quarter of a mile on the opposite side of the road and ran straight south between a patch of woods and a small field reclaimed from the swamp. At the end of the woods, her drive curved around to a small two-room shack, which was hidden from the sight of anyone who might be passing by on the main road. Nellie lived alone, and I loved walking over to see her. Sometimes I wondered what it would be like to live with her. She had a nice couch that made into a bed, and we were expected to sit quietly upon it while she told us long stories about her past. Sadly, she no longer had children to play with.

Nellie had raised seven children in this tiny house about the size of a cow stall, and she'd done it without running water, an indoor toilet, or even electricity. It made me respect her. We had electricity, a working well, three rooms—not two; and six kids—not seven. There was another small, old building about two hundred feet from her house where some of her boys had slept when they were young. This eased a bit of the crowding. When we knew her, all her kids were grown and gone. Even Harry, her husband, had left her. For years they fought furiously over so many things, he finally tired of it. "If you know so damn much about farming, you can do it yourself," he fumed, and he packed a small suitcase and went south to Chicago where he got a job building coffins. Nellie was left to survive on a tiny social security check and the rent money Simon Roth paid to farm her fields.

We met Harry once when he came back to see her about some legal matters. He was tall, thin, and silent—the exact opposite of Nellie, who was short with soft, round bosoms resting on her stomach, and thin graying hair pulled back in a French knot that escaped its bobby pins and hung in little wisps about her smooth face. She never stopped talking and was amused by most things in life, except Harry; just the way he looked made her seethe. She never learned to drive a car so she depended on others to give her a lift into town when she needed groceries. Every fall she closed up her house and moved into Baudette to live with one of her daughters until spring.

We saw a lot of Nellie because she needed to get water from our well several times a week. She did collect rainwater in a wooden barrel beside her porch; whatever drained off the roof she used for bathing and laundry. There was an iron pump still sitting on a wooden platform above a hole in the ground beside her flower garden, but it never brought up water. This was very odd. It didn't seem possible, really. Our county could have exported water to the Sahara, with plenty left over. At one time the little town of Williams claimed eighty-eight artesian wells.

I was proud of our well. It was one hundred feet deep, and our electric pump brought up the coldest, sweetest water a human could drink. For several years after I moved away, I craved this water. Whenever I came home from college on break, I filled jugs and hauled it back to Minneapolis. Then one Christmas, after being away for months, I drew a tall glass of ice cold water from the tap and stopped suddenly. I could smell it even before I lifted the glass to my lips. It was so full of minerals and sulphur it could have passed for a hot spring had it been a hundred degrees warmer. The sweet water of my childhood actually stank.

Randy and I were sure we could make Nellie's well work if we just tried hard enough. Each time we visited her we hoped that today, perhaps, by some miracle, we could bring up water, and wouldn't she be grateful. We primed it with rainwater and stood at the handle pumping it up and down, up and down as it screeched and screed like a donkey. Nellie ran out of her house holding her ears, ungratefully yelling, "Stop that! Stop that! JUDAS PRIEST! You'll wake the dead!"

When Nellie walked to our house we watched her come down the road carrying two buckets, one leg slightly shorter than the other, her head bobbing left to right. She filled the buckets at our well and then came into the house to "set for a spell" while Mom served her a cup of coffee and a piece of cake to revive her. Though her sleepless nights never varied, she always told Mom about pacing the floor, drinking baking soda and water for heartburn, and wishing she hadn't eaten the onions that so disagreed with her. In a stage whisper she would say, "The gas I had! It was frightful! Judas Priest! I thought I was going to die!" Randy and I exchanged smirks. We knew what gas was. He produced it on command. And when natural means failed he effortlessly cupped his palm and pumped it from his armpit.

Sometimes on an afternoon when the heat was stifling and there was nothing else to do, Randy and I wandered over Nelly's. She made grape Kool-Aid and snickerdoodles—about the only kind of cookie Mom and I never baked. Together we sat on the steps in the shade of her plum tree, eating cookies and watching her. She sat in her rocking chair and embroidered as she gossiped to us about Simon Roth's wife, her needle flashing, threads hanging from her teeth as she bit off the ends. Pillowcases, doilies, and dresser scarves flowed from her hoops in avalanches of pink and orange flowers. She told us about the old days and her children, especially her beautiful, teenage daughter who died of polio and who still smiled at us from a faded sepia portrait.

One day as Randy and I rounded the corner at the end of Nellie's drive, we caught sight of something white moving in her garden by the porch. At first, I assumed it was a lilac bush laden with white blossoms, bending toward the ground and shifting in the breeze. Nellie had two lilacs the size of small trees that bloomed in early summer, and every year she reminded us they were French. "French lilacs," she said. One was deep purple, and the other a soft white. We didn't have lilacs in our yard so she let us break off large fragrant bouquets to take home to Mom. But this white was moving too much to be flowers, and it was singing "Waltzing Matilda." We crept closer to peek around a tree, and there was Nellie standing in a galvanized wash tub, bathed in sunshine, and scrubbing her back with a long handled brush. Stunned, we watched for a minute; and then, ashamed of our spying, we ran home laughing and didn't go back for several days, giving her plenty of time to dry off.

From then on Randy and I called her "Nellie Belly Button," which easily morphed into "Nellie Jelly-Belly Button." We so liked the sound of it we all chanted, "Here comes Nellie Jelly-Belly Button" when we saw her coming down the road with her water pails. It was poetry, and we howled until she came within earshot, then we shut up. That name nearly cost us our friendship, because one day as she came into our yard, Jan couldn't resist sharing the joke. "Hi, Nellie Jelly-Belly Button," she said, and we stood with silly grins on our faces waiting for her to get it and laugh like she did about most things. "Well, I never," she said. Tears sprang to her eyes, she spun around, and without getting any water that day, she walked home and didn't come back for several weeks.

Mom and Dad began to wonder why she wasn't coming over to get her water. They saw her walking all the way to Simon Roth's, her closest neighbor to the west, which was farther away. At last, I told them Nellie might have heard Jan call her a name, but she didn't mean for Nellie not to get her water from us anymore.

"What name?" they asked.

"Nellie Jelly-Belly Button."

"Who thought that one up?"

We weren't sure anymore. "It happened by itself," we said.

That evening Mom and Dad walked over to apologize for their children who would insult her in such a way, and they promised to "deal" with us. Nellie graciously forgave us, came back for water, and we were glad.

—————

A little north and west of us, perhaps one and a half miles as the crow flies, through dense woods on barely passable trails, there lived two men—brothers who were very reclusive. Hermits, I guess you'd say. I rarely saw their house deep in the woods, but we often passed the track leading back to it when we went to the beach.

No one lived along the old beach road and eventually all that land between our farm and the part of the lake shore where we went swimming became a state park, a park Dad was eventually hired to manage. Two-track trails that led off the road, occasionally used by hunters or berry pickers, had been around since the earliest settlers came to the area. The settlers had long gone—their small homesteads burned or sunk back into the forest without a trace except for the occasional rusty tin can or piece of barbed wire sticking out of the ground. One of these overgrown tracks led deep into the forest to the Grovum place where two Norwegian bachelors lived. Sometimes it felt like the eyes of Carl and Otis followed us from the undergrowth as Randy and I slowly bounced over the ruts on our way to the beach with the tractor, our brothers and sisters riding on the trailer, and clouds of dust billowing behind us. (We were allowed to drive this rig to the beach on hot days when Mom was busy, which was pretty much all the time. Looking back now, this freedom, with all its attendant risks, is almost impossible to imagine. And on most days there was no one at the beach at all, just us five kids and water to the horizon. Mom kept Roxanne home—if you couldn't walk, you couldn't go.)

I don't think Carl and Otis Grovum could be called true Norwegian Bachelor Farmers because they didn't farm all that much—although, in their dirty bib overalls, they did look like the gaunt, depressed farmers of the Depression era. They shared a small, wood-frame house they built together but never painted, which gave it an abandoned, moody look. They had no electricity, and no modern conveniences. They kept a vegetable garden and Carl did some hunting. At one time they kept a cow or two, no other animals. Dad suspected that Carl poached deer off the land when he needed meat. Both of the brothers knew how to sew, because we saw neat patches on their worn overalls. We also knew Otis could knit because Carl wore woolen mittens in the winter, and he once told us who made them. A man who knitted? I only knew women who knitted. I don't know how they survived without visible income. Perhaps it was more remarkable that they survived one another. According to Carl, the more sociable of the two, they fought continually. In fact, he said Otis became so offensive he had to draw a line down the middle of the house to keep Otis on the other side.

Otis rarely emerged from the woods, but Carl came out more often to collect mail and buy their supplies in town. Occasionally, Carl stopped by our house for coffee and a chance to air his grievances against Otis and the rest of the world. For several years in a row Mom invited them to our Thanksgiving dinner because she pitied their isolation.

Otis was strange, not just because he was nervous around people, casting side glances and constantly clearing his throat, but because he had a lump about the size and shape of half a large egg growing from the left side of his forehead. Of course, we stared. Was it a horn bud? Had Carl hit him there during a fight? Were his brains pressing through his skull? He didn't talk much when he came, but he seemed very pleased to eat Mom's cooking.

One year as we sat down to eat the Thanksgiving meal in our crowded kitchen, Otis cleared his throat. The sound was initially a prolonged snort in the back of his nose as he sucked in air. When he made the transfer deep in his throat, the moist and loaded air rattled with gathering force toward his mouth. Our eyes widened; everyone could see what was coming. Just in time, Carl gave a strangled yell, and in an amazing reversal Otis swallowed it all! At home they were used to spitting on their floor, or at least in the direction of the wood stove where it hissed and dried with just a trace of white ash. Everyone exhaled with relief, and Dad blessed the turkey and mashed potatoes so we could dig in.

Clearly, Otis wasn't the only person who crossed Carl's boundaries: Carl complained a lot about trespassers and had posted their land with handwritten warnings. As the years passed, Otis grew more reclusive and Carl more eccentric and angry with the world. He threatened to shoot anyone who came on his property. So I thought it was courageous of Mom to take them a plate of cookies and tell them we would be picking chokecherries near, but not on their land.

Carl got around the countryside on a motor scooter he'd made from spare parts and a motor from a gas-powered washing machine. On a still evening we could hear its strange pitch—the sound of an amplified kitchen mixer on high. We knew from afar that Carl had driven out of his track in the woods, headed south down the beach road, and turned onto the highway across from Simon Roth's. When he stopped by in the early evening after supper, Mom served him leftovers and listened as he raved to Dad in his lilting Norwegian accent about the evil Democratic Party and the crimes the state was committing against him. They were trying to take his land away. He decried neighbors who poached deer off his land and picked his wild berries, and the law that chose to look the other way. He didn't trust anyone, he said, especially the county assessor. He sometimes smiled at Mom and Dad, but he frowned at us kids before he left in the waning light to ride back down his dark trail.

One evening Carl came by when Mom and Dad had gone to visit Grandpa and Grandma Block. I was ten, and as the oldest, I ruled with militaristic might when our parents were gone. At least, I imagined I ruled. Or I tried to rule.

This was before we had a telephone. The phone company didn't think there would be enough customers to bring lines down our county road. Anyway, Dad said we couldn't afford one if it was available. But just five miles away Grandpa and Grandma Block had a phone hanging on the wall beside their dining room table. It had a hand crank on the side and a funnel you placed against your ear to listen. You yelled your message into another funnel attached to the box. You shouted for two reasons. One, how else could someone far away hear you? And two, the connections were poor due to so many people listening in—that was called "rubbering." When a call came through, it not only rang at its destination, it sounded in every house all down the line. You were only supposed to pick up when you heard your particular ring, but it was difficult to hear one long and two shorts and know you might find out if the Bitzers were expecting yet another baby—didn't they know what caused this? If the person rubbering wasn't really stealthy you could hear them breathing, or hear background noises that could identify them. However, Grandma had other reasons for picking up when she heard a neighbor's ring: it could be helpful to let the caller know that Fran and Calma Swanson weren't going to answer because they'd gone to town and wouldn't be back until chore-time.

When I was home alone with my brothers and sisters, I couldn't call for help if we faced an emergency while Mom and Dad were gone. We could run a half-mile down the road to the Beckers, which I did once when our milkhouse was burning down, but they were only marginally helpful, since they were slow about deciding things in a crisis. Nelly was closer, but she didn't have a car and couldn't even walk fast. So we were on our own, if you didn't count help from God, which actually I did, believing he sent his angels to hover, unseen, over our barn and around the places where we played, preserving our lives on many occasions.

On summer evenings after supper we always went back outside to play. On the evening when Carl stopped in, Roxanne was already in her crib for the night, and the rest of us were in the yard playing "Five Hundred" with the softball and bat. Randy hit the ball as we scattered across the field. We had a point system for flies and grounders and the first person to get five hundred was the next batter. Between hits we slapped at mosquitoes and argued over who should retrieve a missed ball from the tall weeds by the fence. In the setting sun our shadows were thin giants running back and forth across the yard and up and down the roof.

When Carl coasted down the driveway, his long legs skimming the gravel, we gathered around politely to find out what he wanted. He didn't want anything. Only to visit, even though Mom and Dad weren't home.

In contrast to the disrespect we showed one another as children, we were required to respect adults. It was errant to think of joining a conversation. If you had an opinion on whether a Massey Ferguson was better than a John Deere, or felt moved to ask a person about his deformity or when his wife was coming back, it was best to leave. Go outside and play, so you didn't need to be reminded that "children should be seen and not heard."

Children also needed to anticipate the help an adult might need and not stand around gawking like we didn't know where Dad kept the shovel or when Mom needed fresh water for the coffee pot. We had to support our parents' hospitality, but were supposed to hesitate before receiving it at someone else's house. It was complicated; you couldn't seem too eager for the hot cinnamon roll, dripping with glaze and cooling on the counter, even though you were dying for it. You might have eaten at noon, but when offered "a little lunch"—which could be anything from a piece of pie and a cup of coffee to a table loaded with bread, salami, bologna, pickles, cheese, cookies, and canned fruit—it was important to hesitate, and then politely say it would be too much trouble. If your hostess insisted it was no trouble, and you must eat, then it was okay to accept. Even at our own Grandma's house, we couldn't study a plate of old-fashioned raisin spice cake and take the piece with the thickest brown sugar frosting. This was as bad as taking seconds and eating the last one on the plate which my brothers always did anyway.

With Carl standing in the driveway beside his scooter on that evening and with Mom and Dad gone, I had to decide if it was my responsibility to show him hospitality or not. I really didn't want to leave the ball game and offer Carl "a little something." But I was almost a grown-up. I needed to do what Mom would have done, so I invited Carl into the kitchen where I heated left-over coffee and served him a piece of the cake Mom had made that day. Carl sat in a kitchen chair, crossed one thin leg over the other, and jiggled his foot. I could feel his eyes on me as I moved between the table and the stove. My siblings hung around snacking on cookies until they got bored, then they went back outside to play, leaving me alone with him. I wished they would stay. I wished he would leave. But he continued to sit, silent and staring, sipping his coffee.

When at last he was finished, as I gathered up the crumbs and the dirty cup, Carl reached for my hand saying, "Dat wuss goot, you're a goot girl then, aren't you?" He grasped my hand firmly, not letting go. Then, he pulled me onto his lap, insisting I sit there for a few minutes so we could talk. Torn between honoring an adult's request and a rising dread, I decided that no matter how repulsed, I should tolerate this poor man's knees for a minute. He smelled of cigarettes, sweat, and something I couldn't identify. I quickly made an excuse and pulled away to check on Roxanne, who was in the bedroom. I stood beside her crib watching her peaceful sleep for as long as I dared, praying, *Dear Jesus, please, could you make him go away?* At last, I heard the screen door close and his motor scooter sputter to life as he rode off.

All his life Dad had a gift for observing the little details in life that most people would miss. It was almost magical in its power. For example, I could remember every day for weeks to latch the pasture gate after I closed it, but on the one day I forgot, Dad would notice. This power also gave him the ability to tell who had driven into our place while he was gone. Dad wouldn't simply notice a fresh tire track over his old ones on the driveway—he would startle us by knowing whose tires had driven over his tracks. He would walk into the house and ask, "What'd Tom Howard want?" Tom was another bachelor who lived in a shack at the northeast corner of our fields, and though he didn't own a large farm, he always drove a new, baby-blue Ford pickup, which stood out among vehicles in our county. When I asked Dad how he knew they weren't his own tracks from two hours ago, he looked at me like I was crazy and then he dismissed the skill, saying anyone with a brain between his ears would know. This helped build his reputation. He could not be fooled. He was omniscient.

Later that night when Mom and Dad drove into the yard, the first thing he asked when he got out of the car was what did Carl Grovum want? "Nuthin," we said. Jan added that I had given him coffee and cake. I hoped to be praised for this, but Dad swiveled round to me and said, "What else?"

"What else *what*?" I asked.

Then I thought of the peculiar revulsion I felt when Carl took my hand and pulled me onto his knees. "He made me sit on his lap," I blurted. Mom and Dad went into the house, and a few minutes later Dad called me in. He looked angry, and my immediate thought was, what have I done now?

"You get this straight in your head," he commanded. "When you kids are alone, don't ever let Carl Grovum in this house again. You hear me, young lady?"

I nodded, confused. I had no idea why he would make this rule, but I didn't think it would be a good idea to ask right then.

I had forgotten all about it, until another evening when Mom and Dad were again at Grandpa and Grandma's and Roxanne was in her crib. The rest of us were in the yard playing "eenie-einie-over"—half of us on one side of the house and half on the other side, throwing the ball over the roof, catching, chasing. Suddenly Randy stopped mid-throw, listened intently, and announced, "I hear Carl Grovum's scooter." From far away we heard the sound of his washing machine engine climbing an octave as he gave it more gas on the open road.

That's when it came back, Dad's intensity as he said, *"When you are alone, don't ever let Carl into this house again."* I had always thought there was something sinister about Carl. Maybe he was going to kidnap us or kill us. Whatever it was, I knew I had to protect us. But I didn't know how to face Carl, or any adult, and say no coffee for you today, Buddy. Dad said not to let you in the house.

As the sound of the motor scooter drew nearer I decided the best thing to do was to hurry up and hide. It would solve both my moral and social dilemma. I could do what Dad said, and if Carl didn't think we were home so much the better. I wouldn't offend him by not showing hospitality or respect for an adult. Perhaps he would just go away. Or maybe he would ride right past our house on his way to somewhere else. Perhaps I was wasting my worry on nothing.

"Everyone get in the house *now*," I screamed.

Normally when I barked out commands my siblings acted like pigs who'd just been told you're going to market, so get on the truck. Right. But this time they stampeded inside as if they sensed the danger.

I urgently explained, "Carl is going to get us if we don't hide. Get under Mom and Dad's bed."

They rushed into the bedroom.

Hiding five kids in our three-room shotgun house was a joke. The bedroom at the front of the house had windows on three sides and a door that led to the yard. The windows had sheer curtains, but they were tied back all the time. Our only closet was in the living room, and it was stuffed with clothing and boxes. Even more problematic, our doors could not be locked. Keys for doors simply didn't exist for most homes in our county. We never locked anything, except the outhouse door, and even that depended on how much community you were in the mood for. We couldn't keep anyone out of the house if he really wanted to come in. The only thing I could do to keep Carl out temporarily was to use the flimsy hook and eye locks on the inside of the screen doors.

The only person in our family who locked those doors was Mom. She used the locks when she wanted to take a brief nap, which was unbelievably rare given how early she rose and how hard she worked. When she got a chance to rest, the moment she was lying down, her children materialized from all parts of the farm to join her on the bed even though we detested naps. We only wanted to be near her. It was tough to be her companion when she was up. She moved too fast. We told her knock-knock jokes, wrestled, tickled each other, and created such a writhing mess she would send us outside. And to keep us from banging in and out of the house she latched the screen doors until she got up a few minutes later. We considered banishment most cruel. We'd rather be spanked. Those few minutes seemed like hours as we stood on overturned buckets to peer through the screen watching her, pushing each other off, whining and waiting until at last she unlatched the doors to let us back inside. At which point we suddenly decided to be off playing again anyway.

That night I did something I'd never done before. I latched both the front and back screen doors to keep an adult outside. Then I ran to join my brothers and sister as they tumbled and rolled under the double bed. Randy and I pushed Rex and Dallas farther under, then Jan crawled in. Just as Carl turned into the driveway, Randy and I stretched out side by side under the fringe of the bedspread, which hung to the floor. I was panting, trying hard not to breathe, and praying, *We made it, thank you, God. Thank you.* The engine slowed and the gravel crunched as Carl rolled down the driveway and leaned the motor scooter against the yard-light pole. I heard his footsteps as he approached the house, and still I hoped he would just get back on his motor scooter and leave. It was obvious Mom and Dad's car was gone and no one was around, but he banged on the back screen door anyway and yelled, "Hello, anybody home, then?" The screen door rattled as he pulled on it. Rex and Dallas stirred as though they wanted to crawl out and go to the door. I whispered through my teeth, "Lie still! I'll kill you forever if you move another inch!"

We lay motionless. Waiting. There was silence outside, and Randy was getting restless. "This is dumb," he whispered, "I'm going to look."

"Please. Don't," I begged him.

Then Carl was at the front door, right by the bed, banging and yelling, "I KNOW YOU'RE IN THERE, NOW OPEN UP!" How stupid of me! I had failed to realize he'd know we were home because the screendoors could only be hooked from the inside. I lay rigid. Then we heard him scratching on the window screens above us.

I couldn't stop Randy who thought anything rash was worth the risk, and who, Dad said, would be dangerous if he had a brain. He peeked over the edge of the bed to find that Carl was looking straight at him through the window, his long face cupped in his hands and pressed against the screen as he strained to see us. Randy dove back under the bed and we hugged each other.

He was there for years. Which gave me plenty of time to confess all the bad things I'd done and prepare for death. But in case it wasn't quite yet time, I pleaded, *Dear Jesus. Please bring Mom and Dad home right now, please, please.* Finally, we heard the springs on Carl's seat squeak. The sound of the scooter leaving our yard was the sweetest thing I'd ever heard. We slowly crept out from under the bed.

I had forgotten about Roxanne; she'd slept through it all. I tucked the blanket around her, and only then did I realize that Carl would have easily seen her from the window.

We stayed indoors the rest of that night and didn't unlock the screen doors until Mom and Dad came home. Even in the dark, Dad spied the single tire track and knew Carl had been there. He wanted a report, which Randy, Jan, and I gave in unison.

Not long after that Carl stopped by when Dad was home. Randy and I were accustomed to hanging around and following Dad wherever he went when he was working outside. Repairing the fence, greasing the cultivator, dehorning calves, we were ready to run errands for him. We watched him trying to repair the hay baler. "Get me the ball peen hammer!" I'd run to the old granary where the tools were kept and run back. "*Not* the *claw* hammer, you numbskull, the *ball peen* hammer!" Repairing machinery put him in a foul mood, otherwise, he liked our company as long as we didn't get in the way, and could figure out what he wanted. The only time he sent us away was when the Northwest Breeder arrived to inseminate a cow. That was too intimate a thing for children to watch. So we waited in the yard while the two of them disappeared into the barn with the cow and rubber gloves.

When Carl arrived that day I was shocked when Dad told us to "Get outta here. Go play," Then he told Carl to come into the barn and he shut the double Dutch doors. A few minutes late, Carl emerged looking pale and angry. He spat on the ground, threw his leg over the scooter, and spun gravel as he left. He never came back, and Dad never told us what happened.

I didn't associate Dad's reaction with protection for me personally until years later when I learned that Carl had a reputation in the county for being too interested in young girls. (I never heard or read about any details.) It didn't substitute for Dad's love, but it deepened his complexity making it impossible to simply assign him the role of cruel disciplinarian, though he could be that. As is the case with all of us, none are one-dimensional, cartoon villains, we, all of us, carry traces of God's divine image however faint they might be.

Even though I knew we should try to love our neighbors as ourselves, I couldn't love Carl. We paid him back for scaring us that night. When we heard him coming, any of us who were old enough to walk, hid in the tall grass by the side of the road, waiting for him to scoot by at twenty-five miles an hour. When he was almost even with us we'd jump out screaming like wildcats. It could have killed him because, every time, he swerved and nearly wiped out.

———

The thrill of trespassing on Carl was still with me when, as an adult, Dallas talked me into riding horseback along the trails through the woods to spy on the Grovums' clearing. By this time Dallas, an undercover expert, was well into his law enforcement career which would eventually make him sheriff of the county. I didn't know whether to feel safe or crazy doing this with him. We spotted Carl working in the garden behind his shed. I felt like Peter Rabbit watching Mr. McGregor scritch-scratching with the hoe. We made the horses stand quietly as we watched through the brush and pine branches. Dallas grinned over at me and mouthed, "Let's go up and say hi." My response was to flee for home. Turning my horse, I galloped away, sticks cracking, branches whipping me in the face, and making such a racket Carl surely ran for his gun.

## Swedish Pancakes with Chokecherry Syrup

2 cups flour
2 tsp sugar
3 tsp baking powder
1/4 tsp salt
1/2 cup whipping cream
Milk
Melted butter
Chokecherry syrup
Sour cream

Combine dry ingredients in a mixing bowl. Add cream and one cup of milk. Beat just until most lumps are gone. Add more milk to make a very thin batter. Heat frying pan to medium high. Add 1/2 tsp butter or shortening, even if it is a nonstick pan. Pour in a small amount of batter and turn pan to spread thinly. Fry until edges are crisp and lacy. Turn and brown on other side. Add more butter to the pan for each pancake.

Drizzle with melted butter and chokecherry syrup. Spread a tablespoon of sour cream and place a second pancake on top. Roll up together and serve.

HINT: To keep up with demand, try to keep two frying pans going at once.

# Wild Rice

In the sheltered, mineral-rich waters of rivers and bays where
a gentle current runs and the environment is exactly right,
North America's only native cereal grows in watery, green beds.
Wild rice or *manoomin,* as the Ojibway call it, is more nutritious
than any grain white men introduced to this country. For centuries
wild rice was harvested by Native Americans, who paddled or poled a
canoe through waving tall grasses with a partner. The partner bent the
full heads over the edge of the canoe with one wooden "knocker" and
gently tapped the stalks with the other, causing the ripe kernels to fall
into the bottom of the canoe. Two hundred pounds was a good day's
harvest. At the end of each day the rice was parched in a cast-iron
kettle over a wood fire. This loosened the husks and turned the grains
to shades of black and brown. It was then placed in large, flat-
bottomed reed baskets and jigged or kneaded by moccasined feet,
which removed the husks from the kernels. Then, batch-by-batch,
the roasted rice was winnowed in round shallow baskets.
Women tossed it into the air and the wind blew away the dry
husks, leaving the smoky brown rice to collect in the bottom.

Every fall Grandpa Frolander bought rice from the Ojibway as they
came off their summer camping grounds on Lake of the Woods. He
gave us a supply that lasted the winter. The rich kernels stuffed wild
fowl and filled Mom's casseroles and soups with a lush, nutty flavor.

The natural beds are mostly gone now—killed by pollution and
water control. Most of the wild rice bought in supermarkets today
has been tamed by technology and harvested by white men.

# RIDING LESSONS

I was eight years old when Dad began teaching me to ride. His philosophy of education was, "Throw 'em off the dock enough times and they'll learn to swim." Accordingly, one afternoon he brought Dolly, his big bay mare, from the barn with just her bridle. He called me over and asked, "Do you want to learn how to ride?" That was like asking a stud if he liked mares. Dad threw me up on her broad, bare back, and showed me how to neck-rein by laying the reins flat against her neck so she could feel the gentle pressure to turn left or right.

Dolly was trained Western-style, so that reining could be done with one hand, leaving the other free so the rider could rope a calf, whack a steer, or twist a lariat around the saddle horn when it was needed to lead or drag something. Dolly was also trained to rear on her hind legs and paw the air with her hooves like Trigger, the movie-star horse. It was a useless talent for a farm horse, but still, it was impressive. I'll never forget the thrill of standing beside her while Dad made her rise to her full height and come crashing down to the ground with a grunt and a discharge of flatulence that could have launched a rocket.

Dolly was a calm, easy-going horse in the pasture, but when she was saddled up she fizzed with an energy that made her dance like a boxer. Mounting her was like trying to do the polka with one foot in a stirrup and the other still on the ground. We watched Dad hop on one leg and holler, "WHOA! WHOA! STAND STILL!" as Dolly jigged back and forth until he finally threw the other leg over her back and made her stop.

As I sat alone, high on her bare back for the first time, Dad told me all I had to do to make her move forward was nudge her with my heels and give a click-click with my tongue. It was the same noise my brother made when pretending to cock a pistol. I was afraid there might be some correlation because Dolly seemed eager to shoot off. Stopping was easy, Dad told me: just pull back firmly on the reins and say, "Whoa."

"Where's the saddle?" I asked.

Me and Dolly.

"You'll get one once you learn to ride."

With that he gave Dolly a slap on the rump. She crow-hopped twice and took off at a bone-crunching trot. As we turned out of the driveway and onto the road, he yelled, "Take her down to Nellie's driveway and back, but be careful on the way home." The trail that led back to Nellie's little shack was about a quarter of a mile down the road.

I didn't have time to wonder what Dad meant about being careful. Dolly went on her own accord, and my goal was to stay on her back and, thus, alive for the time it took us to trot down the road and back. Dad also warned me that if I should ever, at any time, God forbid, fall off a horse, I should never, ever, under any circumstances, let go of the reins. Glancing at the ground three stories below, I couldn't understand how a 60-pound runt like me was going to hang onto a horse a hundred times my weight and strength if I should fall—which seemed likely to happen at any moment. I had a killer grasp on a shank of mane in my right hand and a tight grip on the reins with my left. When I tried to slow Dolly down by tugging back on the reins, my hand drew even with my ear and made no significant contact with the bit in her mouth, which left her with no idea how much I would have preferred walking to trotting. I tried to think how to get a shorter grip on the rein. It didn't seem possible. If I let go of her mane with my right hand in order to hold the reins while I shifted my left farther forward, I was sure to fall off. It seemed prudent to give up the idea and just concentrate on staying aboard, since I was listing dangerously from side to side.

We made it to Nellie's driveway, and to my relief Dolly headed home without a signal from me. For a fraction of a second after the turn, I sat up straighter, shamelessly thinking I might be ready to star in *Black Beauty*. Then an alarm greater than any I had yet experienced in my short life descended upon me. Dolly picked up speed, moving from a fast trot into a thundering, Kentucky Derby gallop—her ears laid back and her neck outstretched for home. The gravel road sped past at a terrifying rate as I observed it closely from first one side of her neck and then the other.

We rounded the top of our driveway, and the g-force of the turn put me in a prone position, my head on her rump. I confessed my sins as we pounded past the house, and I heard Dad yelling, "Keep your head down!" We were heading for the barn, the doors standing wide open, and decapitation was imminent. Dolly hurtled through the doorway and slid to a stop. The frame of the door passed inches above my eyes. In slow motion, I rolled off her back into the straw of a stall and lay gasping at her feet, but still, I held the reins in my sweaty hand. That was lesson number one.

Dad trotted into the barn. "Now you see what you done? You gotta show a horse who's boss or you'll never make a rider."

With that, he led Dolly outside, threw me back up, gave me a shorter grip on the reins and led us up and down the driveway. Now stopping, now turning. Walking. Trotting. Helping me get the feel of it.

Days later I was riding Dolly and urging her from a tooth-breaking trot into a slow canter when a miracle happened. I suddenly found I could move with her rather than against her. Relaxing my body at the hips, and gripping her sides with my calves and knees, I rose and fell with her gait. I worshipped with a rush of joy. I knew then what conquering kings must have felt as they rode home from battle. To have a living surge of power between your legs, to control it, and yet become a part of such grace and beauty—I knew I could launch a kingdom or at least jump the ditch without falling off.

From my earliest memories I dreamed of becoming a horse if being a girl didn't work out. I loved their large eyes, soft noses, and shapely ears that constantly flicked to catch sound impressions from the air. Their coats gleamed in the summer sun, and they danced with arched necks and tails. Imitating them, I whinnied and galloped about the house in Mom's spike heels, but it was never quite the same as the musical *click-ka-click* of their hooves on the cement floor of the barn. Horses ran like the wind, such a valuable trait in the unpredictable affairs of life. What could be handier than running away from danger or, on the other hand, running straight into it and becoming the hero? What better way to serve God and love his creatures with all your heart?

When I was very young, all I could do was watch horses and offer handfuls of clover as they stood with their heads over the gate. I could reach high enough to pat the bottom of their soft lips as they leaned down to explore me. But as I grew taller, Randy and I climbed to the top rail of the gate and waited for Dolly to pass close by; then we would try to slip onto her back. A few times we made it, but when she moved away from the safety of the gate it was suddenly clear that the ground was far away, and we had no control over what this beast might do. Once up there, how does one get down? What if she decides to run and buck? Randy and I spotted for one another, sliding off in graceless dismounts, catching each other, and falling to the ground in a heap.

At that time I didn't know that many horses have a mysterious affinity for children and are often gentle with them. Once, my youngest sister, Roxanne, ventured into the pasture and managed to get herself between a rowdy, unpredictable stallion and the fence. He was famous for kicking and striking with his front hooves. Alarmed, Dad quietly called for Roxanne to come out of the pasture. He instructed her to go around the horse and motioned with his hand. "Around, around," he ordered. Being only three years old, she misunderstood, and putting one hand on the stallion's rear flank and one on his front leg, she ducked under his belly. "Like this, Daddy?" she asked. The horse stood stone still, simply bending his neck to watch.

Because horses were Dad's second love in life after Mom, he always kept a menagerie of them—from Shetland ponies to Belgian draft horses. Whenever he worked with the horses I was there, watching and waiting to help. There was always a gate to open or close, a lead rope to hold, or a halter to fetch. Manes and tails needed to be cut. Coats needed to be brushed and curried. Our horses were not ridden on hard surfaces, so they were never shod, but their hooves needed regular trimming.

Some horses refuse to stand quietly during this procedure, so Dad taught me to use the twitch—a braided leather loop attached to the end of a short pole. It was a method of management through pain. The loop of the twitch was fit over the horse's upper lip and twisted tight with the pole until that piece of tender flesh was firmly held in a circle of leather. This exposed his long yellow teeth and gums, giving a grotesque appearance to his head. If the horse fussed and fidgeted while Dad tried to work with his hooves, the twitch was tightened until all the horse's attention was focused on the painful distraction at the end of his nose. A horse quickly learned that if he stood quietly, the twitch was eased, but if he tried to kick or move, it was tightened. I felt sorry for him and tried to squeeze back the tears. Even though I wanted to help Dad, I didn't want to be the one to hurt a horse. One day as I stood holding the twitch on Thunder, who was tossing his head and rolling his eyes, Dad heard me sniffling. So he asked: "Which is worse? A little pain now? Or cracked and split hooves that can lame a horse for life? Tighten it up."

He taught me many things about horses. Never feed them too many oats—horses are greedy for them and will eat themselves sick. Never feed them moldy hay—it causes rales, a lung disease. Never let them have their own way when riding or they develop bad habits and become difficult to handle. Speak gently to them when approaching from the rear or you might get yourself kicked. Handle their legs and hooves often so they learn to tolerate trimming.

My first privilege was leading a horse out of the barn to the rail fence where Dad trimmed Dolly's mane and tail. I soon learned what knots to use when tying a horse to a post. Currying them was allowed if I put the combs and brushes back when I was done. Eventually, I could handle their hooves, but I was never strong enough to actually trim them. But I could scrape dirt from the inside wall and cut off part of the frog, the soft, smelly cushion that pads the center. Our dog eagerly waited for this stinking, cheesy delicacy to fall to the ground so he could snatch it up and run away to eat it.

Did I admire Dad? I think so. He was a powerful man with horses, able to train them, command their respect. He was no horse-whisperer, that was for sure. He shouted most of his commands especially when they were a bit out of line, just as he did with us kids. But he loved them; one way I knew was the careful attention he paid to their needs and the grin he'd get on his face as he watched them come when called. One day he came home after stopping at another farm for something, I've forgotten what, and he was flushed, angry—he'd seen horses suffering, barely able to walk because their hooves were so split and overgrown. From then on he despised that farmer. Did I love Dad? I don't know. I feared him. He might have respected me more if I'd shown some spirit, but I never dared. I hid it behind stony sulks, enduring his constant criticism of how I held a horse's lead, how I raced them too much, how I did this or that wrong. I had a big enough personality to control horses, but I sure never stood up to him.

Around the time Randy and I learned to ride Dolly, Dad began to board ponies for a friend. By then my brother and I were old enough to care for them. The good thing about ponies is that they can't be dropped and left in the yard like a softball or a bike. You learn to be responsible. They must be put away. They must be kept. We cleaned them, fed them, saddle-broke them, and loved them. In return, they allowed us to star in rodeos, win contests, and vanquish enemies.

For a long time I rode a chocolate-brown and white pinto named Pixie. She was big for a Shetland with long, lanky legs and a delicate head. Randy rode Patsy, also a pinto, but she was stocky and pot-bellied as Shetlands tend to be. Both ponies were strong and stubborn. Their natures required—no, demanded—we learn both patience and skill if we wanted to ride.

When friends came to play, the first thing they wanted to do was ride our ponies, which was okay with us. Riding a pony looks way easy to the novice, and ours were gentle, quiet, and not too far from the ground. How difficult could it be? The first challenge was Patsy, who always took a deep breath just before the saddle cinch was tightened. If Randy didn't catch her on an exhale, she could make the entire saddle slip under her belly just as the rider mounted and she let out her breath. You would be left hanging upside down, humiliated, and in danger of being accidentally kicked in the head.

When they were securely saddled-up and ready to ride, we gave some basic instructions and then helped our friends mount up. With visions of The Lone Ranger and Tonto in their heads, most kids wanted the pony to instantly hurl herself from a standing position to a breakneck gallop. But our ponies stood in one place with strangers on their backs, their legs splayed, heads down, eating grass, refusing to budge, and pretending they heard nothing and felt nothing at all. We called out, "Pull up on the reins. Click your tongue. Nudge them in the side with your heels." When that failed, "Snap them on the rear-end with the reins." All this was performed awkwardly, but the slap of the reins usually caused the ponies to raise their heads, move forward at a walk, then increasing to a fast trot. Shrieking and laughing, the rider bounced up and down and side to side in the saddle. If it was a hot summer day, the ponies were likely to head down the driveway, break into a canter at the road, cross directly, slowing down at the wide shallow ditch on the other side, then proceed straight down into the water. The laughing would change to screams of "STOP! STOP! WHOA!" and desperate yells to us: "How do you get her to stop? "Turn her! Turn her!", we'd cry. But it was no use. They were headed for the water like a hog to its wallow—not to drink, but to actually lie down. To get them out of the ditch, you had to dismount as the ponies went down in the warm water and mud, and try to push and pull them out of their bath.

If the ponies did not head for the ditch or stop to eat more grass, and if a lucky rider managed to get the pony a good distance down the road and then turned back, a universal horse trick possessed her. Unless you were a seasoned rider, it was hopeless. All you could do was try to stay on her back. A pony can run surprisingly fast, and never faster than when she's headed home. I felt powerfully grown-up and arrogant as I watched them return hanging onto the saddle horn with both hands. This was exactly what happened to me on my first riding lesson, only I'd been bareback on a big horse, not a pony. I was way past the runaway-horse stage.

Thunder was another horse I valued, for he had a gift for amusing us; we wouldn't have traded him even for a television set. Thunder was a tawny brown and white gelding with a sense of humor and more brains than some of our neighbors—at least that's what Dad said. Thunder opened so many gates and unlocked the barn door so many times, Dad had to keep inventing new ways of securing them. The back barn door, which led to the pasture, had to be latched with a leather strap from the inside. If we forgot to close it properly, Thunder always found out because he checked on it several times a day. He would turn the handle on the outside and nudge the top half of the door open. Then he would reach down over the bottom door and unlatch the inside hook. Backing up, he would pull the door open with his head, stroll through the middle of the barn and out the other door into our backyard.

Escaping the pasture didn't mean a better life; he had all the space and care a horse could want on the inside, including all his pals. It was the challenge that attracted him. When he got out he usually headed for Mom's garden, where he trampled cucumber vines and ate sweet corn. Then he would run along the outside of the fence making the other horses concerned and jealous. They would cry out and gallop back and forth. We enticed him back with oats in a three-pound tin coffee can. That was his downfall: he just couldn't resist the musical sound of oats being jigged in a can and always came for them, snorting and blowing, his lips reaching for the treat.

One day when Mom and Dad were gone, Randy and I were entertaining ourselves with him, and he always enjoyed the attention. At one and a half years he was big, but still too young to ride, so we had him in a halter and lead rope because he was starring in our Wild West Show. We pretended he was a wild mustang, an Indian pony we captured, and only we had the power to tame such a tremendous beast. We led him to the center of the corral so the crowd (our younger brothers and sisters sitting on the fence) could get a good look at him. We trotted him as fast as we could run around the ring to show off his beautiful legs and carriage. We climbed to the top rail of the fence and flopped our bodies across his back like a sack of grain. We pretended there were cheers when he allowed us to handle every part of his body. We picked up his hooves and cleaned them. I braided his mane and tail. He patiently endured as we bent his ears back and forth awkwardly, and took his halter on and off about a dozen times.

It suddenly occurred to me that bringing him into the house might offer some new diversion. We could pretend he was a member of our family, like the Arab sheik in *Ben Hur,* who kept his Arabian horses in his tent. To our surprise, Thunder was eager to climb the steps of the back porch and enter the kitchen. Although the floor proved hazardous as he slipped on the smooth linoleum, he merely regained his balance, and continued his inspection of this new space. We already knew he loved people food. He ate anything he could persuade us to give up: watermelon, cake, cookies. He'd never tried Mom's dill pickles so we got them out of the refrigerator to see if he liked them. To our delight, he crunched down half a jar of cucumbers and left a huge puddle of drool on the floor before we led him back outside.

The next time Mom and Dad went to town, they were barely out of the drive-way before Randy and I brought Thunder and Patsy into the house. Thunder felt even more at home this time. When he saw the eight loaves of bread Mom had just baked, still cooling on the table, he took an enormous bite from the center of the nearest loaf. Above the laughter and shouting, I yelled for Rex to hurry up and get out the dill pickles to distract him from the bread. Like a dog, Thunder followed him toward the refrigerator. He was so impatient to eat one, he knocked the quart jar out of Rex's hand. It broke, sending glass, pickles, and juice flying across the floor. I handed the lead rope to Randy and told him to take Thunder into the living room while I cleaned up the mess. Rex took Patsy, who, as a pony, was smaller and theoretically more manageable, but as the two horses turned together in the small kitchen, they lost their balance on the slick floor. In a cartoon scramble of Bambi on ice, the pony fell down, but Thunder emerged from the chaos and headed for the living room.

Randy led him past the large mirror hanging above our old waist-high wooden radio. Staring at himself in the mirror, Thunder saw someone he did not like. He laid back his ears and bit the top of the radio, leaving four deep teeth marks in the wood. The scars Thunder left on the radio sobered us for a moment, so we quickly got the horses out of the house, cleaned the mess on the floor, divided and ate the one loaf of bread, flopped down in the grass to laugh, and then swore our younger brothers and sisters to secrecy, telling them we would beat them up every single day their whole lives if they ever told Mom and Dad what we did. Later, when Mom noticed the deep scratches on the radio, none of us knew how they got there.

The horses seemed to enjoy their trips into the kitchen as much as we did. But one evening when we were eating supper, I decided we'd better quit. Thunder had opened the gate and escaped from the pasture. No surprise. He trotted up to the porch with one of his pony sidekicks. They both placed their hooves on the top step of the porch and peered into the kitchen through the screen door, waiting for pickles and bread. All of us kids froze. Rex began to grin, and Jan put her hand over her mouth to stifle a giggle, while I scowled ferociously at them. Dad was surprised but laughed.

"Look at that, would you?" he said. "Looks like they want to come right inside."

———

It was midwinter, bleak, and nearly dark on the afternoon Dad brought Ginger home. My brothers, sister, and I arrived shortly afterwards on the school bus. We trudged down the driveway, glad to be out of the swaying bus with the smell of exhaust and the heater blasting away at freezing toes. We walked into the house, threw down our books, and reached for Mom's crinkly molasses cookies. She was peeling potatoes for supper. Dad was sitting at the table drinking coffee, and suddenly turned to me. "Go to the barn and get me my lariat."

That seemed odd. "What for?"

"Just do as I say!" he yelled. He often told us, "Don't do as I do, do as I say." It was the unassailable position of many fathers. I put down my milk and cookies and slouched out, griping to myself.

I opened the Dutch barn doors and heard her before I saw her—a shrill whinny. I stopped short and caught a flash of white in the dim light. A slight filly stood tied to the center pole in the middle of the aisle—a strawberry roan with a white blaze down her face. She had delicate dark legs, perfect little round hooves, and a small Arabian head. I reached my flattened palm to her nose and she nuzzled it. I wondered whose she was and why she was in our barn. I stroked her face and nose and bent to kiss it, thinking all my happiness would lie in owning this creature. Then I remembered. Dad wanted his lariat, so I grabbed it off the hook and ran back to the house. Handing it to Dad, I asked, "Whose colt is that in the barn?"

"Yours," he said with a grin.

I hadn't dared hope she could be mine. It was the best thing he ever did for me. I thanked him, and that night I thanked God over and over again and promised to be his best girl.

———

Dad was a horse trader at heart, and he'd got her in a good deal. Even when a horse presented with a mangy coat, skinny ribs, and owner's neglect, his practiced eye could see value. Just looking at a beautiful horse was enough to thank God you were alive. I wonder if, for a moment, a horse helped him forget he had six kids to support and a farm that was failing. Dad loved to trade them and break them; he even relished cutting colts. His father, Earl Block, taught him how to throw a colt with ropes, sharpen and sterilize a knife, and castrate the poor devil. Dad would splash the area with Lysol solution, and with a deft motion, cut off the offending organs, sprinkle on a bunch of antiseptic powder, and a genderless creature would rejoin its mates, blood painting the inside of his flanks.

Cutting colts was an honorable profession in an area where veterinarians were scarce and horses were a part of everyday life. Few stallions are worthy of standing at stud, and their aggressive nature makes gelding a horse a good idea for all but the best of them. In the company of a receptive mare, a male horse can quickly move from your beloved pet to a dangerous animal unless you're a strong, competent handler. As one of the last of his kind, Dad reserved Sunday afternoons for colt cutting. As such, he earned a little extra money or the option to trade for the likes of Ginger, the lovely filly that stood in our barn.

At first, she was too young to ride, but there was plenty to do while I waited for her to grow stronger. She wasn't halter broke, so the first thing was to teach her to walk beside me on a lead—to stop when I said whoa, and to follow when I clicked my tongue. She learned fast, and we were soon at perfect ease with one another. For hours I played with her and watched her. She trotted with such grace; she ate and drank with perfect manners. She called to me when she heard my footsteps. When I brushed her coat, she watched me, her ears flicking and her head following my movements. I knew there'd never been a horse so smart and beautiful as Ginger.

What I didn't learn about horses from Dad I learned from *The Western Horseman,* a magazine that came to our house. Each month I read it cover to cover, and one month it totally paid off because they published an illustrated article titled "How To Teach Your Horse Tricks." I doubt many self-respecting cowboys read that and seriously thought, my horse needs to know this. But I couldn't believe my good luck. I envisioned some sort of lifetime career for us—the featured act in rodeos, maybe. In the next few weeks all my spare time was spent on Ginger's education. First, I taught her to shake hands. This was done by giving the command "Shake hands, Ginger" and poking her lightly in the shoulder with a pin so it resembled the bite of a fly. She would twitch her skin and paw the ground. As soon as she brought her leg forward I was supposed to grab it above the knee, lift it up, praise her profusely, and reward her with a sugar cube. After one week she was shaking hands on command.

Next I taught her to lie down. Teaching a dog to "lie down" was plain unimaginative. I anticipated the admiration I would get when I told a large animal like a horse to "lie down." This trick was a little more complicated. In quick succession I had to tap her front leg, give the command "lie down," then pick up her front leg, bend it to her body, grab her halter while still holding her leg, then pull her head around toward me and take a step backwards. If this was done all at once it was supposed to throw a horse off balance just enough to make her gently lie down. Sometimes it worked, sometimes she stubbornly kept her balance, and sometimes we simply fell down together. Then she got in the habit of simply leaning against me until I was the one who fell down. She might finally do it if it suited her and if she thought I had a reward. Somehow the trick lacked the elegance I'd envisioned. By far, her best trick was kissing me. She did it ever so gently, her soft lips pressed against my cheek—I was sure she knew it meant love, especially since she refused to ever kiss my brother even though he issued the command over and over.

When at last she was old enough to ride, getting her accustomed to the bridle, then the saddle was easy. But still, I mostly rode bareback, enjoying the freedom. Sometimes we slowly crossed the fields and woods, noticing wildflowers and scaring partridge from the tall grass. Other times Randy and I raced our horses, running breakneck for home, pretending the wolf pack chased us.

I thought Ginger would prove my natural love for horses, and that that love would bond me to Dad. It would be something intimate we shared. Sometimes I think he was pleased in a way, like when I won blue ribbons at the county fair. He fingered their smooth satin and smiled a little. Most of the time he deleted joy and spooked me into anxiety. When I learned to barrel race he accused me of thinking I was hot stuff. "You're just like the Sorensons," he'd say. I didn't know why he referred to my real father's family with a sneer. What was wrong with me, I wondered?

He assigned us jobs, and I was eager to do them. Often Randy and I rode around the pasture fences looking for breaks. We repaired and re-hooked wires to posts and insulators. Some of our fence was electric—one strand of wire strung around an entire field. We had to whack away the weeds that shorted the electric charge. Even with enough electricity to burn a cow's nose, they still managed to break out occasionally. During calving season, I was sometimes sent to search out a stray cow. Some cows went through the fence no matter what, driven to find a hiding place away from the herd where they could give birth—usually in the state forest north of our fields. It wasn't easy to bring home a dairy cow who was resentful and ready to charge anyone who came near her precious baby. But if they were left out too long the timber wolves would find them and kill the calf. I was determined not to fail Dad in any of these things. Then we got sheep.

The year Dad decided to raise a few sheep, he began with a small flock of ewes. Everyone knows sheep are dumb. But most people don't know how dumb. I didn't. Soft white lambs are adorable as they leap and play, but they do grow up to be sheep. If there was an animal award for being The Creature Most Unlikely To Think An Independent Thought, a sheep would win. Sheep do everything together. They eat together, run together, jump together. This behavior gets them into trouble together. Like a school of four-legged fish they will suddenly reverse direction, every last member of the flock, at the same instant, for God knows what reason. Their eyes reflect the world in dumb, hypnotic stares: yellow pools of cornea with black vertical slits. They never change expression. They never comprehend.

Our sheep were pastured near the farm buildings until fall, when they were turned out to eat on a fenced alfalfa field. That was when their troubles began. Earlier that summer we heard stories of livestock being attacked by timber wolves. A nearby farmer lost some turkeys, and another found a partially eaten calf carcass. At night we could hear the pack, howling deep in the swamp south of us, but so far they hadn't been around our farm. Then one afternoon after school, Dad sent Randy and me out on horseback to check on the sheep. We found two of them dead, partly eaten, and big wolf tracks around the area. The sheep were extremely nervous and ran from us until they hit the fence and bounced off, panting. We reported this to Dad, who hoped the wolves had moved on to other territory. The next day when we checked, two more were dead. This time only one had been partially eaten. The other one lay where it had bled to death with its throat slashed.

We herded the sheep closer to the barn thinking this would make the wolves stand off, but the next morning all the sheep had disappeared. They had been driven through the fence and onto the far field of an adjoining farm. We could see them from the bus as we drove by on the way to school—tiny in the distance. There they huddled, their numbers dwindling, right next to the dangerous woods that stretched two miles back to the lake without a break.

After school Dad sent Randy and me out again to bring home the remaining sheep. Challenged by this mission, we set off in high spirits to save our flock from the cruel wolves. I exhaled the stale air of the classroom and breathed in the crisp air of fall. We rode past yellow aspen, their golden, heart-shaped leaves rattling in the wind. The shadow of the woods stretched long across the open fields. A covey of grouse exploded from the ditch and flew into the brush nearby. Miles away a farmer burned off his flax fields, and the white smoke billowed into the sky, tinted pink by the setting sun.

When the sheep saw us coming on horseback, they all ran in the opposite direction. We split and galloped in a circle around either side of them and headed them toward home. We stayed to the rear on either side trying not to spook them, gently urging them to safety. To get there, we had to herd them past the field where the wolves had attacked. The closer we came to that place the more nervous they became. We drew even with it, and the collective memory of ripping teeth and tearing claws flipped their switch. They bolted past us, running all the way back to where we had started.

"Son of a bitch," my brother yelled. I thought worse, but didn't say it aloud. We started over again with the same result. By then it was too dark to see, so we had to let them go, and slowly we rode home. Dad was angry.

For two more days it was our mission to bring the dwindling sheep flock home. Each day we found another one dead, and each day they were farther from home. Each night we approached our farm, and they raced for miles in the opposite direction. I was failing at a simple task: Bring The Sheep Home.

Dad was working a job for the county during the day and was counting on us. He was frustrated to see his investment and hopes for a little extra money being eaten by wolves. That night he said, "What's the matter with you? Do I have to do everything myself? How tough can it be to bring in a few cockeyed sheep?"

I longed to deliver them so he could say, "You might not be my real daughter, but you sure can ride, and you saved our sheep." On the other hand, I was miserable enough to kill every remaining ewe myself to spare ourselves having to repeat this exercise forever and ever.

On the final night Randy and I made a new plan. We would bring them home a completely different way. About two miles from home, we would take them across the road and ditch and down the opposite side of our fields. Maybe we could fool them by easing them past the spot where they'd first been attacked. We had to hurry, as the days were growing shorter and there was not much daylight left after school. By this time there were only nine ewes left, and the carcasses of their mates were scattered over acres of land.

We found them about three miles west of our farm. We had seen them from the bus as we drove past on our way home from school. As we cantered around the little band and began to move them, I breathed, *Dear God, we are the sheep of thy pasture. Please make this work.*

By this time I was a teenager and had memorized many portions of the Bible and one that remains beautiful to me to this day is the twenty-third psalm—David's shepherd poem. His sheep ran all through my hours of searching on horseback. The notion that life is dangerous, but that a Shepherd God leads us through desperate, difficult paths—even through the dark places of death—wasn't just a poetic notion. It was about real life. We are relentlessly herded home to a place where we can throw off our clothes and lie down in complete safety: "Surely, goodness and mercy shall follow me all the days of my life, and I shall dwell in the house of the Lord forever" (Psalm 23:6). I believed it, I just didn't know for sure where that home was.

Our strategy almost worked. We were nearly there. We were across from our house and barn. All we had to do was turn them into the ditch, which was dry, chase them up the bank, across the road, and be home. Just as we attempted to do this, every surviving ewe bolted past us and raced back the way we had come. The clatter of little hooves and the rustle of dead leaves faded into the twilight.

The next day Dad brought the remaining sheep home. I don't know how he did it.

———

Dad sold Ginger after I left for college and it grieved me, but what did I expect? I was no longer living there. No one loved her like I did. And it costs money to keep a horse even when you own a farm. I hope he sold her to someone who took good care of her. Dolly, however, he kept until she was too old to bear the cold winters and too weak to chew her food. Then he sold her to the processing plant for a few dollars, but I saw him cry as she quietly walked up the ramp into the back of the truck.

Everything about horses was sweet. Even the odor of mucking out a horse stall is a pleasant memory, a healing gift. For years after I stopped riding—because urban life and finances made it impossible—the only time I rode was in my dreams, flying bareback across countryside on a magnificent horse. In the morning, I would awaken, startled to hear a city bus pull away from the corner, leaving a trail of diesel fumes drifting in the window. The creak and smell of leather, the sweat, the sweet alfalfa breath, the fields and thud of hooves slowly faded from my life.

---

## Thunder's Garlic Dill Pickles

Pickling cucumbers (approx. 4 inches long)
3 cups cider vinegar
1 cup water
1 cup sugar
1/4 cup pickling salt
Garlic cloves, peeled
Onions, peeled and quartered
Dill heads
Red pepper flakes

Wash cucumbers and soak in cold water over night. Sterilize jars. To each quart add 2 cloves garlic, 2 heads of dill (one on bottom of jar and one on top), 1/4 onion, and 1/4 tsp red pepper flakes. Pack cucumbers in tightly.

Bring vinegar, water, sugar, and salt to a boil, stirring to dissolve sugar and salt. Pour over cucumbers in jar. Make more brine as needed for amount of cucumbers and jars. Seal. Store in cellar for 6 weeks to cure.

---

# Morchella Esculenta

In the aspen woods west of our barn and corral, an elusive
mushroom called *Morchella esculenta* grew in the damp litter of
leaves and rotting vegetation. Living on decay, the morel mushroom,
as it is commonly known, is found during the month of May, after a
spring rain followed by a warm, humid day. Mysteriously, they spring
up overnight and blend so well with their surroundings you can stand
in an entire group of them and not notice. Their season is short;
morels quickly shrivel into small black globs that melt back into the
earth. Their dark, phallic caps with wrinkles and ridges make morels
an odd-looking treasure. And yet, when batter-dipped and fried in
butter there is nothing so succulent. My mother taught me to gather
this holy little treasure when I was a child. I thought they were too
ugly to eat, but I loved finding them for the challenge of it and for
the joy they brought my mother. To this day they remain rare,
but I've seen them in places like the farmer's market in Madison,
Wisconsin, where they appear for a week or two in the spring—
heaps and heaps of them for twenty-seven dollars a pound.

# THE COST OF BLOOD

In the same instant I raised my voice to scream, "Don't hit him!" Randy lofted through the air and landed with a soft thud on the ground. Lying crooked in the dust he looked a little like my cousin's broken doll thrown on top of her toy box—he didn't move or make a sound. I slowly approached and the hope that he was just faking leaked away; there was blood dripping from his mouth. That was the first time I thought I killed him. He was five and I was almost seven.

We were playing in the chicken house, an old building sitting in the pasture not far from the barn. Dad had nailed one board across the doorway, which allowed the chickens free range but kept out the cows and horses. We climbed over the board and scooped up handfuls of oats from the chicken feeder in our cupped hands and carried them back to our favorite heifer who stood patiently at the door. She watched us with her big cow eyes and licked up the oats, leaving our hands wet with slobber and tingling from her sand-papery tongue. We wiped our hands on our pants and ran for more.

When the horses noticed free oats being handed out they trotted over, ears laid back and teeth bared, to chase away our calf. Dolly and Keno leaned in, straining the board, and nipping one another for a better position. Horses love oats like some people love chocolate and will do almost anything to get them, including allowing themselves to be caught and ridden. I stomped my feet and ran at them yelling, "HEY! GET OUTTA HERE." They backed off except for Dolly's colt, Duke, who was by then a large, rangy bay. He was curious and not easily intimidated—the same horse who later kicked Bing in the head.

I saw a stick lying on the ground just outside the door and told Randy to get the stick and chase Duke away. He clambered over the board, picked it up, and walked over to Duke, who had turned his rump to us. It presented a large target, and Randy whacked it smartly—which, of course, startled him. The natural reaction of a startled horse is instinctual: I'm going to kick whatever this is to the planet Mars. That is what Duke did, with both hind legs.

Blinking fast, I wiped my eyes on my shirtsleeve and tried to think what to do. The horses gathered around in a circle, their ears pricked forward, watching expectantly. First, get him out of the pasture so they can't step on him. I dragged him into the chicken house, tugging his limp body under the board. He moaned a little, then flipped over, his face in the dirt and chicken shit, which instantly clung to his bloody cheeks and mouth. That was when I knew he was badly hurt—no one would ever, ever lie on the chicken house floor like that unless he was dying and couldn't help it. I had never felt so sick a about time; I wanted to reel it back in and throw a new cast like I could with my Grandpa's fishing rod. Why hadn't we done something else? We could have climbed trees or crawled under the haystack to find the new kittens. We weren't even supposed to feed oats to the calves. I didn't want to leave Randy alone. I didn't want to tell Mom and Dad. But what choice do you have when your brother is dying? I ran to the house, my voice rising in a wail: "Duke kicked Randy in the head. Come quick!"

I watched as Dad ran toward the chicken house and vaulted the gate. Later as he told the story, he said the first thing he saw was Randy's little red cowboy boots sitting on the ground, empty, a sock dangling over the top of one. They were lined up side by side, as though some strange power had carefully lifted Randy right out of them, like the tornado that blows the roof off a house but leaves the pies cooling on the counter. Dad knew Randy didn't like going barefoot and would not have willingly taken them off. It was a signal that made him dread what he would find in the chicken house. He turned Randy on his back and gently picked him up. Randy's head fell back and his eyes closed, their great fringe of black lashes matted to his cheeks. His mouth was open, and blood drooled out the side. His face was coated with smears of chicken manure and wood shavings.

I followed along behind as Dad ran him to the house and laid him on the kitchen table while Mom brought water and a washcloth to clean him up. When the blood coming from his mouth stopped, from where I was standing, I could see that both his upper front teeth were missing and I began to silently cry. Mom and Dad continued to feel him up and down and move his arms and legs. Nothing appeared broken, and Randy began to move and whimper as Mom held a cold cloth to his mouth.

I heard them decide he'd probably been knocked out for a few minutes and if nothing else was wrong, he would merely have a swollen lip and gap in his teeth until the permanent ones grew in. Mom and Dad looked at each other and nervously laugh. It was then I knew Randy was going to be okay.

I was so happy for him to be alive I didn't even care that I might get a whipping for giving chicken feed to the calf and for causing my brother to get kicked in the head. But all I got was a good talking to about how you never, ever walk up behind a horse and hit it on the butt, which I already knew was a stupid thing to do. I just didn't know Randy was too little to know better. For three days straight I filled the wood-box by myself without being asked. I even took out the slop bucket without being told.

Later Dad went out to search for Randy's teeth and his missing sock. He never found the sock and concluded the teeth must've been kicked right down his throat. It became a story Dad told again and again about how Duke kicked Randy right out of his boots and left them sitting there as if Randy had just stepped out of them.

The second time I almost killed Randy we were having one of our rock-throwing contests. We were a little older then because I remember Rex was out there with us. Jan was closer to Randy and me in age, being number three in the line-up, but she preferred to stay indoors. I have fewer memories of her, whereas Randy and my three youngest siblings (as soon as they could walk) were always outside and up to something. Usually we aimed the rocks at one another, dodging bullets that crashed into the stock tank or glanced off the sides of the metal granary with a clang. We rarely hit one another. I don't know what to attribute this to. It might have been God's grace or poor timing, I can't be sure. On this occasion we were lobbing rocks up to the peak of the barn roof and watching them roll down. They bounced off the hip, rolled, bounced again, flew off the edge, and landed on the ground with a satisfying ka-thump. Their descent had a musical rap-rhythm when we had three or four rocks going at once. We weren't allowed to throw rocks on the barn roof because it gouged the shingles, but Mom and Dad weren't home that evening and the damage we couldn't see might not exist.

We began competing to see who could launch the biggest rock without throwing it completely over the barn. I had worked up from pebbles to stones about the size of my fist when the winner crashed down on Randy's head and dropped him. He had his eyes on the ground looking for a bigger rock and wasn't paying attention to what was falling off the eaves. He was out cold, eyes rolled back in his head and blood pouring from a two-inch scalp wound. "His brains are coming out!" Rex yelled.

"Naw, they're not!" I screamed. "Get over to the milkhouse and turn on the pump."

The thought of losing my brother, or worse, being the one responsible for killing him instantly crushed my heart, and I began an internal litany calling out to God. *Please, please, dear Jesus, save Randy's life. I'm so sorry. I'm so sorry. Don't let him die.*

I was familiar enough with the Bible by then to know that bloody stories and all-hell-broke-out events were no strangers to God. In fact, if I had been the one writing the history of God's dealings with people, I would have left out some of the mayhem and failure, like the fact that Cain, the first son born into the world, killed his brother, Able, and it was no accident. At the same time, it seemed that in the very darkest hours of life God was likely to be there caring about and loving hurt people. I had no idea that my childhood practice of calling on something greater than myself would become a way of life, a sweet comfort, giving more shreds of wisdom than I'd ever find on my own. And here was a simple enough start: don't throw rocks on the barn roof anymore.

I had read about reviving the unconscious with cold water. Women who fainted were always sniffing salts or getting water sprinkled in their faces. So while I staggered backwards, dragging Randy by the arms from the barn across the yard to the stock tank, his head lolling back on his shoulders and bouncing along the ground, Rex turned the pump on full blast so we could save his life. By the time I got him to the hose, the water was coming up strong and cold enough to break your teeth. Our well was a hundred feet deep and came directly from the Arctic Circle. I sprayed it full on his face, praying, pleading with God to spare him. I was so grateful when he sputtered to life, I didn't even mind when he stood up, drew back his fist, and tried to sock me in the jaw. I ducked, and then tenderly wiped his face and pressed a rag to his head to stop the bleeding.

It was true there were times I wanted to hurt Randy, but I never really wanted him dead.

Did I want him disadvantaged? Yes. Did I want him outwitted? Always. I once tricked him into sniffing a cow pie, arguing they smelled good when they were whole and fresh. I pretended to inhale deeply as I bent close to one so new it was still steaming. "Aaaahhhh, wonderful," I breathed, "the fresher, the better. It's like new-mowed hay." He looked extremely skeptical. "You have to try it," I argued. "What can it hurt to try?" Finally he bent over, and as he sniffed, I buried his face in shit. Flicking it off his nose and lips, and shouting all the while that he was going to kill me, he got a stick, wadded a gob of manure on the end, and began to run after me. He chased me around the pasture for about twenty minutes before he gave up. The best thing about Randy was once a fight was over he never thought about revenge, and a few minutes later we went on playing like it never happened. I wasn't that forgiving or forgetful. It wasn't easy being God's good girl.

Had I thought of it, I may have pushed him headfirst into the carcass of a dead Holstein Dad had dragged to the far end of the pasture. When Randy accidentally fell into the cow on his own—no help from me—it was pure art. She'd been dead for a week and we were chucking rocks at her. Her stomach had blown up so large her legs stuck up like four huge pins in a cushion. The stink was so powerful we had to circle around upwind before we attacked. We were taking turns seeing who could be first to explode the stomach, but the rocks merely bounced off her tough hide. We were getting bolder, using larger stones and drawing a few steps nearer each time. Then Randy picked up a rock that required both hands to lift. He got a running start, and about six feet away, as he was getting ready to heave and run, he tripped. He fell forward at the same time as he hurled the rock. A dull "poof" sounded as it sank through the hide, releasing a geyser of gas and putrefying juice, some of which fell on his hands and shirt. He peeled off his shirt and threw up even as we both backed off laughing—he for having beat me in a contest, and I for his matchless timing.

Some of our quarreling came from a basic difference in worldview. It was true I worked for love and acceptance, but I also loved work for its own sake—it helped heal my need for purpose and significance. When I looked at life I saw stuff that needed to be done and people who needed to be doing it. Due to proximity, Randy was the most obvious recruit for any job: he was younger and theoretically more manageable.

"Here. Stack these bales over there. I'll move the loose hay, and then we'll have a castle where I can live."

"If we curry the horses and braid their tails they'll look very pretty."

"Let's clean up the yard; I'll mow, you restack the woodpile. It'll make Dad happy."

Randy's love of freedom and play made most of what I wanted to do look like Egyptian slave labor. He was always saying, "What *for?*" and running away to roll in the grass with the dog or do wheelies on the bike.

Sometimes I convinced him work was play, but there were many days when even games were a battlefield for our differences. When playing bat and ball became too work-like for him, which is to say, when I was telling him how to stand and swing every time he touched the bat, he would casually hit the softball over the fence into the stinging nettles in the ditch where I fumed and searched for it by myself. When he was tired of paying rent for my Boardwalk hotel, and before I could completely bankrupt him, he casually dumped the Monopoly board on the floor.

When Dad sent us out on a job, to my way of thinking, play was not even a remote option. It was then I resented Randy most for his terrible lassitude. And he detested me for my domineering, self-righteous attitude. There was another basic difference though: as first son, handsome and secure, he didn't have to prove anything, while I still naïvely hoped my contributions would help the farm be more successful, and more importantly, would make my stepfather like me. My intentions piled up like the mounds of brush and downed wood I dragged from the pasture, like the strips of bark we peeled from the cedar fence posts. All of it for Dad.

When we were no older than ages six and four, Mom would tell us to fill the wood-box beside the kitchen stove. With my intense desire to please her, too, I began with the fervor of a chipmunk storing nuts. Run to the woodpile in the backyard. Load arms with chopped birch. Stagger to house and up steps. Dump in box with crash. Back to the woodpile. Do it again.

Randy sat on the back steps petting the dog and staring at the sun until he was dizzy with spots. I stood in front of him with my hands on my hips and used my most compelling argument to get him up and working: "I'm *telling!*" He would sigh and look at me mournfully with his great blue eyes and say, "I's too tired ta work."

When we were old enough to do it, Dad offered to pay us a dollar to pick the sweet clover out of the red clover field. I loved this arrangement and thought, surely it was a benefit to all parties. Our red clover fields bloomed with a thick carpet of purple flowers eighteen inches high, but scattered throughout the fields were sweet clover plants. These tall tough weeds needed to be pulled up by the roots before they went to seed. If the field was harvested and the sweet clover seeds mixed in with the red clover, the crop's value suffered. Pulling them out was tedious and had to be done by hand. When the ground was dry the deep roots were reluctant to give up. Feet planted on either side, you grabbed the stalk with both hands and pulled with all your might. In a shower of flying dirt, the sudden release sent one crashing backward. When the soil was wet, the sweet clover pulled out easily, but the clay stuck to the soles of one's shoes until we teetered up and down the field on stilts of mud. Either way, we did it.

The thought of a whole dollar, perhaps even two, kept me focused. In Baudette—if we ever got there—one could go to the soda fountain at Rexall's Drug Store and get a Bridgeman's chocolate ice cream cone, one scoop for a nickel. Or two scoops for a dime. Think of it! At home we only had the kind made with real cream and fresh strawberries in a hand-cranked ice cream maker. I did the arithmetic: a dollar meant at least ten double-dip chocolate ice cream cones. Or one could go to the Ben Franklin Store and buy a Donald Duck comic book for fifteen cents. Maybe I would do both. I could feel the weight of four heavy quarters in my pink plastic coin purse.

After breakfast, when the dew on the grass dried enough to walk through without getting our tennis shoes sopping wet, Randy and I headed through the woods and across the pasture to the back field. We carried a MSason jar of water and a roast venison and mayonnaise sandwich for a mid-morning snack. It usually took us the better part of two or three days to finish forty acres. We began moving parallel back and forth across the field, taking it in portions swath by swath.

We waged war about particular plants. "That one's on your side," I'd say.

"No, it ain't."

"Yes, it is. Definitely. Now get it."

"You better get it. It's yours."

"I'm not gonna."

"Then just leave it and you'll see. I ain't gettin' it."

"It's yours!"

"Is not."

"Is too."

"Nuh-uh!"

"Uh-huh!"

He sauntered directly past a big sweet clover plant. Sighing, I went back and pulled it even though it was completely, definitely, on his side.

A few minutes later, I glanced over, and he was gone. At first I didn't understand how anyone could suddenly disappear in an open field. I scouted the horizon and yelled for him. No answer. I walked back to where I had last seen him and nearly stumbled over him. He was sunk in clover, watching the clouds, and listening to bumblebees hum through the blossoms. "I need to rest a minute or two," he grinned.

I grabbed his arm and jerked him to his feet. He flopped back down like a rag doll. I left him there, saying, "Okay, fine, but I'm telling and I'll get my dollar plus yours." Thinking murder, I went on alone.

On my way back across the field, I was already tired of being a martyr. When I found him lying in the same spot, I fell on him, intending to beat him up until he started working again. I sat on his chest to give his arm an Indian burn, but he grabbed my leg and flipped me over. We rolled together, and I stood up with him clinging to my leg. I made a fist and hit him with the knuckle of my middle finger. Right in the center of his biceps. Which he was always flexing and telling me to feel this, feel this. He screamed and bit my leg, clamping down hard on my calf. I tried to pull his hair, but he had a buzz cut and it was too short to get a grip. The bite was sending spikes of pain all the way to my spine, and I was bawling like a calf. Since he refused to let go, I stuck my finger in his mouth and raked my nail across the inside of his cheek as hard as I could. He released me instantly and stood up crying and spitting blood.

"Good," I said. "Serves you right. I probably got rabies from you and I'm gonna die." I stalked away, and we worked until the sun was overhead and we knew we could go home for dinner, our noon meal.

When we got back to the house I showed Mom my calf. His bite left a perfect impression of his upper and lower teeth, which was white at first but gradually turned to red and then to a satisfying, swollen purple lump. I got half his pay, and he got a spanking for biting and being lazy.

Duffy was the only pacifist I knew growing up. He was my favorite dog after Bing and could have passed for Lassie's twin. We got him from a family who lived in town and no longer wanted him. He was too much bother, and they thought the country would be a better place for him. His coat was matted and dirty with missing patches where mange revealed inflamed scabby skin. He was thin and his breath stank like a rotting corpse as he leaned over the front seat of the car and panted on our heads all the way home. Even in this shameful condition Mom detected his sweetness. She brought out the horse shears and clipped his coat, cutting out the cockle burrs, bits of mud, and sticks. She shaved his ruff and the stinking fur under his tail and gave him a bath by the pump. Dad treated his mange with kerosene and spread Bag Balm on his sores. I used the horse currycomb on the rest of his coat, pulling out gobs of hair. We fed him in an old aluminum pot by the back steps where he politely waited for table-scraps: leftovers of hot cereal with milk and cream, beef bones and fat, potatoes and gravy with bits of vegetables, and chicken skin. Dallas and Roxanne lay on the ground beside him, their little faces right at his dish while Duffy carefully ate his food, his plumed tail gently waving as he paused to wait while they examined his teeth.

I had a habit of running eveywhere I went, whatever I did. Now I had a running partner: from the house to the barn to the swing set, Duffy ran beside me. His shepherd's instinct for herding made him leap at my arm, barking, nipping at my heels, or gently grasping my wrist in his effort to lead me to safety, wherever that was in his doggie mind.

Duffy was a healer and a peacemaker and he expected us to share that calling. It was like living with Mother Teresa in a dog's ruff. He thought rings were toxic and gently tried to bite off my dimestore rings that turned my fingers green. He never fought. He was never aggressive. He never killed a thing, except frogs. He could not tolerate any quarreling between us kids. If we even wrestled in play he would get between us, tripping our feet, barking and tugging on our clothes and arms, trying to separate us. If Dad spanked one of us in the yard, Duffy came running to grab his arm. Dad would throw him off and yell at him. Duffy would back off, but Dad couldn't stop his barking and whining. No one else dared confront Dad like this.

As Duffy's coat grew back, he emerged shining and graceful—his pedigree so obvious. He was kind, smart, and beautiful. "We have a purebred collie," I bragged to my friends at school, fervently wishing I'd inherited the same lovely blood.

———

Some things on the farm are destined for death. That's just how it is if you want to keep your family alive. Early in the fall of the first year we owned Duffy, Mom and I learned that butchering deeply troubled him. The roosters who had arrived in a batch of mail-order chicks in the spring were ready for the freezer. From tiny balls of yellow fluff to fully grown Rhode Island Reds with shiny, arching tail feathers, bright red cockscombs, and spurs on their legs, they weighed anywhere from seven to ten pounds. By this time they were aggressive toward the hens, which they mercilessly mounted and pecked in the head. They fought one another, flying at each other with beaks and spurs. They shrewdly attacked anything they could get the better of, including young children who accidentally wandered across their path. Their crowing was never limited to a poetic greeting of the sun in the morning: it was a loud, tiresome competition conducted at all times of the day.

I didn't feel very sorry for them—there is hardly a more stupid animal than the chicken, unless it's sheep. It's different now; I might even give up eating chocolate forever if I could be amused by a little flock of free-range hens and eat their eggs besides. Even back then, it wasn't fun to butcher them; not that I was ever a vegetarian or anything. I disliked it because it reeked of blood, wet feathers, and burning hair, and because doing sixty in a day was a long wearisome job. Then Duffy arrived and added another layer to the complexity of life. He made the work disturbing. Even sorrowful.

Early in the morning on butchering day, Mom brought water to boiling in a large copper kettle on the gas burner in the milkhouse. While it was heating up, we went to the chicken house with a sharp axe and a long, heavy-gauge, wire hook with a narrow U loop on the end. Reaching in among chickens under the roost, I could single out a rooster, slip the hook around his leg, and drag him out. Then, with feathers and dust flying, I grabbed both legs, held him upside down, and carried him to Mom, who firmly grabbed the head and stretched the neck across a chopping block. With a quick motion she chopped off the head and tossed it. Before the spurting neck stump could spray me with blood I threw the body into the grass. There the headless rooster leaped and bounced aimlessly—like, well, a chicken with its head cut off, finally coming to rest with a twitch.

At first we thought Duffy was going to eat the head he picked up, but that wasn't it at all. Amazed, we watched as he carried it over to the body and laid it on the ground, nudging it closer, like, "Here it is. I've brought it back. You're going be okay now." He made repeated trips back to the chopping block, picking up heads and carrying them to the bodies scattered around us, so it wasn't random. How could a dog do this? How could he know what he was seeing? It didn't make us stop. I still loved Mom's fried chicken and the scrapple she made from cooking all the backs and necks, but from then on whenever we butchered chickens we locked Duffy in the barn to spare us all the grief.

After the chickens bled out we carried them to the milkhouse, dipped them in the hot water, and plucked them. The stink of wet feathers and burnt hair from singeing the skin clung to our clothes and hung in the air as we ate our noon sandwiches.

After lunch we began the gutting process. Mom was so fast—in about two seconds she could cut a hole around the anus and, with a sucking sound, pull out a pile of steaming entrails. I tried to keep up with her like this was the Kentucky Derby. Life was a race of speed and endurance. If you finished, you were a good person, and you got the prize: Mom's undying love and gratitude. But it was no competition to her: she was always grateful for help, and it never mattered that I was slower.

One day I did do something, which felt as good as winning the barrel races at the county fair. I liked to think I did it for her and Dad, too. I saved the life of a cow. She was as good as dead and I saved her, not like I paused to think of all this at the time.

Mom had some kind of terrible back pain and could barely walk; otherwise she would have dealt with the crisis. It was rare to find her lying down, but she was on the couch that day. She was reading her Bible, and I knew she was praying because she closed her eyes some of the time. There was a lot of stress in the family because the farm wasn't bringing in any income, Dad was gone working on road construction somewhere in the county, and Mom had been doing a lot of the field work that summer while I took care of my siblings. She rode the tractor for hours, pulling the cultivator over our summer-fallow fields. I didn't want her to be in such pain, but I was so happy to have her home even if she had to stay on the couch. It made the day feel glorious and free with her there.

The previous summer had been a bad one for her. It began with a cold and sore throat followed by weeks of exhaustion. She felt feverish every day and when her hands and feet began to swell and her chest hurt, Lou, her friend and spiritual mentor, wisely told her she needed to get into the doctor right away. He immediately hospitalized her with rheumatic fever: her heart was enlarged, which was serious enough to require a month's stay at least. Bed rest was absolutely mandatory.

After two weeks, Dad brought us to visit her one Sunday afternoon. I can't remember where we all stayed while she was hospitalized. I think I was home with one or two siblings and the rest must have stayed with Grandpa and Grandma Block. Children weren't allowed inside the hospital, so we stood out in the parking lot, a scruffy lineup of motherless kids, a little dirty, our clothing awry, and she waved to us from the window of her second floor room. I remember looking up at her with a choking feeling, worried she might never return home. As far as

I knew no one went into the hospital unless they were going to die like my father or have a baby like my mother.

Reflecting on that time, Mom says she couldn't stay any longer, even though the doctor wouldn't sign her out. The next day she left. There was so much work to do at home, she couldn't fathom how it would get done unless she did it, and seeing us in the parking lot looking so forlorn with Dad crying as he held up Roxanne, the baby, and pointed—"Wave to Mommy,"—made her decision to leave the only solution.

That night in bed I prayed that God would make our mother well again. The next day he dropped a huge deposit in my faith account when Grandpa Frolander delivered her home. Just like that. I couldn't believe it. I didn't know until many years later that Mom also believed God had healed her. When she returned for a check-up two weeks later, the doctor was amazed to find no evidence of disease.

It was on a day about a year later, as I cleared the breakfast dishes, that I looked out the window and noticed one of our best dairy cows had escaped from the pasture into the field next to the yard. She was mowing down dew-drenched alfalfa as fast as she could.

This is not a good thing for cows. Wet, green alfalfa forms a volatile mix in a cow's first stomach, the rumen (they have five altogether), and it causes bloat. Green alfalfa, plus water, plus enzymes, plus bacteria, equals a powerful bovine gut-bomb. An enormous amount of gas and foam builds, and if something isn't done quickly to neutralize the process, she will die. Her stomach expands until it crushes her heart and lungs. As I approached her, I could hear her heavy breathing and the rip of the alfalfa as she continued to wrap her tongue around bunches and tear them from the earth. Her stomach was already looking more round than normal on the left side. I chased her through the yard, into the barn, and hooked her up in a stanchion. I ran to tell Mom about it and to ask whether I should treat her. She said to do it, and as fast as I could. The loss of just one cow was unthinkable—her value, her weekly contribution to our income, the nourishment she gave.

I knew how to prepare the remedy, though I had no idea why it worked. You took a Coke bottle and filled it with half kerosene and half milk. You shook it up and forced the mixture down the cow's throat. This isn't so easy for a man, let alone a girl. The cow does not want to drink kerosene and milk. She does not feel well and wants to lie down. Her pain makes her toss her head, streaming saliva in all directions. She groans and kicks at her belly, trying to rid herself of pain. But I tried. I grabbed her lower jaw, lifted her head up, forced the Coke bottle into her mouth, and began to pour the liquid down her throat. The cow threw her head against my arm, knocked the glass bottle from my hand, shattering it against the cement manger. I ran to prepare another dose, brought it back, and forced the second mix down her throat. She coughed up the entire thing. It spewed across my face and down my front. I spat and made myself stay calm. It looked like she was going to fall, and if that happened it would be too late for help. Dripping kerosene, I ran back to the house to ask Mom whether she thought drastic measures should be taken. She was unequivocal: "Yes, the cow is dying. It's worth the risk."

My habit of reading every single piece of literature, though most of what came into our home would not strictly qualify as literature, was about to save a life. Dad subscribed to a magazine called *Successful Farming*, and I was so starved for reading material I read every word of it every month. I knew about crop rotation, Bang's disease, and wheat rust. All seemingly useless information for an eleven-year-old—until now. I remembered an article titled "When It's Too Late For Oral Remedies." The author described the worst-case scenario when you have a bloated cow, the vet cannot be reached, and you've tried the antidotes, which haven't worked. Although it is rarely done, you can take a knife, punch a hole in the cow's stomach, and release the gas.

Thinking bigger is always better, I grabbed the largest butcher knife we owned. It was more like a machete with its wide, eight-inch long, steel blade. I ran back to the barn with Duffy at my heels trying to trip me. This time my brothers and sisters followed in our wake, eager to witness anything involving blood sacrifice. Even Mom hobbled out to watch, bent over and clutching her back. By this time the cow was swaying and appeared about to fall down. As I approached her side I saw a problem *Successful Farming* had not addressed. I didn't know exactly where to stab her because the illustration in the article showed the only correct place to insert the knife was a depression right in front of the cow's pelvic bone. The cow used as a model stood calmly chewing her cud with a normal-sized belly, and clearly, in the photo, the depression was obvious. Our cow looked like a giant beach ball about to pop. I had no idea where her depression was. I held my arm up to stab her, aimed for the most likely spot, and brought the knife down. The tip merely bounced off her hide.

Mom shouted, "Do it again! Harder! Much harder!" I was shaking and praying in my heart with a sustained yell that filled the barn and the entire sky above us. God must have heard. With both hands, I held the knife above my head, and with all my strength plunged the point into her side. The knife sank to the hilt and a geyser of foul gas and foam blew into my face and hair. The lips of the cut reverberated, making the most prolonged farting sound we'd ever heard. We all stepped back, gagging from the terrible smell, and laughing with relief as gas continued to hiss through the hole.

The article suggested that after performing this life-saving procedure, a cow should be walked for half an hour in order to work out any remaining gas. As Randy and I took her back to the pasture, Mom told us to come back to the house when we were done. As a family we said grace at meals, but we rarely got on our knees to pray together. That day Mom asked us to kneel beside the couch. In a row, we knelt beside her, our hands folded, our eyes closed, and she thanked God, who cares for us in all things, and who helped us save this cow from certain death. Reeking of kerosene and stomach acid, I thanked God, too, because of my great happiness in doing something heroic. And because now I knew what I wanted to do for life: I had performed my first surgery. I was destined to become a doctor. I would treat injuries and heal people.

This, I knew would merge perfectly with my dream of becoming a hero, and possibly an inventor of great, life-saving devices at the same time. It would make Mom and, especially, Dad, proud of me. There was another reason, less noble. I rather liked broken bones, blood, guts, and accidents. I just did. I knew this interest was a little strange when later that summer Grandpa Block injured his hand while harvesting corn. The picker had jammed up with corn stalks, and Grandpa reached into the machine to pull them out. He was a tall, bull-necked man who could palm a fifty-pound keg of nails like it was a two-pound can of Folgers coffee. Once, with his back, he held up a wagon loaded with hay while someone else changed a flat tire. And one time he got his bib overalls caught in the hay baler, which tore his pants completely off, forcing him to sneak back over the fields and into the house in his underwear. In his mind, this was practically the same as being naked. Farmers loved that story, and everyone knew that most men would have been dragged into the baler and killed, but Grandpa withstood the force until the denim seams popped and his pants gave way.

On the day Grandpa was trying to free up the corn picker, it grabbed his hand, and he pulled back so hard and so fast that the machine only tore off his index finger and the tendon that ran up his hand. The next time we were at their house, Grandpa said, "You want to see something?" We nodded dumbly. You never knew. Once it was little brown balls of rabbit poop that he tried to convince us to eat because they were vitamins. He went to the freezer and pulled out a plastic bag containing a fat gray bratwurst with a long, whitish egg noodle attached to it. But when he turned it over we saw the finger nail. Everyone else clapped their hands to their mouths and backed off. Grandma said, "For heaven's sake, Earl, get rid of that thing." But I stepped closer. It took my breath away.

That the cow lived was more of a miracle than we knew. The next time the vet came out to the farm Dad showed her to him, and they looked at the scar, which was healed over by then. The vet raised his brows and asked about the size of the knife I used. Dad brought it out and the vet thoughtfully turned it over in his hand, feeling the edge. He shook his head and said the knife was way too big, and given the spot where I stabbed her, there was no way I could have missed hitting a vital organ or cutting an artery.

I thought of a picture of Jesus in Mom's King James Bible. It was a color illustration—a reproduction of a classical painting, it may have been Rembrandt. It was protected by a thin, transparent sheet of onion-skin paper which, when lifted, made the picture jump out. There were other illustrations, but I always returned to this particular one of Jesus on the cross. There were women crying, and other folk gathered below him. The sky was dark with frightening black clouds. No one could save Jesus now from what was happening. In the picture he was already dead, but a soldier was making sure. He stabbed Jesus, leaving a gash in his side, and blood and water ran down his leg. The soldier hadn't missed the spot, and I wondered how it felt to press the point of your blade into the side of the Son of God. Was there a sudden give as it sank through the skin and ruptured his stomach and heart? I wished I'd been there because I was sure I'd have tried to save him. I didn't like to think that his dying for the sins of the world included some of the evil little things I did. I had fallen in love with him and fervently wished there had been a way around the cross.

There was another time I might have healed a bloated steer by stabbing him, but it was not only too late for milk and kerosene, it was too late for the knife. In the end I had to kill him. It was after the evening dew had fallen and he'd gotten into the alfalfa field nearby. As Randy and I drove him into the barn, he fell down across the gutter, giving a deep groan. There was nothing to do then, he was dying. I ran for the big butcher knife again. I didn't know that if you knew precisely where the vessels were you wouldn't need to practically saw off his entire head to hit the jugular vein and drain off the blood. Randy helped me, holding the head, stretching it back and back as I cut through hide and muscle, slashing across the heavy esophagus and trachea, continuing on and on nearly to the vertebrae, it seemed. The steer's eyes were open like he was looking at me pleading, but I kept going until I finally hit the big vein and the blood gushed. Poured out. Quarts and quarts of it. We looked in wonder at the steer's life floating there in the gutter—a glistening river of red, and I saw his eyes glaze as his body drained.

When Dad came home he said we'd done right. Bleeding the steer right away meant the meat could be salvaged for us to eat, so it wasn't a total loss.

## Scrapple

One pig's head, washed
(Chicken backs and necks may be substituted for pork)
Oatmeal
Water
Salt
Pepper

Place head in a large pot. Cover with water and bring to a boil. Simmer
for two hours or until meat is tender and skin slips off bones. Cool.
Remove head from pot, reserving the cooking liquid. Separate meat from
skin, cartilage, and bones. Discard brains and tongue. Dice meat into small
pieces and save in a large mixing bowl. Be sure to include some of the fat.
Measure amount of scraps and make an equal amount of oatmeal: bring
reserved cooking liquid to a boil in a large pan and for each cup of liquid
add 1/3 cup of oatmeal. Simmer until oatmeal has thickened. Add meat
scraps and fat to the oatmeal. Mix well and season with salt and lots of
pepper. Spoon mixture into bread pans and refrigerate until set. Unmold
from pan, cut into 1/2 inch slices and brown in frying pan until crisp.

Serve for breakfast with maple syrup. May be frozen until needed.

# The Common Loon

The common loon, a water bird found in the northern regions of our country, nests on the shores and islands of Lake of the Woods. As an adult it weighs close to eleven pounds and has a wingspan of five feet. With its distinct black and white plumage, it looks as though it were designed by a Native American minimalist. The loon rides low in the water, sleek, elegant, and perfectly made for diving after fish, its main diet. Loons mate for life. Each spring they renew their bond in a love ritual of transcendent grace. They are devoted parents, raising one or two chicks each season. The chicks take to the water as soon as they are hatched and are allowed to ride on the backs of their parents when threatened, cold, wet, or for any reason at all.

The loon is Minnesota's state bird and the subject of every local wildlife artist. It is carved, drawn, and painted on everything from mailboxes to electric switch plates made of birch bark. Walk into any store that sells Northwoods ambiance and you will hear a CD playing in the background—an orchestra accompanied by the manufactured sound of waves breaking on the shore, punctuated by the tremolo call of the loon. The loon has been romanticized, trivialized, and over-marketed. But encounter it in real life when it rises from dark water twenty feet in front of your canoe, looks at you with its red eye, and calls—well, naturalist Charlton Ogburn describes it like this: "It raises a cry that wells up out of the quiet in a clear falsetto and falls off to drift away . . . into silence, a silence profound and intense. God only knows what you would think if you did not know the origin of that voice . . . The effect is devastating."

It is filled with such mournful beauty that, for a moment, your heart dreads and involuntarily thinks of eternity.

# N IS FOR "NEEDS IMPROVEMENT"

I could see the yellow school bus a mile away, flashing along the road toward our house. I was five years old, it was the first day of first grade, and the bus was coming to pick me up. For the hundredth time, I checked: I was carrying my lunch in a brown paper sack—a venison and mustard sandwich, a chocolate chip cookie, and an apple. I had a pencil box containing a jar of paste, a pink eraser, two yellow pencils, and a box of Crayolas with eight colors. I smoothed the red gingham skirt of the school dress Grandpa Frolander had bought me when we were in Kenora, Ontario. My white anklets were neatly folded down, and my new saddle shoes were tied in double knots. I wore my red sweater buttoned to the neck, because the sun hadn't melted the chill from the air. I was ready.

Randy, who was at the window watching with me, announced to Mom and Dad, "The bus is coming!" I ran for the door, already anxious about missing it, even though the driver, Dad's uncle Johnny Block, was a patient man. He had to turn around in our yard to go back the way he had come, so he wasn't likely to leave without his passenger. As I ran past Dad, he grabbed me, cupping my elbow in his big hand. "What's your hurry?" he asked. "Aren't you going to give me a good-bye kiss?" I gave him a kiss and hopped up and down, trying to escape. Mom patted my head and assured me I would do fine. Bing was barking, and Randy was now howling, "He's turning into our driveway!"

Finally, Dad released me, and I ran outside to wait as the bus rolled to a stop in our yard. I climbed up the steps, and as the door shut behind me, I felt a wave of nausea. The long aisle of the half-filled bus stretched out forever as every eye inspected me. Mom had explained that when I got on I could sit anywhere, so I fell into the nearest empty seat, right behind the driver.

We arrived in Williams, a town of 250, with a fleet of other buses, and parked in front of the school. I got off the bus and stood on the sidewalk while kids of all ages rushed past, talking and laughing. They swarmed across the schoolyard, down the walks, and through the doorways of a building so large I felt invisible standing before it. Until then, I don't think I'd been inside any building larger than our barn. Two hundred students were bussed in from surrounding farms and townships to attend grades one through twelve, and I seemed to be the only one who didn't know how to find my classroom. Mom had tried to prepare me for this moment by telling me to ask for directions; she claimed anyone would be happy to help me find the first grade, but I was speechless. I clutched my lunch sack and pencil box tightly to my chest. I'd never seen so many people I didn't know. I wished I were home playing with Randy and Bing. As my eyes began to water, two big girls stopped and asked if I was a first grader. Delinda Peterson and Pinky Bergen were in second grade, and being the smartest girls in their class, they knew everything about everything, and that included where I needed to be. "C'mon," they said, "we'll take you to your room." It was the kindest thing anyone ever said to me.

The main building of the school was three stories high with worn wood floors and polished oak banisters. Cloakrooms with hooks and shelves annexed each classroom. On the way to lunch that first day, we passed the gymnasium, where echoed shouts and stale sweat already hung in the air. Giant boys with squeaking tennis shoes were bouncing balls and firing them at a basketball net. Bleachers ran along one side of the gym opposite a stage framed with heavy velvet curtains. Five years earlier, my father's military funeral had been held in this gymnasium, his flag-draped casket on the stage we now crossed; the Congregational Church hadn't been large enough for the crowd that attended.

In the cafeteria I ate my sack lunch and drank a bottle of milk that cost five whole pennies. I soon envied students who had a quarter and could buy hot lunch every day—except Fridays. No one wanted hot lunch on Friday, because the kitchen always served baked salmon cakes with white sauce and canned peas, on account of Catholics who weren't supposed to eat meat on Fridays. The smell of canned fish wafted through the school and penetrated classrooms long after lunch was over, reminding us of Hal Bitzer's comments: "It looks like puke and tastes like dog poop."

For twelve years school was a world where I tried to blend in. Although I hid them when possible, poverty and religious beliefs made association with me a social risk. No one in our county was considered rich, but there's a relative scale of wealth anywhere in the world. At school, if you were really poor the students didn't like you, and teachers felt sorry for you—that is, if you were poor and smart. If you were poor and stupid, then, the teachers didn't like you either. I soon figured out that compared to most other families, we were near the bottom.

For one thing, most girls wore a different dress to school each day of the week; most had three pairs of shoes, and for another thing, their socks looked fresh and new. I learned to move fast when changing into tennis shoes for gym class, hoping no one would notice my toes sticking out the ends of my socks and my bare white heels. Their fathers drove big John Deere tractors and combines. Their mothers drove four-door sedans and stopped having babies after three or four. They had indoor bathrooms and telephones. Some kids even had their own bedrooms.

Each December I was reminded that our religion didn't allow us to go to the movies when I missed the long-awaited treat for the entire school. The local theater sponsored a free Disney movie and everyone attended the annual event. At the end of the movie, Santa Claus distributed a brown paper bag filled with treats of red and green Christmas hard candies, salted peanuts in the shell, popcorn balls, and a red apple for every student. In first grade, only myself and one other boy, Stanley Zook, a Mennonite, stayed behind. The two of us sat at our desks glumly coloring mimeographed images of holly wreaths and candles, and I wondered if the chaperone would remember to bring a sack of treats for us, too.

As we watched the afternoon sun sink lower and lower, Stanley leaned across the aisle and whispered, "What are you? What church?" I didn't know what to say because I wasn't aware that there were other churches in the world. When I was a little older it seemed embarrassing to explain we were part of a group that claimed it was not a denomination, that denominations were man-made institutions and wrong, and that we were just Christians, and the church (small "c") was the people of God, not a building. A few years later when someone asked, I just said we're sort of like Baptists, which made people nod and change the subject.

When Mom became a Christian somewhere between my first and second grade, this small rural gathering of people became our community. This is where I learned that people must keep themselves holy and unspotted from the evils of the world, which were mainly drinking, dancing, and movies, all of which had the power to chain your heart and ruin your life. Most of the time the difference between us and the rest of the world didn't stand out much, and being part of a loving church community that took care of one another's needs and had services on Sundays, as well as picnics, baptisms, baseball games, and potlucks, made our beliefs plausible.

After first grade the annual Christmas movie didn't matter so much, because anyone who didn't go to the movie was allowed to skate all afternoon without supervision. No teacher wanted to monitor an outdoor ice rink for that long in temperatures below zero. The few of us who stayed back didn't care about the cold, we went in and out of the skating shack, warming our hands in the dark by the smelly oil burner, returning to the ice to play pom-pom pull-away, and crack-the-whip, which often launched the end skater over the board fence, and plunged her headfirst into the snow-banks on the other side.

At first, the two best things about school were chocolate milk—I'd never had it before—and the girls' bathroom. Each morning the janitor came down the hall, pushing a cart stacked with wooden milk cases full of little bottles: half-pints of milk, regular or chocolate, clinking together, announcing the arrival of our mid-morning break. The janitor left them by the door, and milk monitors passed them out. Sometimes Mom gave me five nickels, which paid for a chocolate milk every day for a week. Billy Thompson and Dale McGuire never got any. They watched the rest of us sitting at our desks with unopened bottles waiting for teacher's permission before we carefully tore off the foil, pulled the cardboard seal from the mouth of the jar, and drank. The sweetness in those bottles couldn't match anything I'd ever drunk in life.

After milk-break came my second favorite thing: a trip to the bathroom. It wasn't that I'd never used an indoor toilet. Grandpa and Grandma Frolander had one. It was just that my everyday experience was the outdoor toilet. It was a stinking little hut, which could be rocked on its foundations and even tipped over when some poor kid was inside, with her pants down around her ankles. One might never even know who to get even with for daring to interrupt elimination. So for revenge, you just got into the habit of rocking the thing whenever you were passing by and noticed the door was latched from the inside. It was a dark inferno in the summer and a fierce freezer in the winter. I hated the flies that careened past, flicking off my bottom, and I rarely exposed it without a vision of wild animals living down that hole just waiting to sink their teeth into my soft, white flesh. Checking it was profoundly unpleasant, but an absolute necessity before sitting down. Most of the time an old Sears & Roebuck catalog served as toilet paper; we tore off a page at a time, crinkling it up to soften it a little.

At school, bathroom behavior was strictly enforced: we were sent in with instructions to do our business, wash our hands, and get back to our desks without talking. I loved the bathroom because it was clean, white, and boy-proof. It smelled good, like bleach and industrial soap, not human waste. There were not one, but two sinks with running hot and cold water, mounted waist high so a girl could easily reach the warm stream of water with her hands. There were three open stalls, each with a clever, dwarf-sized porcelain commode that flushed. When I sat on the little toilet I felt like Goldilocks sitting in Baby Bear's chair—it was so just right.

On the way to the bathroom, we passed a cot set up in the hallway. This was where they put you if you got sick during the day and your parents didn't have a phone so your mom could be called to come get you. Sometimes I saw someone fevered and tossing, trying to sleep amid ringing bells and students' stares.

We relished the news of someone throwing up on the floor, and reviewed how disgusting it was when the janitor mopped up the chunks. When my turn came to lie hot and dreaming on the cot all day, I didn't know what was worse, being sick or getting gawked at.

Kindergarten was not offered in our school district, and Mom must not have thought about teaching me the ABCs before I started first grade. Maybe it didn't occur to her because she was simply young, only twenty-two at the time I started school. Or perhaps she was overwhelmed with everything else that needed to be done. At first, it didn't bother me that I knew nothing about the alphabet or counting. I still don't know much about numbers, but it doesn't trouble me much anymore. Other children in class proudly called out letters and numbers when the teacher pointed at them with her long pointy stick. Some of them even knew how to print their names. The shapes that made my name were a torturous code, and I was astonished when our teacher, Miss Edwards, expected me to transfer them onto every paper I was given. Until then I hadn't given letters any thought. It was a shock to learn that they were the main point of school, and the key to happiness and success in life.

She divided our class into three sections for special reading times in the circle at the front of the room. Students who already knew how to read were in Reading Group I. Those who recognized letters and knew the sounds they made were in Reading Group II. The rest of us were assigned to Group III. Our names were all listed on the blackboard under their assigned group. I was pleased when Miss Edwards carefully pointed them out. There on the board were my special letters. M-a-r-g-i-e. Everyone could see how nicely they looked together.

Long after the other groups had moved on to other readers, Group III began the painful journey through the first Dick and Jane primer. *See Dick run. See Jane run. See Spot run. Run. Run. Run.* The pictures were colorful, but plot was woefully absent. I might never have finished it, except I began to notice the other picture books Miss Edwards brought from a place called the library. She read aloud to us: fairytales, fables, stories about orphans so poor they lived in a boxcar. I began to think reading might have some potential.

I was still oblivious to class standings on the day Delinda Peterson and Pinky Bergan peeked into our classroom and saw my name on the board under Group III. That noon hour I went outside to play with them as usual; Delinda and Pinky allowed a few specially chosen first grade girls to help them in the store they'd set up on an old wooden bench beside the skating shack. We collected bits of trash—Almond Joy wrappers, Juicy Fruit gum packets, empty Coco Cola bottles—and sold them to customers who paid with used milk bottle caps. But that day they told me, "Dummies can't play with us." I was stupefied. I was a good gatherer. I didn't mind walking all the way to the ball field looking for candy wrappers blown up along the fence. Then, in a chorus they said, loud enough for the entire world to hear, "You're in Reading Group III—nanny, nanny, boo-boo, stick your head in poo-poo." I didn't immediately get the connection, but I understood the humiliation of getting fired in front of the customers lined up at the store. I quickly left for the far side of the playground where I sat in the dirt, pretending to concentrate on making a row of pebbles.

That was when I decided to work on reading. Words began to light up in spellbinding stories. I was like the one who flew away to the window in a flash, "tore open the shutters and threw up the sash." I beheld far more than eight tiny reindeer and Santa Claus on the breast of the new-fallen snow. Books exploded into talking horses, trolls living under bridges, and the poetic order of "In an old house in Paris that was covered with vines lived twelve little girls in two straight lines."[1] At first, this progress was noted in Ns for "Needs Improvement," which was slightly better than the rows of Us, for "Unsatisfactory" that I'd been bringing home on my report card. The teacher's comments moved from "Does not recognize letters or numbers" to "Needs to work on comprehension." Then, my report burst into rows of the coveted Ss for "Satisfactory." And best of all this: "Margie has been moved from Reading Group III to Reading Group I." Miss Edwards could have added, "And she's been rehired as a clerk in the playground store."

Here was proof to my sweaty little soul—if you work hard enough? You win. You win it all! Teacher, friends, and parents. Mom was proud of me. I wasn't so sure about Dad. He called me Miss Smartypants, and I didn't need to know the word sarcasm to get what he meant.

I began to read everything from picture books to cereal boxes. I even read the Sears catalog as I sat in the outhouse: MIRACLE FABRIC! 100% Nylon! Women's Shirtwaist Dresses, Our Lowest Price Ever—$7.29. The only books we had at home were a set of Childcraft books Mom bought from a traveling sales-man after he convinced her that any responsible mother who cared about her children's education would make any sacrifice to buy these books. She later re-gretted paying the ransom month after month when she couldn't afford to buy sanitary napkins. But I was glad to read the stories over and over. By the time Roxanne, my youngest sister, learned to read, they were broken and tattered from long years of use.

Students in our school weren't allowed into the library until third grade. Until then, "Library Day" meant going to the table at the back of the classroom and choosing two books from the armload the teacher hauled down from the third floor.

So it was Mrs. Cole, our third-grade teacher, who introduced us to the library. I liked Mrs. Cole for a lot more than this, and in spite of her ability to say, without turning from the chalkboard, "Margie, why don't you stand up and read that aloud to the rest of us" in such a conversational tone, you'd have thought she was just telling us to get out our math books and turn to page forty-six. I knew that during recess I'd be standing shame-faced at the chalkboard writing "I will not pass notes in class" about a hundred times, but I liked her because she understood the things that could terrify a child's heart.

One day during December, Mrs. Cole called me out of the classroom into the hall to ask if something was wrong. That week Randy and I were staying with Grandpa and Grandma Block because Mom was in Warroad staying with Grandpa and Grandma Frolander while waiting for the birth of our brother Rex. It seemed magical and a little alarming that an adult could know something was amiss when I didn't think I had said or done anything to betray my feelings. That day I was so scared my heart felt like it was getting crunched by an oat grinder, and I didn't trust myself to say anything aloud. I stood silent, not speaking until she knelt down, put her hand on my shoulder, and waited. At last, I told her, "My brother, Randy. He was taken to the hospital last night cause he was coughing blood. Grandma says he has pneumonia."

I knew this meant he was going to die like my father had. When we were sick with ear infections or had tonsillitis and couldn't swallow for days, we did what we could with home remedies, like having Dad blow cigarette smoke into your aching ear canal or getting your chest smeared with Vicks VapoRub and a handkerchief pinned around your neck. Mrs. Cole's glasses hung on a chain around her neck, and she paused to put them on so she could look straight into me. "Randy will be just fine. Today doctors have medicines that cure pneumonia. He'll be back home in no time. Okay?" She patted my head and sent me back to my desk.

I loved her for that reassurance, but I loved her as much for taking us to the library. Unaware of worlds about to unfurl before me, I was more excited by the journey to the library, which took us through the entire school. We lined up at the classroom door and headed out—down the elementary grades' hall through the double doors to the back of the stage. We marched across the stage and through a dark passage, past the door to the band room, where we heard a man's low, urgent voice—"Again from the top, ah one, an-dah two, an-dah ..." —followed by the screeches of an I-didn't-know-what. Around a corner, down more steps, and past the locker rooms on the right, then up three flights of dimly lit wooden stairs to the very top floor, passing classrooms filled with big kids.

We arrived at a large, oak door with an opaque window marked LIBRARY in gold letters. Mrs. Cole placed her finger across her lips in a warning and slowly opened the door, motioning us to tiptoe in. We entered a cavernous room where sunlight streamed through high-ceilinged windows, glancing off large oak tables, and across polished wood floors giving a golden glow to the room. The dry smell of paper and old cardboard with hints of leather and mimeograph ink hung in the air. Then I saw the shelves, case after case rising to the ceiling on every wall. They were filled with what must have been all the books of the world. Shiny titles glistened on spines of brown, red, and green, all of them gathered right in this room.

As I gazed at this miracle, quite by accident, my glance fell on a familiar name. *Bambi.* I held my breath as I pulled the thick, rusty-brown hardback off the shelf. The head of a buck was embossed in gold on the cover. I had read the Little Golden Book about a fawn who grew up to be a stag, and from my class-mates, I knew about the Disney movie called *Bambi,* but I didn't know it was based on a story long enough to fill a book this size. I turned to the first yellowed page and began to read until I heard, "Children, two minutes left. Make your selections and check out your books." For the rest of the day I reached inside my desk fingering the book and wishing the day would hurry past so I could go home and read. *Bambi* was my first book without pictures. As a child I so com-pletely missed the author's animal rights message I thought the book was only about my favorite theme—life is dangerous and hard, but if you work at it and do what is right, in the end you meet your soulmate and live happily ever after, even if you're an animal.

I began feasting on books, gobbling everything like a pig happily rooting in the kitchen slop. My new habit irritated Dad, and he began a refrain I heard many times: "Get your nose out of that book, you cock-eyed bookworm. The house could burn down around you and you'd never know. Get outside and do something!" I put the book aside, but when he wasn't around, I read until my head ached, and my eyes hurt. I read on the bus, in class, at home, and under the blankets with a flashlight. Stories took me to worlds where children were good and beautiful, and even if they were poor and in danger, they got rescued, married the prince, and their father came home from the war.

I loved books about horses. Beginning with picture books about Blaze, the super-colt, who could save a kid, stop a forest fire, and love you 'til death, I moved on to my first real horse book: *Black Beauty.* What a hero! Intelligent. Loyal. Lost and suffering. Even though he was beaten and starved, he struggled to please his master unless it endangered someone's life—then he heroically refused to obey. When it looked like he would die a broken, lonely horse, he was reunited with his original owner, who restored his health and beauty. It was tragic, but so beautifully ended. I wanted to be a black mare so I could marry Black Beauty.

During the fourth and fifth grade the *Black Stallion* books by Walter Farley refined my fantasies, and I became the gorgeous girl who solved crimes, per-formed amazing rescues, and won the love of the most handsome boys—whom I, of course, ignored, being solely devoted to my Arabian horse. My favorite fantasy could have been a movie complete with stunt doubles and special effects: my school caught on fire, and no one could enter the building to rescue trapped children. Flames and smoke drove the firemen back. Brave men wrung their hands in despair. Helpless teenage boys gathered around to watch. Then, during that moment of collective despair, the sound of hoof beats. I thundered onto the scene riding my chestnut stallion. With an intelligent glance and incredible slo-mo grace, I assessed the situation. Signaling my horse to kick down the doors, we leapt, as one, up the stairs, and down the hall to the sixth grade classroom, where several of my classmates, including the handsome Lloyd LaValla, were trapped. Grabbing them onto the back of my mount, we flew out just before the roof collapsed. Our picture was featured on the front page of *The Northern Light,* our town's weekly newspaper—circulation two hundred. The headline read: "Mystery Girl on Chestnut Stallion Saves Children."

At thirteen, horses were still headlining my dreams when I chanced to read the legend of Lady Godiva—that ravishing, mysterious woman from England. She had a cruel husband who crushed his people with heavy taxation. Lady Godiva was so moved by her people's suffering that she went to him and begged him to ease their burdens. When he would not, she threatened to ride, naked, through the streets—proving that the power of illogical debate, a form I still use and admire, may have pre-modern roots. I'm sure he did not believe she would carry out her threat. The book I saw had a classical painting of her, all very modest, in a Renaissance sort of way, but to my amazement, she really was nude. She was only covered by her long red hair that fell discreetly over her full breasts. She rode in a red velvet saddle on a prancing, white warhorse!

As I pondered how it might feel to be so free you would dare to ride a horse naked, I decided to try it myself—on Ginger, my little roan mare with the white blaze. She wasn't an Arabian stallion, to be sure, but she was pretty. Early one morning before anyone else was awake, I stole out to the barn. I carefully laid my pajamas on the manger and bridled Ginger. I didn't even throw a blanket on her back, so nothing could interfere with the experience. I didn't have a cruel husband or a people to rescue, but my father was dead. I headed out to the pasture to bring the milk cows in from where they'd grazed all night.

Because we lived in a remote part of the county, and because most of our pastures lay through the woods toward the back of the farm, I assumed there was little danger of being seen, even if someone did drive by that early in the morning. On the other hand, it would have been a little tricky explaining this to my parents if I were caught.

As we galloped across the field, every stride wounded my romantic notions a little more. It was freezing cold and her back scuffed at my bared skin. It also made me dirty. When I arrived back at the barn with the cows and dismounted, my thighs were caked with dirt and hair from Ginger's hide. Dismayed, disillusioned, dis-everything, I wiped myself off, put my pajamas on, and went back to bed.

It was about a year later when I sat alone in Ginger's manger, crying about Victor. Ginger eyed me passively. "Kiss me," I demanded. She indifferently put her soft nose against my cheek, then continued to nibble hay, pulling wisps out from under me. I was certain that if my real father were still alive I wouldn't be having this problem; he would allow me to date Victor Krull—the redhead-ed boy who played basketball on the varsity team. His sister Janet and my best friend Rita finally convinced him to focus on me long enough to notice I was no longer a little girl, and oh, joy of joys, he asked if I wanted a ride home after the basketball game on Friday night. I imagined everyone admiring us as we walked down the hall between classes holding hands and gazing deeply into one another's eyes. I looked forward to paradise, a place of smoldering glances, passionate love letters, and crushed-in-his-arms embraces. At the same time I knew Mom and Dad were hopelessly illiterate and would be completely unco-operative about dating. As I sat crying in the manger, I couldn't believe what a scourge they were on my life. I was already in the eighth grade, and this was, surely, my only chance to date a boy.

I scoured my girlfriends' comic books, *Confessions of the Lovelorn*, for hints on how to conduct a romantic relationship that led to eternal soulmate love, but most of them ended in tragedy—the young heroine with the waist of a wasp, a heaving bosom, expressing a tear from the corner of her eye. The only authors available at the library were the maddeningly vague nineteenth-century spin-sters, like Jane Austen and Charlotte Brontë. My favorite book was the saccha-rine 1867 novel *Little Women* by Louisa May Alcott. There was a section I read over and over, trying to guess at details the author so annoyingly left out:

> If he had any doubts about the reception she would give him, they were set at rest the minute she looked up and saw him; for, dropping everything, she ran to him, exclaiming, in a tone of unmistakable love and longing—"O Laurie, Laurie! I knew you'd come to me!" I think everything was said and settled then; for, as they stood together quite silent for a moment, with the dark head bent down protectingly over the light one, Amy felt that no one could comfort and sustain her so well as Laurie, and Laurie decided that Amy was the only woman in the world who could fill Jo's place, and make him happy.[2]

I practiced speaking in a voice of "unmistakable love and longing." I imagined Victor's red head "bent down protectingly" over my mousey brown one. I wondered what Laurie and Amy were doing during that moment of silence. Kissing? Did he put his hands on the small of her back and pull her to himself, and did she tip her head back and pucker her lips? My chances of personally experiencing this looked pretty grim. When Dad called me "Straight Hair and Curly Teeth," I pretended to laugh. There was nothing I could do about getting braces, and no perm could ever change my hair to flaming waves of glory. My shape was becoming more womanly, but he also made a point of ridiculing my "harnessed peas" and commented on my "bullet butt." I was fourteen years old, poor, plain, and naïve. I was in the barn with a horse, and Louisa May Alcott's Laurie wasn't going to show up at our garden gate anytime soon.

Even my reputation as a horseback rider, which I clung to, had been ruined by Thunder. When this easy-going pinto was ready to saddle-break, I knew it would be a cakewalk. I rode him in the fields and trails around our farm using a jointed training bit that was gentle on his mouth. I soon thought he was ready to ride along the road to get used to traffic, which was a vehicle about every thirty minutes during rush hour. The moment I headed him up the field driveway and turned onto the road, a pickup load of boys chanced to drive by. They rolled down their windows to holler and honk, though I didn't recognize them. Thunder reared wildly, gripped the bit in his teeth, and bucked. I yanked hard on the reins to make him release the bit, but he had it clamped in a death grip. After his initial fright was over, he hurtled down the road toward home, bucking every few strides. I knew he was no longer afraid; he was having fun, and I wasn't strong enough to stop him. By the time we drew even with our yard, I knew I was going to be thrown, so I just let go. On his next buck, I catapulted over his head, landed in the ditch, and he galloped over the top of me. A hoof bruised my waist and another grazed the side of my face.

Dallas saw me fall and ran to the house to tell. I lay in the knee-high grass wondering if I was paralyzed until my hand moved to touch my face. I was already mad at myself. I don't know why riders are so ashamed of getting bucked. Cowboys get thrown by broncs all the time. But then, I'd also let go of the reins, which was another thing Dad said you shouldn't do. When I made it back to the kitchen, I washed my face and looked in the mirror. The entire right side looked like a hamburger patty. I wanted to cover it with a bandage, but Mom said there was no way without wrapping my entire head, which would look even more ridiculous. Dad caught Thunder and rode him in the ditch for two hours, slogging him through hoof-sucking mud. Thunder came back lathered and exhausted, glad to be home and probably promising himself he'd never shy at traffic again. In church the next day, my twin cousins smirked at me, and Paul Olson, the quietest, gentlest elder, grinned at the hoof-print on my swollen cheek and said, "I heard Thunder threw you." At school on Monday, even the teachers asked what happened to my face.

One by one the things upon which I'd built my self-esteem were demolished. It seemed to me that, if you let up on your vigilance for one second, life effortlessly wrecked the image of coolness you worked so hard to create—even getting to the high school basketball game in an old Buick driven by your Mom on a winter night could be dangerous. During the time of my infatuation with Victor, one evening she dropped me off at the school so I could play with the pep band. I lugged my trombone up the snowy sidewalk and through the front entrance.

My girlfriends played tiny feminine little instruments like the flute, but I wanted to be unique. Learning to play the trombone, I hoped, would enhance that image. At the same time I wanted to look ravishing, I wanted to sound like a virtuoso and be discovered by, I didn't know who—someone who had something to do with Hollywood or the Top Forty, perhaps? On summer evenings I practiced outdoors where my bellowing notes echoed off the woods and carried for miles. I imagined far-off neighbors pausing amidst chores to muse, "How extraordinary, how beautiful. Now who could be making such heavenly music?" I practiced John Philip Sousa marches until my lip looked like a red bubble escaping my mouth. Then I went inside and used the instrument as a weapon—a more gratifying, much more attainable goal. I called Randy into the bedroom, and as he innocently came around the corner, I blasted such a note it knocked him to the floor clutching his heart. He always threatened to kill me.

The school door I entered for the basketball game opened onto a wooden landing and a staircase that descended to the gym. On that particular night, there was a crowd of students and cheerleaders gathered at the bottom, watching as I descended toward them. I unwrapped my scarf, shouldered my purse, and on the top step, my snow-packed tennis shoes slipped, and, like one of the Three Stooges on a banana peel, I slid down the entire flight on my back. My trombone hurtled down ahead of me and people jumped out of the way as it shot across the hall and hit the opposite wall with an explosion, my sheet music fanned out beside it. I followed a fraction of a second later coming to rest at the feet of the first chair trombonist, a senior whom I had been trying to impress. I lay for a moment, smiling at their laughter, as though this was how I intended to arrive, so what if I'd bruised my tailbone and dislocated several ribs? I got up and bowed. It wasn't until Monday in typing class when I couldn't lift my arm to return the carriage that I finally admitted I had been hurt.

I think I know why infatuation is called a crush—it sucks all the air out of your lungs, which is what was happening whenever Victor so much as looked at me. At the time of my crush, he was a junior who played on the starting line-up for the basketball team. He slicked back his red hair with Wildroot Hair Oil, but some of it still fell over his forehead in the most appealing way. He walked loose in a sort of forward strut, his muscular shoulders swaying side to side and his head thrown back. I believe this is what Tom Wolfe later called the "pimp roll" in his book *Bonfire of the Vanities*, something I read many years later. Victor drove a 1949 Chevrolet Coup he'd restored, which was so cool even back in 1961 it could have been a movie prop for *West Side Story*. Victor stopped by my locker between classes one day, and leaning his elbow on the top of my door, asked, "Hey, Baby. Wanna ride home after the game Friday night? We can stop by Johnson's party for a while if you want." He ran his fingers through his hair and it felt like someone sat on my chest. I barely whispered, "Sounds okay to me, but I'll need to check with my parents." Then I rushed to the bathroom, slammed into a stall and sat down with my head between my knees. "Hey, Baby"? Couldn't I ever think of a clever response? "Sounds okay to me"? "Check with my parents"? It was devastating.

By the time I was in junior high my parents held strong convictions, which made them cautious about their children getting too close with anyone who didn't share our beliefs—especially if it could lead to marriage. They wanted us to be careful, to love and obey God, which meant remaining pure and virgin until marriage. To encourage that, I wasn't supposed to date until I was sixteen. I asked what I was supposed to do while the entire rest of the world went to parties and had more fun than I had ever dreamed possible in this dump.

Victor's invitation meant I urgently needed to change their minds or convince them this wasn't a date, but more a matter of convenience—for them. They wouldn't need to arrange to pick me up after the game. An indirect approach to Mom and Dad seemed the best plan. I reasoned that not telling them everything would spare them worry. I would emphasize that if I got a ride home, it would relieve them from driving ten miles back to town again after the game to pick me up.

I chose supper as a safe time to bring it up in the midst of family chatter and the clatter of eating. Dad usually concentrated pretty hard on his food and didn't say too much during mealtime. Halfway through the meal I mentioned, "Oh, by the way, you won't need to pick me up after the game tomorrow night. I've got a ride home."

Mom put down her fork, and Dad looked up. Everyone stopped and stared at me. Dad asked, "Who's going to drive you all the way out here?" Was I stupid enough to think they wouldn't ask who was bringing me home? I couldn't think fast enough to tell a credible lie. All I managed to croak was the truth: Victor Krull. Immediately, just hearing the name set Dad off on a tirade about tough-guy teenagers with fast cars, who did they think they were, which led to the degenerating condition of our country, which led to communists controlling everything from the local farmers' union to the price of wheat. The answer was no—end of discussion. Mom would pick me up as usual.

I hurried through the dishes, ran to the barn, and climbed into Ginger's manger. I wished I'd told them it was time for them to face the fact that I was very mature for my age. And what's so magic about sixteen years? I wasn't going to be sixteen until halfway through eleventh grade, and by then life would be over. I wished I had cruelly insulted them with—"What's the matter, are you afraid I'll be just like you? That I'll get myself knocked up? I could have spent the night with Rita, gone out with Victor, and you would never have known." Why was I such an idiot? How could I face Victor and my friends at school the next day and say, "My parents won't let me"? They would think I was such a baby. I would be a complete moron. I was very nearly that already because my family was poor and religious. Victor had been my one chance and now my parents, especially Dad, had ruined my life forever.

I wished desperately then for my real father, Keith Sorenson. I thought I might have felt more at ease and at home with him. He loved my mother, I knew that; and surely he would have loved me. After all, he was the one who insisted if I were a girl I should be named after her. I was sure he would have understood how important Victor was. I wasn't even thinking about what lay beyond the chemistry of holding hands and kissing. I just wanted a boyfriend because my heart longed for one, and it was what I thought all the most popular girls had. If I had been honest, I might have admitted that in a tiny corner of my heart God was telling me: "Your Mom and stepdad may be right—Victor might not be good for you in the most profound sense: he likes your body, but he's not really interested in you and your romantic idealism." If I'd had the insight I might have realized that what I really wanted was to simply, fundamentally, belong to someone other than my mother, to have the option, like a baby loon, of riding under the wings of my father at any time, for no reason, only because I could.

As the things I based my worth upon were erased, I had to face that I didn't have compelling beauty or enough intelligence (I looked up my IQ one day while I was working in the principal's office, filing; my score fell just below the genius level), and I didn't have enough wealth to buy me social status. This lack of power was painful, but the worst realization was that I couldn't seem to satisfy my hunger for unconditional and unfailing relationships. Even though I was spiritually naïve, this emptiness forced me to turn inward toward God in a search for something deeper and more lasting. I was learning that these desires would never be met perfectly by others. I was asking for things only God could do— soothe me, comfort me, and affirm me in the most profound ways. Although I knew God's love for a person was not limited to issues like which psalm shall I read before bed, I wasn't exactly sure how to get him out of the confining box of do-not-do-this-or-that and into the real life of a teenager who needed some help living in the real world. Like, okay maybe I was a tiny bit nervous about sitting alone with Victor in his souped-up Buick late at night.

Not so many years later, I could look back and see that I was spared all sorts of agony by not being allowed to get involved with that young man. It took longer to realize that no amount of good parenting could have satisfied the longing in my heart. Observing my own children as they grew up, I experienced a kind of déjà vu pain. Remembering my own teenage angst, it pierced me again on their behalf. As much as I wanted to spare them, I couldn't seem to stop the hurt they experienced as they urgently searched for ways to satisfy their intense needs. I believed that my inability to protect them from injury could be used by God to touch and turn them to the only source who can completely heal the disappointment of finding out no one truly loves or knows us like God can. My stepfather unwittingly assisted this process, and I turned toward a deeper love. I know that the failures, even the abuse of others, or my own failure to be the perfect lover or parent is not the end of the story. To me, the ways of God are often counter-intuitive, and beyond me. They bless me in a way that can leave me nearly speechless with thanksgiving and hope.

So on that night, when my parents refused to let me date Victor, and as I prayed urgently for God to get me out of school the next day, a sense of his presence filled the manger—obviously not the first time he'd visited a manger--and my heart was consoled.

I can't say it was God who gave me the idea when I left the barn with a plan to avoid total humiliation. But he may have been the source. Even though it meant lying, I hoped he would overlook it, since I was considering myself an orphan for the time being, and as everyone knows God loves orphans.

The next morning when Mom called me to get up for school, I groaned and turned over. She came back to check on me a few minutes later. I flapped the blankets. "I'm so hot, I'm burning up, I think I'm sick." She put a thermometer in my mouth, and while she was gone I reached over to the lamp and held the tip on the light bulb. When she returned, I watched through half-closed eyes as she checked it. A puzzled expression came over her face as her eyes moved to the top of the glass column. The mercury had traveled to the end and burst.

"Hmmm. It must be broken." Cautiously, she put her hand on my forehead, then she looked at me kindly and said, "You can stay home today, but you have to stay in bed."

And so I did. With the weekend, it gave me three days before I had to see Victor or my friends at school. In a way, I never really saw him again. My moment had passed, and he had moved on.

Mom could do that sometimes—let me stay home, make daily life the right place to be, and though I wasn't aware of it then, she planted a love for simple pleasures. Holy, everyday ones that comforted me—like sitting on the steps watching the swallows dive off the barn roof in the evening sun. Or, years later in my own kitchen, stealing leftover manicotti from the refrigerator, and eating it cold right out of the plastic container. Or sitting in a lawn chair slowly turning the pages of a novel while the freshly mopped floor in the kitchen dried, and my children ran through the sprinklers on a hot afternoon.

———

The thunderstorms that blew across our flat northern land were often preceded by an unnatural stillness. We watched them build in the west—magnificent clouds glowing like distant mountain ranges, spreading up the sky, until they rolled over one another, bank upon bank, braiding themselves together in long, creamy-white strands and seething, purple ribbons. The rising wind bent small aspens halfway to the ground, and lightning cracked horizon to horizon. As it grew dark, distant thunder boomed, and Mom would yell out the kitchen door, calling us home. We emerged, running from all corners of the farmyard. She joined us to turn off the water pump, close the chicken house door, tie the barn doors shut, roll up the car windows, pick the ripe tomatoes, get the clothes off the line, and bring in dry wood for the stove. We did it, breathlessly laughing, trying to beat the rain. We made the final dash to the house, our arms loaded, as large drops began bouncing in the dirt of the driveway.

In the kitchen, Mom mixed cocoa, sugar, cream, and a little vanilla, brought it to a boil in a saucepan, then slowly stirred in milk for hot chocolate. I took the last batch of buns from the oven, and Mom pulled them apart for us while they were still too hot to hold. She spread them with the butter we had churned, and sprinkled them with brown sugar, which melted into a fragrant confection that made you believe home was the place to be after all, and that maybe, someday, you would get a life in spite of it.

We watched the heavens fall on our farm. A bucket rolled across the grass and hit the foundation. In the front yard a tree split and half fell on the swing set.

## Mom's Half-Time Buns

3 pkgs yeast
3/4 cup water
1 cup shortening, melted
3/4 cup sugar
2 1/4 cups milk, scalded
1/1/2 cups cold water
1 tbsp salt
6 eggs
12 cups flour

Preheat oven to 350 degrees. In a small bowl, dissolve the yeast in warm water. Set aside. In a large bowl mix melted shortening and sugar. Add scalded milk and cold water. Let it sit until it is lukewarm, then add yeast mixture. Add 3–4 cups of flour and beat well, then add eggs two at a time, beating well after each addition. Add remaining flour. Dough will be very thick. In a warm place let dough rise until doubled. Punch down and with oiled hands; form dough into buns and place on greased pans. Let rise until double in size. Bake for 15 minutes until golden brown. Brush tops with butter before cooled. Makes 4–5 dozen.

# Aurora Borealis

The Aurora Borealis, also called the northern lights, appears most often on winter nights, igniting the sky from end to end. All northern cultures have myths and legends about the lights. On clear winter nights they rose above our farm in the northern sky from low on the horizon, lighting the countryside with a ghostly aura. They shimmered in corridors of white and shades of green and blue, sometimes tinged across the bottom edges with red. Sometimes they spiraled up like heavenly staircases and disappeared as though drawn up into the Pole Star, only to reappear, pulsing, alive. They could emerge from deep space, moving toward us at incredible speed from pinpoints of light, and then unfold in layer after layer of waving curtains the size of continents. Then they rolled back and back, revealing a vast stage of darkness and sank silently like exhaled breath. They made my hair stand on end and tears of fear spring to my eyes. At any moment I expected to see angels descending. Despite scientific explanations of charged particles and the earth's magnetic field, the northern lights made me want to be on the good side of whoever made them.

# PATHS OF DARKNESS

In northern Minnesota the summer sun hangs below the horizon for hours, leaving a long and lingering crack between day and night. This was the time when daily work was over. The milking finished. Cows turned out to pasture. Supper dishes dried and put away. The wind died down, and in the hush of evening, sounds carried in damp air: the hum of mosquitoes; the trilling of frogs; the far-off voice of an unseen neighbor; the bark of a dog; an occasional gunshot. It was our time for playing games: tag, softball, five hundred, kick-the-can, or seven sticks. When darkness finally came, a moonless night on our farm was so black you had to feel your way along the paths, taking care not to step in a depression or turn your ankle on a rock. We had a yard light set high on a utility pole halfway between the house and the barn, which shed a small circle of light, but that only made the curtain of darkness beyond more intense.

On summer evenings I had one last chore to tend: shutting the chicken house door. Forgetting to shut the door at night, Dad said, could mean losing chickens. That would mean a loss of income from the eggs we sold, and a loss of food, since we ate both the chickens and their eggs all winter.

We kept Rhode Island Reds, a heavy, hardy breed of chicken. They ranged in color from a lustrous chestnut brown to a pale cinnamon and, compared to the nervous White Leghorns, they were pretty calm. If startled, however, they still created a storm of dust and feathers. The hens laid large mocha-colored eggs that needed to be gathered every day. I often gathered voluntarily; it felt like treasure hunting. Inside the chicken house, the hens had a wooden box with enough room for several at a time to sit in quiet darkness on nests of straw, adding to their pile of eggs or just keeping them warm in fowlish hopes of hatching babies. I lifted the hinged door and reached beneath a hen, pulling out the eggs one by one, cupping them gently, touching their warm, chalky surface before placing them in a basket. Then I looked for other places where a hen may have started a clutch. Sometimes in the corners of the dirt floor there would be two or three eggs in a rounded hole. Sometimes a lone egg would be lying under the roost as though a hen accidentally dropped it during the night. A quick turn around the outside might reveal a crater full of eggs nestled in the tall grass. A nest could be hidden for days until betrayed by a hen that had just laid an egg and announced it with delirious squawks. A nest like this might hold valuable rotten eggs.

The test for a rotten egg is simple. Shake it. The insides of a fresh egg, held firmly in place by strong strands of protein, make no movement when shaken. On the other hand, a rotten egg sloshes around as the protein has begun to decompose, turning the white albumen and golden globe into a dark fetid liquid inside the shell. These pungent grenades won battles, plundered money, and extracted secrets for the one who owned them. There was nothing so beautiful as a direct hit with a rotten egg, which could cause the victim to vomit on the spot.

In the spring Mom ordered baby chicks through the mail—a mixture of pullets (females) and roosters that the mailman dropped off in a heavy cardboard box ventilated for air and lined with wood shavings. The week they arrived someone had to meet the mailman every day or they would be left on the road beside our mailbox—which was fatal for the chicks on a cold day. Our job as children was to watch and report to Mom immediately if they arrived. Then she hurried out to carry in the box filled with seething, peeping, yellow fluff. When we looked inside and gently moved aside the yellow mass, we always found several suffocated victims where the chicks had stood on top of one another for too long.

For several days the chicks stayed in a large cardboard carton in the kitchen while they recovered from the stress of their journey and gained strength. A light bulb with a reflecting shade was suspended over the box to keep them warm. Water was placed in dispensers and small feeders were filled twice a day with chick mash. We watched them line up to gorge themselves and then collapse on the sawdust, their opaque little lids closing over their eyes. There was always one who wandered off to a corner and suddenly thought she was lost in the universe. She made loud shrieking peeps until someone gently lifted her to the middle of the crowd a mere eighteen inches away.

When they began to stink from spilled water and filth, Mom moved them to the chicken house, where they lived until butchering day. That came in about three months for the roosters. Hens could expect to live up to three years if they could avoid predators or cannibalism.

Chickens have several weaknesses. One, they are almost as stupid as sheep. How can anyone get lost in a box? Another is that peculiar sense of pecking order that makes chickens single out one of their sisters and, in a cruel fashion, pick at her until she begins to bleed. At the first taste of blood they fall into a frenzy of pecking that won't stop until the hen's bottom is bleeding, her entrails dragging on the ground, and she is dead. Sometimes I would sit in the sunshine watching the hens and holding out my hand with a little grain in my palm. They would cautiously approach, softly questioning: praaawk-praaawk? Eyeing me first with one beady golden eye then the other. When the grain was gone, quick as lightning one would try to pinch off the end of my little finger as if it were a fat grub. I wondered if I were to lie quietly in the grass beside them how long it would take these heartless hens to peck through my eyes all the way to my brain.

The hens made the most of the long twilight hours, scratching for bugs in the dirt outside the chicken house door and stirring lazily in their dust baths. They didn't go inside to roost until the final moments before dark. Night was a dangerous time for them to be out, but chasing them inside so I could close the door early never worked. If I tried to gently shoo them in, the lingerers would alert the rest, and soon twenty or more would be heavily flapping, squawking, and disappearing into the tall stinging nettles behind their house. I had to wait for them until that moment—that tiny window of time just before twilight turned to real night. Only then did they go inside. I didn't like this nonsense because I also considered nighttime dangerous.

Sometimes if I forgot—being lost in a game of softball or pelting Randy with rotten tomatoes from the garden—then I had to feel my way to the chicken house in the dark because it was located far beyond the safety cast by our yard light. Dad said flashlights were for sissies. He always seemed to know when I had forgotten this chore. As I came in the house, he would ask, "What did you do after you shut the chicken house door?" There was, of course, no satisfying answer to that question.

Our chicken house was set against the north woods of the pasture at the end of a narrow path that led from our house, past the milkhouse, over a small slippery ditch, and through a stand of alfalfa, or corn depending on the year, heavy and wet with dew. I had to leave the warm glow of the kitchen, the voices and sounds of the family fading as I walked toward the chicken house. Like walking into a lake, I pushed a wave of night sounds before me, and they closed in a wake behind my back. The trilling of peepers and leopard frogs were silent within the vibrations of my steps, but if I dared stand still for sixty seconds, the chorus slowly approached on all sides, converging in the darkness and drowning me in their nighttime anthem.

Often I did stop, frozen like a rabbit hunted by an owl, pupils dilated, my body poised to run, listening to the sound of whatever was out there. The wind trembled the aspen leaves. The garden corn rustled together like someone crept toward me. The grasses swished and hissed together. Bats silently flicked past. Ahead of me a mound of Canadian thistle looked like something slipping under the fence.

I was afraid of wolves, bears, and ghosts like The Axeman. The Axeman had worked in a lumber camp south of town early in the twentieth century—even before settlers arrived in our county. One day he'd gone crazy and killed everyone in camp with his double-bladed axe. The bodies were found weeks later, but the The Axeman was never found. He escaped into the wilderness. Sometimes you could still hear him howling at night. Some, Randy insisted, had even seen him running naked along the far edge of Dale Bergen's field, swinging his axe, and disappearing into the brush.

But what I feared most was the North American skunk who often found ways into a farmer's chicken house for an easy supper. If he got inside, all he had to do was walk under the hens' roost, where they perched in perfect safety. A skunk can't climb, but when the hens sensed him lurking in the dark below, a rising panic turned the flock into a screaming melee: hens flying into the walls, each other, and his jaws. I wasn't afraid of his sickening stench, though I hated it: I was terrified that he might have rabies—which was a real possibility. I read a book about hydrophobia, another name for rabies, and knew there was no cure. One of its pictures permanently etched itself in my memory: it was a medieval print of a man chained to a tree stump, frothing at the mouth, and trying to bite anyone who came near. His family stood by horrified and helplessly watching.

Quietly, I continued down the path conserving my energy for the bolt back to light. Upon arriving at the door of the chicken house I paused for a tiny second, listening to the hens. If they were softly murmuring, it was okay to shut the door. If there was nervous shifting and frightened clucks, then there might be a skunk lurking in the shadows, in which case I was allowed to get Dad who would come with the gun. And the flashlight.

One night I forgot to shut the door until it was utterly black. As usual, I imagined dark forms lurking in the shadows and skunks frothing at the mouth. This time when I listened at the door and peered into the dark, there was a sudden crescendo of hysteria among the hens. Suddenly, one hurtled past my shoulder, and I saw a small flash of white moving fast across the dirt floor toward me. I turned and ran—praying like a banshee: *Help! Help! Don't let me slip and fall when I jump the ditch the milkhouse. Please, help me!* I could hear its soft feet thudding down the path behind me as I cleared the ditch and ran screaming to the house. Dad heard me coming, immediately guessed what was happening, and was out the door with the .22 rifle as I ran in yelling, "SKUNK!"

By the time Dad met the skunk, it had crossed the ditch. By the time he lowered the gun and aimed, the skunk had attacked the end of the barrel. He blew its head off.

Perhaps Dad burned him like the rabid animals in *Old Yeller*. I don't remember. But I did learn one thing: nightmares could come true.

———

My stepdad, Wallace Block, was the son of hard-working German farmers, a big handsome man, strong and steady like the Belgian draft horses he loved all his life. The first time he saw my mother he was a guest at her wedding to Keith, my father. He and Keith had been classmates for part of high school until Wally dropped out of school at the end of his junior year. At the wedding reception Wally made repeated trips through the receiving line just to kiss the bride. On his third time through Keith noticed what he was doing and stopped him. The next time Wally saw my mother was two-and-a-half months later at my father's funeral. He remembers holding the door for her as she entered the auditorium that day.

Mom took no thought of him until about a year later when she saw him at the Nite Hawk and he asked her for a dance. It was her first social outing after Keith's death and my birth; Wally seemed genuinely nice. At the time Mom was living with one of Keith's sisters and she encouraged her to accept a date from him, telling her it was okay to begin another relationship. By then, Mom had turned eighteen. It's pretty clear that Wally was already in love, and he quickly made it clear he was willing to marry her. Mom remembers feeling like he was a reliable fellow who would take care of her. When she became pregnant with my brother, Randy, it hastened plans for a marriage.

In the meantime, Wally had moved to Lead, South Dakota for a job in the gold mines. He needed a temporary job that paid well in order to make a down payment on a farm, and he figured it would take about two years of saving every penny. Mom and I followed him a few months later. His father, Earl Block, helped pack all our belongings in a car and drove us out to Lead, where Mom and Wally were married before a justice of the peace.

When I became an adult, the first live auction I attended I did not really know how bidding worked. I was shocked when the auctioneer yelled, "SOLD" and pointed at me. I had accidentally bought an antique iron I didn't want because I scratched my head. But when the auctioneer reached for the next box his assistant handed to him, he held up a rare Depression glass vase, and I knew I wanted it. When I won that lovely treasure, I didn't understand I had also "won" the box full of junk that came along with it. It was all stuff no one wants, like Mason jar lids, stained pot holders, and a rusty cast-iron skillet, but I had to take it all, because they wouldn't allow me to leave without it. I think this is how it was for Wally and me—I was that box full of stuff. He had to take me home with the real treasure, my mother, and deal with the rest somehow, some way.

It was our habit to sleep together, my mother and I, until the night we moved into Wally's apartment. I was one-and-a-half years old the first time I was sent to sleep in my own bed, and I cried until Wally pulled the belt out of his pants and spanked me. He told Mom that would teach me a lesson I wouldn't forget. Spankings were rare for me, because from early on, I was determined to please this man. Of course, I don't remember this incident—it was Mom who told me about it years later and what surprised me was that she still felt the pain of it herself.

For the rest of my life I knew him as Dad, but he never became my father. The simple explanation was that he didn't like me. He was never able to say why even though he was confronted, never by me, but by other members of the family. Perhaps it was jealousy; that's the theory Mom and my youngest sister, Roxanne, hold. Over the years the knowledge of his dislike slowly crept in like the northern twilight. As a child there were no words in my language to access such an idea so I didn't know what was wrong. I was fed and sheltered. The skunks were shot. I wasn't abused in the terrible way some girls are. All I knew was I did not please him, and that I needed to work to change this.

As I grew older and stronger, I worked for his approval. I hauled manure from the barn, stacked the woodpile, peeled cedar posts with a draw-knife, remembered my chores most of the time, and tried to clear the pasture of brush and downed wood. Sometimes Dad thanked me for these efforts, but my work didn't permanently change how he felt. Most of the time he ignored me. When he was looking, it was to note my appearance: my dishwater blonde hair was ruler straight, my eyes a pale gray, and some ancestor's large teeth were misplaced among the small bones of my face. I was a Sorenson—so different from my beautiful mother.

There is a mysterious sense in which a man who becomes the father of a child—natural or surrogate, it doesn't matter—participates in the shaping of that child's image of a God who claims to be Father of us all. It's mysterious because we waken in this world longing for the hands of a father who will not only lead us safely down dark paths past rabid skunks, but who will love us and tenderly enfold us. The ache may lie dormant for years or may never be spoken, and yet any child whose father has left or was never there is familiar with those aches. Where do they come from—these desires for fathers who never leave?

What young father expects to set in motion currents of belief, conclusions about fatherhood that stream through the rest of life? As children we were taught to pray "Dear heavenly Father" and "Our Father, who art in heaven, hallowed be thy name." God and Wally shared the name "father," so did they share the same nature? God must, I thought, need to be won by the same sort of hard work and allurement my human father apparently required. And yet, what would God need that I could give? Winning his love seemed as unattainable as winning Wally's favor, but doggedly I kept at it. By the time I was eight years old, the spiritual disciplines of prayer, confession, and Scripture reading were habitual. I remember ironing Dad's western plaid shirts, the iron ticking against the snaps and steam rising. It was not a job I loved, and there were usually five each week, but it doubled as time to memorize chunks of Scripture I had written on little index cards and stacked at the end of the ironing board. Many portions are still with me in the archaic language of King James, which cannot suppress the words of Jesus still coming with power to lighten darknes:

> Let not your heart be troubled: ye believe in God, believe also in me. In my Father's house are many mansions: if it were not so, I would have told you. I go to prepare a place for you. And if I go and prepare a place for you, I will come again, and receive you unto myself; that where I am, there ye may be also" (John 14:1–3 KJV).

Back then, this was my God-work.

At night when the lights were out, and the family was asleep with Dad's snores drifting out of the bedroom, I was especially troubled. I lay awake possessed by obsessions and fears. I wondered if I was in danger of being sent away to live with distant relatives. My failures passed before me. My dreams were filled with crashing planes, and I charged through the under-brush trying to reach the passengers before the fiery explosion. Dark beings visited me. I shouted for someone to rescue me only to waken and find myself whispering help. I was bereft, weaponless, alone.

Each night I reasoned with myself. Nightmares are not real. It is safe to let go of consciousness and go to sleep. Listen to the breathing around you. Hear the whippoorwill calling. You are earth-bound. Say your prayers and don't think too much about the phrase "If I should die before I wake, I pray the Lord my soul to take."

I felt safer when Mom and Dad were at home and in bed, but they were often gone in the evening. Before I could go to sleep, I wanted everyone tucked in and the house quiet. I wanted a sibling close by, and most of the time one was. Sometimes two of us slept in the three-quarter bed with another snuggled in at the other end between our feet. In the middle of the night when I shot out of a nightmare, I could reach out for my sister, Jan, and place my hand on her arm or my foot on her leg. When I was assigned to sleep by myself on an army cot in the living room, sleeping was more difficult.

Making certain our house didn't burn down was part of my sleepless obsession. I could hardly put it out of my mind when the living room where I often slept was dominated by the presence of the iron stove, which, even if I had my eyes closed, I could feel and hear as it snapped and cracked with the heat. Every winter some house somewhere burned down, the children trapped inside. This fact was probably not repeated as often as I imagined, but it was already seared on my heart the day we drove to town and passed a ramshackle house that had caught fire and burned to the ground the week before. All that remained were a few charred beams and a collapsed wall. Part of the blackened roof rested on the twisted metal frame of a bunk bed. Several children had died.

When Mom and Dad were out for the evening and I was babysitting, the responsibility was not too difficult until we were all in bed and I had the time to think. Roxanne, the baby, was the first to go down: double-diapered, bottle-fed, and tucked into her crib. Next were the "little kids." Rex and Dallas had to be chased down, faces washed, pajamas donned, made to pee in the bucket, and sent to their bed. Jan could ready herself, and that left Randy and me with a little extra time to play Chinese checkers or read aloud together before we, too, shut off the lights and crawled into bed. Then I silently reviewed the warnings my parents had given about fire.

Do not play with fire. Ever. End of discussion.

If you use the cook stove, be sure to turn the burner all the way to "off" when you are done.

If you smell gas, check all the burners. Make sure they are off. Check the pilot lights—one for the top of the range and one for the oven. If they are out, relight them.

Don't try to light the oven. That is how some people get their heads blown off.

Leave the wood stove in the living room alone after Dad has banked it. Do not change the damper or the grate. Turning them either way could make the fire burn too hot or too low.

There was the danger of a chimney fire if the fire was not properly controlled. Dad banked the fire with a combination of dry birch and green poplar, which smoldered and burned all night. Every morning he built a roaring fire that cleaned out the pipes and cleared the chimney of any creosote or residue from the green wood.

I didn't think these rules applied on a day in early autumn when Mom and Dad went to town and the temperature suddenly dropped below freezing and the house turned stone cold. We were shivering and I felt responsible for keeping us warm. Randy and I decided to start a fire in the wood stove in the living room. First, we opened the damper on the chimney pipe and the grate at the bottom. Then we crumpled the pages of an old Sears catalog, placed kindling and split wood on top, and lit the paper with a match. Slowly the flames licked up the paper, turning glossy pages of work boots and fur-lined parkas to black ash. Then they died out.

Randy said he knew what to do based on his vast experience and the numerous fires he had started in the pasture, the outhouse, and the stock tank: get the kerosene can, pour a bunch on the wood, and poof we'd have a fire. And so we did. As he was pouring it into the stove, some accidentally spilled down the front and onto the floor. We expected to throw in a match, jump back, and slam the door shut, but while Randy fumbled with the matchbox, somewhere beneath the wood, a spark ignited the kerosene and flames quickly spread down the front of the stove and across the floor.

Kerosene isn't nearly as combustible as gasoline, but it was bad enough. Both of us began to scream and cry. We screamed for the little kids to get out of the house, and I grabbed a throw rug to beat it out while Randy ran for water from the kitchen crock; and I shouted, "No, no, water doesn't stop kerosene from burning," and he grabbed another rug. Together we beat out the fire before it did any real damage. But there was no way we could avoid showing Mom and Dad the charred rugs. We knew how close we'd come to losing everything. So did Dad. He yelled his most eloquent oaths at us: "You cock-eyed pot-lickers. Haven't I told you never to mess with fire when we are gone? *What* were you numbskulls thinking about?"

I should have known not to do this. We should have just put on our jackets.

I took his questions to heart, but it didn't prevent the fire I started a couple years later on a bright Sunday morning in the middle of winter when Roxanne and I stayed home from church with bad colds. Late that morning, as Mom had instructed, I peeled potatoes for our noon meal and took them out to the milkhouse to cook on a burner plate because our kitchen stove was low on propane gas. I lit the burner and put the large pot on to boil. The milkhouse was so cold I also started a wood fire in the barrel stove to take the chill off and keep the pump from freezing. I opened the draft wide for a good fast start and ran back to the house, intending to return in a few moments to check on the potatoes and close down the draft down a little.

Roxanne was three years old then, and we lay down on the floor near the living room stove, in a patch of sunlight, pillows tucked under our elbows, where I was reading her a story. I forgot all about the milkhouse until a shadow passed over the window, and I looked up to see smoke drifting past. It took a moment to identify—too black and too much. I ran outside to look for the source. Smoke was billowing out the chimney and seeping under the door of the milkhouse. I pulled the door open and tried to get in, but the heat and smoke were already too thick. Our only source of water was the pump on the well inside. It was unreachable. I pulled out two ten-gallon cans of cream sitting just inside the door. Flames were licking through the roof and the wind was blowing cinders in the direction of our house just a few feet away. I had to get help, but how? And who? We had no telephone, and there sure wasn't a chestnut stallion riding to the rescue.

I ran back to the house, pulled on my parka and boots, and left Roxanne with strict instructions to stay inside. I hated leaving her alone, but I promised to be right back and told her that she should stand at the window and watch me. I ran a half-mile down the road to the Beckers. Lorraine met me at the door as I tried to catch my breath and tell her I needed help; the milkhouse was on fire, our house was in danger, I was home alone, could Billy come? She blinked her eyes slowly in the sunlight, then said, "Billy's out to the barn, got some cow calving this morning. I could ask him, but I don't know as he could do any good 'cause ain't your water pump in the milkhouse?" I could see that trying to enlist them for help was useless. I shouldn't have wasted time running down there.

I turned and ran back. Seeing the black smoke billow into the sky made me sick. I could hear Dad's guns going off. They were stored in the rafters. I hadn't thought of them. Then a box of bullets exploded. Roxanne was standing at the window waiting and crying as I ran back down the road. *God, God, help us help us please, please save our home!* I ran to the outside corner of our house and felt the outside wall with my bare hand. It was almost too hot to touch, but suddenly, inexplicably the smoke and flames shifted away. They began drifting straight up and then more to the east and finally to the northeast as the wind completely changed direction blowing the exact opposite of the way it had been. Seconds later the family and other members of our church arrived. Having seen the smoke from miles away they came roaring into the driveway, not knowing what they might find. Whether we would still have a home. Or whether Roxanne and I would be alive. I began to cry, first from relief, and then gasping from guilt. I knew how little we could afford to lose so much.

No one blamed me. Mom hugged me and assured me it was an accident. That God would take care of us. Dad didn't say anything, but he didn't need to—I knew he might never be able to replace all of his guns. I was thankful our house hadn't burned, and that Roxanne and I were alive, but this was my fault. It was much later as I reviewed the event and remembered the specific kindness God sent in the midst of a terrible day. I recognized that he was pushing me away from the dangerous belief that I could get or keep his love by being perfect.

I thought of my brothers and sisters as I lay on my cot in the living room. The baby and the little kids were in the bedroom asleep. Randy slept peacefully nearby, his long dark lashes resting against his flushed cheeks and his mouth wide open. I stared at the cast-iron stove a few feet from my head. It burned so frightfully hot I could see the outline of the coals inside as the metal glowed a translucent red. How would it feel to roast and burn in a fire? I touched the wall behind the stove. It was too hot to keep my hand there. At what temperature did wallpaper ignite?

I wondered whether I had checked the burners on the stove in the kitchen. I would check. They were all off. Back in bed I thought I smelled gas. Perhaps I missed one. I checked again. They were all off. Both pilots were on. If the house caught fire how would I get all five of my brothers and sisters out? Should I just carry them out in their pajamas? Should I try to get on clothes or blankets? Wasn't the outside bedroom door banked with flax straw and frozen shut? Would we freeze to death in the arctic air? Would Randy be able to help? He was always so groggy when he first woke up. He was a sleepwalker. I observed him do eerie things in his sleep. One night he opened the stove door and tried to crawl inside. It was summertime so the only damage was blackened pajamas. Another time I heard the screen door slam and followed him outside where, to my surprise, he crawled into the back seat of the car and sat there, his eyes wide open, unseeing until at last he slumped over on the seat. I led him back to bed. Sometimes he went out to the light pole and counted to one hundred like we were playing hide and seek. He never remembered his nighttime rambles the next day.

I got out of bed once again to make doubly-sure. All the burners were off, and the wood stove continued to glow in the dark. I lay perfectly still and prayed the words of the King James. "Come unto me, all ye that labor and are heavy laden, and I will give you rest"(Matt. 11:28 KJV). I was a draft horse staggering toward Jesus pulling a five-bottom plow. "Are not two sold for a farthing and one of them shall not fall on the ground without your heavenly Father knowing?" (Matt. 10:29 KJV). I was a falling bird. Did God notice that my brother shot barn swallows with his BB gun?

Every car that passed our remote farm at night began as a tiny glow on the opposite wall of the living room. The light grew and slowly moved across the wall, the shadows of the poplar trees moving with the headlights first slowly then faster and faster. I prayed each one would be my parents returning home. The light would suddenly reverse direction, flip up the wall, and race across the ceiling. For a brief second a red glow from the taillights flashed through the opposite window and was gone. *The seventh car will be Mom and Dad,* I told myself. I waited. Counting. Praying, wishing they would not leave us at night. And occasionally rechecking the kitchen stove. When Mom and Dad finally came home, I never said anything, just turned over and fell asleep at last.

———

What visited me then in the night was worse than skunks with rabies or houses on fire. Whether the spirits were real or not, I didn't know. In the dark they watched me through the windows of the living room where I lay just below the sill. I dared not whisper or move. I held my breath hoping they wouldn't see me if my chest did not rise or fall under the blanket. Frequently, the same beast came out of the western woods beyond the barn, making its way across a misty plot of grass and weeds, over the rail fence, past the driveway, around the house, and up to the east window where I lay. From somewhere above the house I watched its approach. It only had one leg with a cloven hoof, yet it drifted across the ground in a fluid motion. When it stopped at my window, its single hoof sank into the soft ground.

I knew it wanted me. I watched with unblinking eyes and planned my escape. If I could reach my sleeping parents in the next room, I would be safe. I couldn't leave the bed to run to them, because it was waiting, ready to leap for me if I moved. Then a miracle—the large ten-gallon cream can rolled up to my bed and kindly suggested I crawl inside and he would roll me into the bedroom to my parents. Relief filled my body like fresh air. Inside the stainless steel can, which smelled sour and cheesy, he rolled me over and over to the bedroom where I woke to find myself in my own bed and the black window still staring at me. I wanted to call Mom. I knew she would come, but I didn't dare call. And what would I tell her if she did come? Dad's snoring reassured me that they were at least alive.

One morning I made a rational attempt to control my fear by looking at the ground outside the living room window. To find that nothing stood there during the night could prove that all I imagined existed only in my dreams. In broad daylight with the eastern sun pouring down the side of the house I stared at the single hole in the ground made by a cloven hoof.

———

Some time after Mom's conversion to Christianity, which she places as the summer between my first and second grades, I began a repeating nightmare. Perhaps it started when I was in third grade. All I know is that it came again and again. It was a battle that took place on the floor in the narrow corridor between Mom and Dad's bed and the three-quarter bed beside them. The beds were positioned side by side, each against a wall with enough room to walk between them. This was always the setting for the dream, but I could have the dream wherever I slept—whether I was on the bunk bed, the couch, or a cot in the living room, Mom switched our sleeping arrangements often, looking for what worked better.

I dreamed that in my sleep I rolled off the three-quarter bed onto the floor and awakened on the cold, hard linoleum between the beds. In the dark I saw nothing but a faint outline of the windows above the beds illuminated by starlight. On either side of me was a deeper darkness beneath the beds. My mind sensed danger and knew it needed to wake my body from the paralysis of sleep. It needed to get me out of the dream or back up on the bed before something terrible happened. My limbs were bags of boneless sand, but with enormous effort, I managed to get to my hands and knees. Something moved under my parents' bed, and with a violent effort I heaved myself up toward my bed. I was almost off the floor when a cold hand grasped my wrist and pulled me down. Satan had emerged through the floor from the cellar below. He had come for me. I fought him, grasping air, tearing at the blankets that hung over the edge of my bed, but I was slowly being sucked under. I screamed for help and managed a groan. Suddenly another hand from under my bed reached for me. It felt warm and strong. I don't know how I knew it was God gripping my other arm. My shoulders wrenched. My wrists cracked. I willed every atom of my being toward God. Momentum shifted and I inched toward him. The strain of this slow, breaking battle finally snapped the spell of the nightmare, and before it was won and I was safely in bed with God and a happy ending, I woke to find I was still in my own bed in a real room of a shotgun house.

Then I lay listening to what seemed like the arguments of Satan: "I doubt you've ever really belonged to God. You are going to hell. For one thing you don't have a date of conversion."

I had rededicated myself, confessed, prayed many times, at many campfires upon the urging of counselors and preachers. They warned us you must be sure of your salvation. I carefully recorded the dates of those confessions. *Upon this day (present date), I, Margie Lou Block, received Jesus Christ as my Lord and Savior.*

"You said the same thing last summer. Do you know where liars go? Yes, straight to hell. So"—he folded his arms—"which one was real? When are you going to get sincere about this? Perhaps you should do it again and get a real date. And this time really mean it."

People did ask, "When were you born again?" We were reminded that we knew our physical birth date. (Well, of course.) But the more important date was your spiritual re-birth. Satan was right, I couldn't remember it, which meant maybe I didn't have one. I had loved God since I could think. It began on a winter day with a rat terrier named Bing who had stolen my mitten. But what does a four-year-old know? Not much, I guessed.

Mom remembered the day of her conversion. A lot of suffering led up to it. She hadn't bothered to reflect on spiritual matters until her late twenties when it looked like life might be over. During the nine-and-a-half years between my birth and that of my youngest sister, Roxanne, Mom had six miscarriages in addition to five more children. Years spent pregnant and lactating made her sick and weary. The labor of a farm wife was body-breaking; nothing was simple or easy. During her first spring on the farm she remembered thinking they needed to get a plot of ground ready for a garden. When Dad came home from the fields, he found her trying to push a cultivator through the hard-packed clay. He laughed to think his wife didn't recognize something made to be pulled by horses. Somehow she managed to get her first garden planted. There were days when the slipped discs in her back kept her in bed most of the day, but even then she managed to crawl to the kitchen and pull herself up to the counter to work a little.

The summer Mom had rheumatic fever, she met Lu Block, an aunt to Wally. Lu was an amazing woman—part Native American, mother to seven children, trained as a nurse; she was funny, smart, as poor as we were, and a devout Christian. She began reading through the Bible and praying regularly with Mom. As a result Mom's fears about her spiritual destiny were awakened. She was afraid of what might happen to her soul if she died. She was convinced none of her children could know about theirs either. Who would teach them? She remembered how Darby, her father, prayed for her when she was a child, and how she had put him off and planned to have a lot of fun until she was an old lady—then she might consider whether Christianity had any relevance.

One day on the path between the woodpile and the house she stopped to consider how tired she was of resisting God's offer of finding a resting place with him. Laying her burdens down was appealing. She had carried them from Darby's homestead on the lake; she had carried them whether she was orphaned, married, widowed or remarried, and trailing six children to this wet farm seventeen miles from town. All her days had led her to the place where she stood on this path loaded with firewood, her arms aching. In that moment she made a conscious choice to give everything to God—her life, her children, her work. She simply prayed: "take me, I'm yours." Then she continued to the house and dumped her load into the wood box.

There were no angelic choirs, no miraculous signs—just a long exhale. Her back still ached and the kids still had the measles, but she had found a balm that penetrated deep into old wounds, restoring health and forgiving aches. Years later, she remarked to me, "I wish I had converted for love, but no, I was tired and I was afraid of hell."

That was her spiritual awakening. Her conversion. After that Mom took us to a little country chapel on Sundays and taught us the stories of the Bible. As a young child I never felt the pressure or the urgency to make a choice, the choice to "get saved now before it is too late." Rather, as watercolor spreads across paper, my mother's teachings painted my heart. I absorbed them gradually and naturally, filled with happiness to learn more about Jesus.

Even Dad had a pretty dramatic conversion after a frightening, painful infection in his face that swelled it until you almost couldn't recognize him. Dad became soft and teary thinking he was going to die and Mom thought he was dying, too. He turned to God that night, and the next day the infection was nearly gone. Eventually Dad followed us to church. He quit drinking on Saturday nights. He and Mom stopped dancing at the Nite Hawk and went visiting friends and neighbors instead. The changes in his life were real, but they never quite spread to his relationship with me. Or his way of beating and kicking the boys when he was angry about something they had done.

It was Mr. Sommical who got him to quit smoking by going out to the barn in his suit and tie and confronting Dad about it; Dad smoked several packs a day. I don't remember how many, but he was pretty addicted.

A few visiting evangelists came to our small church on a regular circuit and preached about the fires of hell and warned us to be sure of where our souls stood with God or we'd find ourselves among the damned. At first, I didn't think the message was meant for me because I already loved God. But eventually their arguments for knowing the exact hour when you first chose to renounce your life and follow Christ worked up such confusion and uncertainty I examined every possible date in my life and could not come up with anything definite.

Mr. Sommical, a traveling evangelist from Canada, visited our country church every summer and reinforced my doubts. He was a sweet, portly old gentleman who always wore a tie and a transparent white nylon shirt and the same wool suit worn shiny with pressing, year after year, even during the smoldering heat of July. Underneath his shirt we could see he wore a muscle shirt that struck me as odd since Dad and every other male I knew, including my brothers, all wore crew-neck undershirts. Wherever he went he carried a large, black leather Bible printed on onion-skin paper and hummed hymns under his breath. He said "aboot" when he meant "about." Randy and I also noticed that the name Sommical rhymed with comical, though we never mentioned this to him.

When it was our family's turn to host him for supper before the evening meeting, Mom turned out meal worthy of King Solomon. While she made the fried chicken, cream gravy, and put the finishing touches on a Lemon Angel pie, we children were allowed to quiz him by randomly turning anywhere in the Bible and reading him a verse to see if he could guess where it was found. I read aloud the most obscure passages I could find.

From a minor prophet in the Old Testament: "And he shewed me Joshua the high priest standing before the angel of the LORD, and Satan standing at his right hand to resist him."

"Zechariah 3:1."

From the convoluted genealogies of the Israelites: "Of the tribe of Asher, Sethur the son of Michael. Of the tribe of Naphtali, Nahbi the son of Vophsi."

"Numbers 13: 14–15," he shouted.

He must have memorized the entire Bible.

Each evening of his series he preached a message from a colorful canvas chart hung across the front of the chapel. "From Eternity to Eternity" began with the dawn of time, when God created Adam and Eve, and stopped with the end of time, where all the wicked were shown dropping off a cliff into the eternal flames of hell while the righteous were transported up to the eternal blue heavens, the streets of gold, and God sitting on his eternal throne of light. The chart was split down the middle by the cross of Christ, which filtered out two streams of people. Most headed down a wide-open, easy road. A few squeezed through a narrow gate beneath the cross and were working their way up a treacherous mountain path. Mr. Sommical's sermon began like a volcano with a barely noticeable swelling of the earth that grew and grew until suddenly it burst with frightening ferocity. He leaned over the pulpit and shouted to the small gathering of regular attenders, "Which road are you on?! If you don't know for sure then you are on the road to hell!" So I confessed again and again. I wrote it on the flyleaf of my Bible, crossing out the old date and writing in the new.

I was nine years old the first time I attended a summer Bible camp and found that the leaders and counselors there were all agreed: it was important to know exactly when you had been saved. We heard testimonies from people who had left lives of evil and rebellion. They had committed deeds too terrible to tell, though I fervently wished to hear about them. In each case there was a definite Before: I was a bad person on my way to hell and taking others with me. And a definite After: now I am saved, on my way to heaven and telling others about Jesus.

I noticed the same theme from a program Randy and I listened to on the radio. *Unshackled!* was carried hundreds of miles on the night airwaves from Chicago's Pacific Garden Mission to our little house on the Canadian border. It was a drama throbbing with organ chords and simple sound effects like footsteps running down an alley. Wind howling. Doors slamming. Glasses of alcohol clinking together. We were mesmerized hearing about men, at least I only remember men, who'd lived lives of drunkenness and debauchery. How they'd left their families, committed crimes, become homeless. Until they reached the bottom of misery and heard something—a preacher on the street, the Bible, the Holy Spirit—calling them out of darkness. On their knees, in a cold street, at the front of a mission church, even in an alley behind a bar—it could happen anywhere. Weeping, they heard the voice of God, and responded by confessing sin and receiving Christ into their hearts. Everything changed for them once they were on the right path and living in the light. They were immediately Unshackled! They were certain of heaven and could recall the exact time and place where it happened.

My lack of a date was supported by the parade of failures that passed before me night after night. Though I tried to obey my parents, there was no doubt about it: killing your own favorite dog was a very wicked thing to do. I had done that. In addition, I lied about it.

There were other things, too. School was proof that I could hate—mostly girls—with blistering intensity. Girls examined your physical features and sifted through your belongings to determine whether or not you were fit for their company. They compared test scores, fought to be bathroom monitor, and showed off their "Day-of-the-Week" panties. They said:

"I can go like this on the monkey bars, I bet you can't."

"I got a hundred on my spelling test, I bet you didn't."

"I have a new can-can slip. Look!"

"Oh. Do you *still* wear an undershirt?"

I wanted to give them all the worst Indian burn. Bad enough so they could never raise their little white arms in class again. It was one of the compelling ways in which Randy and I taught lessons to our younger siblings. Grab a bare forearm in both your hands and twist the skin in opposite directions. It burned a whole day if done well.

Boys seemed utterly oblivious to such things. They were content to settle differences with a clean, dispassionate punch to the nose. They wore the same clothes every day of the week and couldn't care less about grades. I liked them.

The year I was in fifth grade I had two corduroy skirts for school; girls were not allowed to wear pants. They comprised my basic no-accessories wardrobe. These were gored circle skirts that flowed in graceful waves around my waist when I twirled. One was a soft raspberry color, and the other a periwinkle blue. I wore these on alternate days with a white, Peter Pan collar blouse.

One day Karen Lee Anderson, the most popular, talented, and well-dressed girl in the class, clicked past me in her penny loafers on the way to the pencil sharpener. I could feel her scrutiny bearing down my neck. On her way back she whispered, "How come you never wear anything different? 'Cause I'm sick of your two skirts." She also suggested I get new shoes since my old tennis shoes were dirty and disgusting. She owned five pairs of shoes and never wore the same clothes twice in one week.

In an instant all I loved about my two skirts, the soft color and fine texture, was destroyed. I hoped to see her burn in hell. I hated my parents who did not give me more clothes.

Which brought up another problem: I was ashamed of our poverty. I pretended to prefer my sack lunch of homemade bread sandwiches, cookie, and an apple—when in fact, we couldn't afford to buy hot lunches. I pretended not to care about my straight hair or worn dresses. I didn't talk about home or invite friends to visit. I was ashamed of my siblings. Anyway, who would want to come way out to our farm to be stared at and spied upon by all my younger brother and sister brats, which they did the only time I invited Elsie Bridges to stay overnight? We still didn't have running water. The outdoor toilet was humiliating. We didn't even have a telephone.

Besides anger, hostility, and shame, running shallow beneath the surface was a bit of malice, that is, intentional ill-will. I was often quite willing to pick a fight with my brother. As long as I had the strength to do it, I wrestled Randy to the ground and sat on his chest, my knees on his little arms, my head hanging over his, a silvery thread of saliva dangling from my lips, threatening to let go before I sucked it up at the last moment, making him repeat the most humiliating thing I could think of. "I want to kiss Linda," or "I suck my thumb." Only then would I get off. I did it just because I could. And when I sensed his male strength growing beyond mine, I quit.

He actually missed our wrestling matches, and when I refused to fight him anymore, he tried to force me. He badgered, pushed, and finally threatened to beat me up. I said go ahead. He got a half nelson on me, pulled me over his leg, and threw me down. I rolled over and went limp, which made him furious. He sat on my back, pulled my hair, banged my head on the floor, and still I did nothing. When Mom and Dad came home, I told on him and he got in trouble. It wasn't fair and I knew it. My quitting had nothing to do with virtue.

In an agony of remorse about my offenses, I confessed: *Dear God, I am sorry I hate Karen Lee so much. I am sorry I beat up my brother and killed my dog. I know it's wrong to want all the new clothes in the Sears catalog. Forgive me for being ashamed of my family and for being a rotten tattle-tale. I know Jesus died for all these things, but I will try hard to be better. Amen.*

I wanted to do something to prove I loved God and could change if I tried very hard. Something big and costly. I thought God would be very happy if I became a missionary. Missionaries had to live in primitive conditions without running water or indoor plumbing. I already knew how to do that. But you also had to eat things you might not like. I heard of people who ate winged termites, waiting for them to emerge from their holes, deftly picking them up, pulling off their wings, and popping them in their mouths. That would be hard, but I would do it. It couldn't be worse than eating morel mushrooms or the testicles of bull calves. I might get speared to death, and maybe eaten, but then I'd be a martyr like the five missionaries who were killed in South America by the Auca Indians. I was willing to do this for God, and I hoped he would love me in return.

One night after another fall-off-the-bed nightmare, as I argued with the same old doubts, a new question arose. It went straight to my heart with the sudden clarity of floodlights thrown on at the ice rink. It was a simple question. Gentle. Clean. Not like the accusations from Satan or my nitpicker self. All my thoughts stopped to listen. The question asked: *Right now, at this very moment, what do you believe?* It was not an audible voice, but I knew it came from God. The answer was so easy. Why hadn't I thought of this before? I felt hope rising in my heart. I answered, "Right now, this minute? I believe Jesus. I love him."

*That's all you need.*

There was a finality about it. That's all you need. The beautiful simplicity of a chord resolved. My salvation was not linked to a particular finite memory of when belief began; God would keep track of that. All I needed to know is that right then, at that moment, he was Father to me.

Suddenly, I was flooded. How could I have missed this path for so long? I relaxed into my pillow smiling into the darkness. I heard Satan say again, "You don't have a date." But the power was gone.

From then on I understood that day or night God lived in a shotgun house, in an isolated county of northern Minnesota, far away from catechisms and churches backed by centuries of prestige and power. Apart from theological centers of renown, God came to me night after night teaching me about divine Fatherhood: it was not my effort, my hard work that kept his love but his kindness that drew me and his mysterious grace that kept me. He came to me, along the very cracks in my person, stopping the poisonous wind that could have left me spiritually ill for the rest of my life.

My place and existence were not accidental. I wasn't lost in a box eighteen inches from safety. I wouldn't be pursued by rabid skunks down dark paths of life or by beasts that emerged from the darkness. I was forgiven and eternally dated. What was said of God in the Acts of the Apostles was true: "He determined the times set for mankind and the exact places where they should live. God did this so that men would seek Him and perhaps reach out for Him and find Him, though He is not far from each one of us." (Acts 17:26–27).

I had reached for God from the time I was four and swore at Bing. For sure, it was he who had found me. Certainly there were other cracks in my soul that would need to be faced one day, but that one closed, and I never fell off the bed or saw the faces at the window again.

---

## Grandma Frolander's Angel Pie

*Meringue Crust*
4 egg whites
1/4 tsp cream of tartar
1 cup sugar

Preheat oven to 275 degrees. Beat egg whites and until foamy. Gradually add cream of tartar and sugar, beating until meringue stands in stiff peaks. Spread in a buttered 9-inch pie plate. Bake for one or two hours or longer until crust is dry all the way through. Turn oven off and allow crust to cool in the oven.

*Lemon Filling*
4 egg yolks
1/2 cup sugar
1 lemon, juice and zest
1 cup cream, whipped, no sugar added

In a saucepan beat yolks until thick. Add sugar and lemon. Stirring constantly, thicken over medium heat.

Spread half the whipped cream on top of cooled meringue. Carefully spread lemon filling as the next layer. Spread remaining whipped cream on top of filling. Refrigerate until served.

---

# Vaccinium Myrtilloides

When fire burns across boreal forests, conifer stands,
muskegs, and peat bogs, one of the first plants to recolonize is
*Vaccinium myrtilloides*—the velvetleaf blueberry. In Lake of the Woods
County, it's a miniature shrub with downy branches and bright green
leaves, often no more than eight inches high. Wild blueberry is smaller,
sweeter, and more flavorful than its domesticated cousin. Its drooping,
bell-shaped flowers are sensitive to late spring frost, and a reduced
crop of blueberries has been connected to a reduction in black bear
reproductive success and an increase in bear-human conflicts. In late
summer its fruit is so highly sought after, human pickers comprise
twenty percent of all visitors to northern Minnesota state parks.

As Mom and I picked across a sandy ridge, dense with windfall,
boulders, and scattered jack pine in Zippel Bay State Park, we kept an
eye out for bear. We'd seen signs: scat dotted with berry seeds, deep
scratches in the bark of a pine tree still dripping with resin,
and blueberry plants mashed down and stripped of fruit. Suddenly
Mom whispered, "Look." She was pointing just beyond a large rock
outcropping. A black bear with his back to us sat like an overgrown
toddler. We were quietly backing away when he turned, rose to his
hind legs, and stared at us with tiny pig eyes. Then he was gone,
his round rump bouncing away in the bracken and brush.

For the deer, fox, mice, chipmunks, squirrels, skunks, birds, and
especially the bear that depend on them, blueberries are life.
For humans, blueberries are lace and truffles. Most years
there were enough for both of us.

# SHAG CARPET FOR A BLUE BATH

A woman stood alone in the wind, tears tracking down her blackened face as her skirts and smoke billowed about her. She watched as a fire burned across the prairie consuming ranch buildings, cattle, and everything in its path, including the hero who was trapped by flames as he rode back to rescue her.

It was a Western, the first movie I'd ever seen, and I was transfixed. I had no doubt these were real people, that what we saw on the screen was real, space-time history. I was five years old when this movie came to the small theater in Williams. It wasn't a children's movie, but Mom and Dad had taken Randy and me into town with them; perhaps there was no one to babysit that night. I don't know. I don't remember them ever going again. Movies weren't optional after Mom and Dad were taught by the church that good Christians didn't support the immorality of Hollywood. I didn't see another movie until I was seventeen, had left home for the university, and hoped that in a city of one million I could sneak into *The Sound of Music* without the risk of being discovered.

The embers of that first movie smoldered in my memory for several years until I made an astonishing discovery as I played house in our wooded pasture with Randy and Jan. Randy was bending young aspen trees to the ground and riding them like a horse, springing up and down on their little green trunks until they splintered and broke. With sticks and branches, Jan and I had carefully laid out the forest floor plan of our new home. It was a ranch house worthy of John Wayne with two bedrooms and leafy fern beds. It had a modern kitchen and, most significantly, an indoor bathroom for the wife. Men were restricted to the barn or outhouse. I knelt at our ground-level kitchen counter, a row of flat fieldstones painstakingly quarried from the rock pile, where I was cooking supper. We were having puffball mushrooms, wild strawberries on leaf plates, granite potatoes roasted in the oven, and fragrant poplar catkins for dessert. A rusty tin can with a bouquet of goldenrod and Indian paintbrush decorated the table.

When it was time to eat, Randy came into the house and actually used the bathroom. "You idiot," I yelled. "Do that in the barn."

As I walked through the rooms, intending to push him through the wall, I suddenly stopped. The toilet he had just anointed was an ancient black stump. It was certainly blackened, not just an old virgin tree stump sawed off by lumbermen. I looked around cautiously. There were others. I rubbed my finger across one and sniffed it. Charcoal. This had to be the very site of the movie I'd seen. The fire had burned right here, across our land! I gazed at the lush grass, the bracken, brush, and young poplar trees, most of which were small enough for my arms to reach completely around. I shivered. If this happened once, what was to stop it from happening again? The next time fire came through, our family would be caught in the midst of it. We would be the ones losing our home, small as it was, and Mom would be left crying in the smoke.

———

For years Mom dreamed and prayed about moving to a bigger house—one with running water, an indoor bathroom, and more than three rooms. The larger the family grew, the more space we required. Eight of us crowded around the table for meals in our small kitchen. Our furniture was worn and broken, our living room couch sagged in the middle from the weight of our jumping on it when Mom and Dad were out. We were no longer able to fit three to a bed. In the winter with the house closed up, the barn clothes hanging by the back door, the slop bucket, and the exchange of air from our lungs and pores made our house smell like boiled kidneys. After we breathed it a while we didn't notice it much, but on first coming in, it hit you.

Our clothing was crushed into the drawers of two dressers, making it impossible to shut them easily. Each of us had one drawer to ourselves, but as our sizes went up, so did the challenge of stuffing everything into a single drawer. It had to hold not only our clothes, but the personal items you didn't want hanging around the house for someone else to steal or comment on. Mom had a rule that we were not allowed to snoop in anyone else's drawer, though that hardly stopped certain people. It was where I saved my money in a little plastic coin purse, the kind that fit in the palm of your hand, with lips that opened like a mouth when you squeezed the ends. It bulged with the folded two-dollar bill Uncle Don, Mom's brother, gave each of us every Christmas, and the four quarters I earned picking field rock for Grandpa Block. At the back of my drawer I filed away birthday cards from Grandma Frolander, and on the very bottom beneath my underwear, I tucked a page torn out of the Sears catalog, which advertised training bras and showed how to measure the chest to determine your bust size. Why were they called "training bras," I wondered? Training for what? There was little privacy for this sort of thing, but I became skilled at running into the bedroom, grabbing Mom's tape measure from the drawer of her old treadle sewing machine and wrapping it around my chest as I took a deep breath and held it. Each time, I hoped I'd be at least size 28 double-A so Mom would order a bra for me. Day after day I stayed the same: 26 double-nothing.

I wished we could move because I didn't like the bats that lived in the walls of our house. At night we heard them squeaking and scratching in the wall between the living room and bedroom. Sometimes we smelled them—an acrid ratty odor. They occasionally found their way inside, coming down the chimney, timing their arrival for right after Mom and Dad got in bed. We heard a flut, flut, flut, and tiny screeches as it swooped through the house, then total silence.

Mom whispered, "Wally, there's a bat in the house." Dad turned on the light and told us to cover our heads, and not peek—he didn't wear pajamas to bed, only jockey shorts, and we weren't supposed to look at him in jockey shorts.

The bat was hanging from the corner of the ceiling above my sisters and me. Dad jumped from their bed to our three-quarter bed, which clanged as the springs hit the metal frame. He swung wildly at it with a fly swatter. Trying not to step on us, he slammed into the bunk then chased it to the kitchen. "It's back here now!" we screamed. He finally caught it and tossed it out to the yard.

We muffled our laughter under the covers, shocked to see this creature with a thick, sunburned neck set on a white, barrel chest, skinny legs, and flapping forearms the size of hams. Our next house would not have bats, Mom hoped. And, God willing, there would be a bedroom just for the two of them.

For a while Mom thought we were going to get the Bruber house. It was only two miles from our farm, set back from the road on a winding driveway, and almost hidden at the edge of the forest. The Brubers had died, or moved away, I don't remember. Mom and I drove by one day and stepped onto the screened-in porch on the side of the empty house and quietly tried the French doors. They creaked open to reveal a dining room with smooth, honey-colored hardwood floors. The sun poured through the six-paned windows throwing a pattern of golden squares across the empty rooms as Mom and I entered, dreaming of how an oak table would look in the dining room. And oh, how we would cook in that kitchen with running hot and cold water. Of course, my sisters and I would have a bedroom of our own with a closet, and we'd never, ever use the outhouse again. In the yard Mom and I would trim the overgrown vines, cut back the lilacs, plant flowers and a vegetable garden. I would never complain about walking a quarter-mile out to the road to catch the school bus, not even in the winter when it was thirty below.

It was difficult to get a bank loan for any reason when the farm crops failed three years in a row. A year of severe drought was followed by two years of so much rain, it drowned the winter wheat planted the fall before and kept farmers out of their fields until it was too late for most spring planting. All summer Dad watched the crops he had managed to plant turn yellow from standing water. The wheat that did grow was spoiled by a fungus disease, and the corn was destroyed by smut. There was no harvest, no savings, and no money in the checking account. Even though Dad had a reputation for honesty and hard work, and was never a spendthrift or deeply indebted like many farmers were, the bank turned down Mom and Dad's loan application to buy the Bruber property.

During the second summer of rain the ground was so saturated, it was wet enough to trap the giant earth-moving machines that slowly rumbled down the road and tried to turn around in our field. They had come with a road-building crew, widening the ditches into gentle slopes, and laying blacktop over the gravel road that ran past our place. The first one that turned into our field got mired in the clay. The second one tried to pull the first one out, but it, too, sank in mud to the top of its giant tires. No amount of male finesse could free them.

For several days men from around the county gathered in celebration, eager to give advice and speculate on what "a guy coulda done" to have avoided this problem in the first place. Finally, Clayton Fadness came with his Cat D12, the biggest bulldozer we'd ever seen, and pulled them out, leaving water-filled craters the size of ice rinks in our field. No one was more fascinated than my six-year-old brother, Rex, who stood at the edge of the field, with muddied shoes and pants wet to his knees, knowing what he would do for life. His eyes brightened and flashed, and he couldn't stop yammering about draglines, gravel trucks, and Tournepols even when we told him to *shut up* about it. Undaunted, he said what he always said when confronted, "You're not the boss of me," and went right on talking.

The day after the bank turned down their loan application, Mom didn't say much, but she stood on a chair and found some old rolls of wallpaper in the attic and repapered the living room. She painted the kitchen yellow and made new curtains for the cupboard fronts. On Saturday, we cleaned house as usual, shaking rugs, mopping floors, sweeping out the one closet, and baking cookies and sweet rolls. When I pestered her about when were we ever going to move, all she would say was, "For some reason, we're not getting the Bruber house. I trust God knows what is best for us."

By the time I was in sixth grade I considered our life squalid and never invited friends home from school. However, my hospitable parents didn't allow three rooms and six kids to stop them. On holidays, birthdays, and informal gatherings our house was like the mail-order box of a hundred chicks that came in the spring—wall-to-wall noise and bodies in motion. In the kitchen I was accustomed to reaching past someone's head to the spice rack, pressing around another to grab a mixing bowl, and beating chocolate cake in a tiny open spot on the counter, while someone else peeled potatoes, shredded cabbage, and set the table. While the women cooked, the men drank coffee and talked as the aroma of fresh bread and roasting beef rose in the air around us. To this day, it pleases me when a crowded kitchen awakens, not irritation, but a sense of closeness and home directly linked to the old shotgun house.

We had our own Early Warning System for the arrival of unexpected visitors. The one who spied a car slowing down and turning off the road yelled, "There's a car pulling into the driveway," which first created a stampede to the window. "Who is it?" Mom would ask. It didn't matter who; her response was predictable. It gave her about sixty seconds to prep the house for company, and she fired off a string of commands: "Jan, pick up the dirty clothes and throw 'em in the closet. Margie Lou, take the baby. Wash her face and comb her hair. Randy, go change your pants, they're filthy. Rex, pick up the toys." We tore around while Mom wiped the table and straightened the rugs. By the time someone knocked on the door, we hoped we looked casually interested—like we'd just been waiting for someone to stop in for coffee.

Occasionally a visitor—like the traveling preacher who unexpectedly dropped by with his wife and another couple from Iowa—asked to be shown the rest of our house, which wasn't much more than what they saw as they entered the back door into the kitchen. For Mom's sake their timing was perfect. Not only had we cleaned the house that morning, it had a rich smell from eight loaves of bread cooling on the kitchen table, and the triple batch of chocolate chip cookies we were still baking.

People exclaimed over how Mom managed in such a small house with six kids, but I was increasingly affronted when anyone dared ask to see our three rooms. What gave them the right? Would I stand at their back door and ask to see their home? I didn't care who this preacher was, he shouldn't have asked.

Mom was always gracious and gave them the tour. They stared at our little bedroom crowded with a neatly made double bed, a three-quarter bed, a set of bunk beds, and a crib flanked by the two dressers and a Singer sewing machine. They commented on how orderly, how clean the rooms, while I seethed in the background, hiding behind a staring phalanx of brothers and sisters. Then they sat in our tiny kitchen eating our warm bread and cheese, followed by hot coffee and cookies so fresh the chips were still melty.

Despite my shame and insolence, and before I had the ability to recognize and be thankful for it, Mom modeled something that leeched into my resentful teenage bones. It was the art of welcoming others to share what you have. The ability to acknowledge that no home will ever be perfectly appointed or free of trouble, but it can still be a place of shelter where human needs and even spiritual longings are met with the comfort of food and the love of God.

Dad continued to get outside work, supporting us with income from the Department of Natural Resources. The DNR planned to develop a state park on land that adjoined ours—a sand ridge left by ancient glaciers covered with old pine stands, groves of birch and poplar that sank into acres and acres of swamp and miles of sandy shoreline along the Lake. Dad was hired to oversee its development. He knew this land so well it was a perfect job for him—clearing campsites, turning trails into roads, and overseeing the building projects. Eventually it became Zippel Bay State Park—and Dad was made park manager, which meant steady income and options like renting our crop land so Mom didn't have to drive tractor when Dad was away working. And owning a telephone—which only slightly mollified me because I was never allowed to use it without permission.

The winter of my the tenth grade, before anyone was sure Dad would get the job as park manager, and while the ice was still thick on the Lake, the DNR moved a single-story building from Garden Island onto the mainland about five miles from us. In the early 1900s it had belonged to Booth Fishery and had been used as a home for the manager and a dining hall for the commercial fishermen they employed. The fishery was long gone, and the state had inherited the island and its buildings. The house was solidly built with a main room and four smaller ones leading off it, but no one had lived in it for years. The DNR thought they could sell it, but who would want a ghostly old house with broken windows and weathered siding? It sat for weeks without a buyer until the DNR made plans to demolish it. A county commissioner who knew of the plan saw Dad in town and told him about the building. He suggested Dad move it onto his place. He said, "You've got a big family, and you know, with a little remodeling a guy could make a pretty good home out of this. I tell you what, if you pay the state a buck we'll make the deal legal. You'll only have to get her moved."

That spring a large truck slowly pulled into our field driveway hauling a faded, white, house-like structure. The men parked it in the alfalfa field east of our house, jacked it up, and left it on blocks where it looked strangely derelict, like it really should have been demolished. It sat there all summer while a basement was dug, a foundation laid, and a septic system put in the ground. Then it was going to be permanently settled onto its new foundation.

After the truck left, Dad stacked railroad ties up to the door so we could climb in to see our new home. Inside it smelled of dust, mice and mold. The empty rooms were draped with cobwebs and strips of yellowed wallpaper. The closets were lined with insect riddled newspapers from the 1940s. Spiders scuttled into cracks, and the worn plank floor squeaked as we walked through. The main room had a hole in the wall where a stovepipe had been. There was no bathroom. The remaining rooms were darkened with age and small windows. It hardly seemed like the answer to years of hoping for the roomy, bright home Mom prayed for and I dreamed of. Dad was not a carpenter who could change any of this, but Mom said, "Wait and see." Grandpa Frolander was coming in the fall after he closed up their resort for the season. I thought about the fragrant log cabins with pine furniture and the sleek wooden boats he built and felt a sliver of hope.

When school let out in May, Mom set up beds and moved four of us kids out to the house for sleeping. We swept and mopped the linoleum floor, which was curling on the edges and worn black through faded patterns of Persian flowers. I put a throw rug beside our bed, and we moved our clothes into cardboard boxes. Roxanne and I slept together on an old bed that squeaked and sproinged when she jumped on it. Randy and Rex slept on single cots in another room at the back of the house. At night, Roxy and I cuddled under our blankets to escape the mosquitoes that crawled through the cracks in the windows and screens. I hugged my five-year-old sister, and pulled the quilt tightly over our heads; it was so odd to sleep without Mom and Dad nearby. The distance from the old house where we heard one another breathe all night long to this silent open space seemed about as far I would ever dare to go from them.

One night I woke knowing something had made a sound that reached my sleeping ears. I stiffened with adrenalin. There was a noise outside, at the corner of the empty house. Something groaned and scratched on the wall. I tried to identify what I heard. Was someone playing a trick on us? I grabbed Roxy and wrapped my arms around her. If this was someone I knew trying to scare us, I was going kill him. Whatever it was continued to moan and claw at the house. I swore to never read the horror stories of Edgar Allen Poe *again*. There *had* to be a rational explanation for this. I wanted Randy to wake up so there could be another witness and to think together of what to do, but he was three rooms away. Anyhow, he slept so soundly you could roll him over, draw on his face with an ink pen, which I'd done many times, and he still wouldn't wake up. Finally, the noise stopped, but for hours I strained my ears listening for footsteps and watching the door in the dim starlight to see if the knob was turning.

The next day I told Mom, but trying to describe it was like a baby screaming, a dog yelping, and an old man's snoring was not it. It wasn't like anything I'd ever heard before. We looked at the outside corner of the house. There were no tracks in the hard, dry ground. We saw faint scratches in the wood siding, but nothing definite. Could I have imagined it, I wondered?

Years later I happened to see a television nature program about bears. The

crew was filming a black bear and taping his sounds when I was suddenly flooded by the same fear I experienced on that summer night. My memory made an
instant connection before my conscious mind had time to identify a threat. I
was back in that bed with Roxanne, hearing once again the surreal noise of a
bear grunting and groaning. I had seen bears—in a distant field eating grain,
disappearing from a blueberry patch, crossing the road in front of the car, and
even one that climbed a tree at my grandparents' resort, but I had never in my
life heard one until that night.

During that summer of separation from our old house, in the long twilight before dark, and in the early morning hours when the sun rose by 4:30, I
read with no one to stop me—old books from a box someone gave us—mostly
Reader's Digest Condensed Books about fatal accidents, miraculous recover-
ies from disease, and acts of heroism. Among the books I found Shakespeare's
plays in Little Leather Library editions. There were no footnotes to explain what
I read. I only grasped enough of him to be vexed. But some things are universally
understood like love and insults.

> PRINCE HENRY: These lies are like their father that begets them,
> gross as a mountain, open, palpable. Why thou clay-brained guts,
> thou knotty-pated fool, thou whoreson, obscene, greasy tallow-
> keech . . . This sanguine coward, this bed-presser, this horse-back
> breaker, this huge hill of flesh.

> FALSTAFF: 'Sblood you starveling, you elf-skin, you dried neat's
> tongue, you bull's pizzle, you stock-fish—O for breath to utter
> what is like thee—you tailor's-yard, you sheath, you bow-case,
> you vile standing-tuck[1]

His exquisite name-calling was shocking and brilliant. It made Dad's insults
(meathead, moron, and pot-licker) almost sound like compliments. I wondered
how someone as old as Shakespeare could be so intelligent and yet so rude. I
assumed that the progress of the human race meant people got a lot smarter at
things, not only coming up with new inventions like flush toilets and tail fins for
Cadillacs, but stories that reflected humankind's growing genius. It was hard
to explain how Shakespeare was able to write works that were considered the
greatest English literature ever written, being stuck as he was in the seventeenth
century. Of course, it didn't occur to me that the Bible, whose words I considered
almost every day, were a whole lot older than Shakespeare.

Before sleep, I often turned to a woman born in the nineteenth century. Amy
Carmichael was a single missionary who went to India and spent her life rescuing

young girls who had been orphaned, abandoned, or given to temple prostitution. She wrote a little book called, *His Thoughts Said, His Father Said*. It was a collection of intimate prayers and conversations with God. I read them, again and again, words identified my secret anxieties. I knew they were meant for me.

> His thoughts said, "My heart is overwhelmed."
> His Father said, "Thou art not the first to feel so. Here is a word for thee, 'When my spirit was overwhelmed within me, then Thou knewest my path.'"
> And his Father poured comfort into him saying, "O man greatly beloved, fear not: peace be unto thee, be strong; yea, be strong."
> And when He had spoken unto him, the son was strengthened.
> Then he remembered how often at midnight, or in the small hours of the morning when all life's molehills become mountains, some familiar Scripture flowing through the mind had renewed his strength. And he knew that in those words was a power that was not of earth.[2]

Not counting the bear episode, for one second that summer I wondered if any of us would live long enough to see whether Grandpa could make anything of the desolate house in the field.

We wouldn't have paid much attention to the Cold War between the United States and the Soviet Union except that signs of it reached us in spite of our isolation. People in northern Minnesota watched the skies and listened for Soviet bombers that, we were told, would come down over Canada to hit us by surprise. Before the web of radar defense bases became operational in bands across Canada and Northern United States, the military selected listening posts along the northern border. A network of civilians was enlisted to operate an electronic listening device that would detect enemy aircraft entering our air space. Grandpa and Grandma Block were chosen as one of the sites because they were located right on the Lake and perfectly positioned to give early warning if a bomber flew over their house. A large antenna was erected in their yard, and a square box with blinking red lights and switches sat in their dining room. It listened day and night to the wind blow across water and land with a constant shoo-oo-shing sound.

It would have made perfect postmodern white noise, except that whenever a crop duster or single-engine Cessna flew anywhere near, the noise that began as a faint insect hum grew until it roared like an entire squadron of warplanes. When we heard one coming, we ran outside and down to the end of the dock to see if the Russians were coming while Grandma called a number to report an unidentified aircraft. The racket annoyed Grandma enough for her to often drop her citizenship duties. Then she'd order, "Earl, shut that thing off. I can't hear myself think."

In 1958 when the Air Force built a small radar base outside Baudette, it made the listening posts obsolete. Military personnel were posted to our remote county where fun was seeing your kid's peewee team play hockey on Friday night and watching *The Lawrence Welk Show* on Saturday. When the young draftees arrived in Baudette—the "Walleye Capital of the World," population 1100—they were greeted by a 42-foot statue of Willy the Walleye staring at them from his glass eye. Willy guarded the downtown with its single stop sign, a theater, Rexall Drugstore, the Red Owl Grocery, and Rosie's Café, where the specialty was hamburger soup. They moved into barracks and manned the station, which we could actually see on the horizon at night from our farm twenty miles away—its north-facing, giant eye flashing as it scanned the skies from east to west, protecting us from the Soviets.

I believed in this protection until a hot day in July when Randy and I had been sent to the garden to pick the green beans. That summer the Air Force tested radar technology with our own bombers. Mimicking what the Soviets might do, a squadron of American fighter jets sortied far north of the border, then they headed south, flying in fast and low over the Lake. They swept directly over our farm at treetop height. The sudden roar of their engines arrived a split second after their giant shadows flashed over us. I threw down my pail and ran for the house thinking, if only I can make it home. If we were going to die, I wanted to burn together. I had only gone a few steps when all about us the land and trees shook with an explosion I felt in my body. I fell to the ground with my head buried in the crook of my arm. Just as suddenly it was quiet, and as Randy and I lay in the grass, we heard the grasshoppers resume their sawing.

It's hard to imagine now how there were no categories, no context in which I could process what had just happened. I'd never seen anything fly that was larger than a single-engine plane, like the one my father died in. Uncle Peter, Mom's brother, flew a small Piper Cub he sometimes set down in a field nearby and taxied up to the house. It was a marvelous machine—touchable, comprehensible. The only jets I saw were in photos or 36,000 feet above us, visible only as a silver cross leading a thread of white vapor across the sky, and trailing about five seconds later, a faint hiss.

Mom heard the jets and felt the boom as we ran for the house. She came out to find us and reassure us it was our own military and they were only testing the radar. She explained the noise came when they broke the sound barrier, but it was nothing harmful. I was so relieved I momentarily forgot I had reached the point in life where I knew so much more than she did. I felt stupid, as stupid as the city person who climbed our manure pile and thought it might be an Indian mound.

In early September our one-dollar house was moved onto the new foundation and Grandpa Frolander arrived with his tools. Soon the fragrance I still associate with him filled the rooms—freshly cut lumber and the metallic tang of hot saw blades. Our bed was moved to the middle of the room and covered with plastic during the day. At night I swept up the sawdust; then Roxanne and I tiptoed across the cold floor and piled on the blankets as night temperatures dipped below freezing.

Grandpa tore down walls, put up new studs, and rewired. Plumbing fixtures and kitchen appliances arrived in large cardboard cartons. He hung doors and built closets. He took out old windows, and replaced them with wall-sized picture windows. Where there had been two small rooms there was now a living room with an entire bank of windows that looked across the fields to the rising sun. He cut a hole in the floor and built a stairway to the basement. The room with our bed became a kitchen with birch cabinets and a built-in desk. Of all things, the desk brought tears to my eyes—to see Mom's worn cookbooks neatly arranged in a row and the black rotary phone sitting together beneath the mirror represented beauty and civility. The south wall of the kitchen had floor-to-ceiling sliding-glass doors that led to a deck. In front of them, Grandpa placed a large, pine harvest table he'd built specifically for us. It sat there, drenched in sunshine, just waiting to comfortably seat up to fourteen people, and still, there was room to spare in the kitchen for serving a meal and chasing the dog. The shining cabinets and Formica counters formed a long, L-shaped work area with enough room for hordes of cooks and bakers preparing food for multitudes of friends.

For the first time in our lives we were going to have an indoor bathroom. For the first time in their married life Mom and Dad would have their own bedroom at the back of the house. We kids would sleep in the basement with a curtain strung up to separate the boys from the girls, which suited us fine.

———

It was unusually dry the fall Grandpa Frolander worked on the house. All around the county, fires were burning, and when the swamp south of us caught fire, memories of the only movie I'd seen were fanned to consciousness again.

The swamp across our road extended for a hundred miles south. Some sections had been drained and cleared for farming, but most of it remained marsh and bog filled with peat moss. Scattered across it were islands of cedar and thin stands of alder and poplar trees. Blueberries and high bush cranberries grew on hidden hillocks among tall marsh grasses and cattails that swayed above our heads. There were tracks and scat from the animals that lived there and sometimes you caught the merest glimpse of movement—a fox or a mink slipping away.

In late July and early August the wild blueberries ripened and we wandered into the swamp with lard pails and buckets looking for them. When Mom was with us we usually found them and never worried about meeting a bear or getting lost. Without her it seemed reckless to enter. All during the picking season Mom made pies. They came out of the oven with a sugary, flaky crust on top and a thin, crunchy layer of crystallized sugar in the bottom. Steam escaped from the lightly browned vents, and inside the dusty-blue berries turned a deep purple. Thick, gooey pies weren't a sign of success in her kitchen. We imagined those were the kind town people made—with appalling, store-bought, canned filling that tasted like sweetened rabbit pellets. Mom's were just right. They dripped juice as a slice was lifted unto a plate and topped with thick sweet cream where it spread across the warm crust and ran down the sides in streaks of violet and blue.

Extra berries were stored in an ancient freezer kept in the old granary turned tool shed. By mid-February when winter seemed to last forever, when we'd altogether forgotten blueberries, her pies surprised us with warm pleasure.

No one in the county paid much attention when the swamp burned; few people lived near enough to be affected. We watched it glow on the horizon after dark. Five miles south of us it slowly burned our direction in the calm autumn evening. I heard Mom and Dad talking about it with Grandpa Block and Tom Howard, our closest neighbor to the north.

"A good thing there's no wind. If it picks up it could jump the road then."

"Yuh. There's no way to get the tractor across the road to plow a fire-break. Wouldn't do no good anyway."

"Clayt Fadness might be able to get back there with his Cat. But he's clear to the other side of Baudette dozing a fire-break for the county."

"So then. Maybe it'll rain."

"Yuh."

I watched the fire from my bed and remembered the movie. If it came up fast and hot, it seemed like our way of escape would be cut off unless we could beat it to the Lake. Our new home would burn to ashes—all the years of waiting and dreaming would go up in smoke. I begged God to stop the fire and let us move into the new house. I pulled the sheet over my head and breathed, but it was hard to ignore the smoky air seeping through the window.

In the still morning a choking fog shrouded our farm. We could barely see the outline of the barn from the house. On the way to school we sat unusually quiet and tense as our bus slowly groped along the gravel roads in heavy murk.

Uncle Johnny Block drove while his son, Peter, stood on the bottom step with the door open guiding his dad slowly along the edge to keep us from straying into the ditch.

After school a hot south wind blew fingers of fire that licked across the bog and up to an old fence across the road. Some of the fence posts caught fire. As we watched, the wind shifted to the east and a cold breeze ruffled our hair. The sky darkened with a layer of clouds racing in from the west against the east wind. That usually forecast rain, and soon the first drops fell, leaving darkened round spots in the gravel, rattling leaves, and sizzling in the fire. It became a downpour—the first in weeks. I ran for a sweater before I put the cows in the barn. By suppertime the air was rinsed clean, and the temperature had dropped. Winter was coming.

In the warm kitchen we sat around the table as Mom brought out blueberry pie and a carton of Land O'Lakes vanilla ice cream. "Cream or a scoop of vanilla?" she asked. We laughed; we were crazy for store-bought ice cream.

Throughout the coming winter months piles of snow would soften and smooth the tortured stumps and burned hillocks. At night the moon would make a shining path across the snow and deep into the smoldering swamp; for months the peat moss would continue to slowly burn. Here and there small caverns glowed red like the lanterns of an underground world, and wisps of smoke drifted like ghosts across the landscape.

In November after the fire, and after Grandpa packed up his tools and went home, two things happened. I shot my first deer during hunting season, and we finally moved into the new house. I was fifteen years old and in the eleventh grade.

Dad let me use a .410 shotgun with slugs—sometimes called a brush gun, because it is light, easy to handle, and best for short distances where visibility is limited. For a fifteen-year-old girl, it was perfect. I practiced shooting tin cans off fence posts and hitting the bull's eye drawn on a cardboard box. The sights on the gun were a little high, so I learned to compensate by aiming low. We depended on hunting to provide meat for the winter, and I was eager to prove to Dad I could help with this. Before opening day, he picked a stand for me in the state park. He walked me down an overgrown, two-track road and showed me where a deer trail crossed. I was to hide in the bushes beside an old Norway pine where I'd be in position to watch the trail.

On Saturday of hunting season we were up at four-thirty dressing in long underwear and sweatshirts. We gulped down breakfast like wolves—bacon, fried eggs, toast and blueberry jam, orange juice, and coffee with lots of sugar and cream. We sorted through blaze orange jackets and hats. I pulled one of Dad's old orange sweatshirts over my coat and stuffed my hair into a red stocking cap. If I could just get lucky and shoot something the first day, it might make

Dad really proud of me. He and Randy were going to meet the men in their hunting party. Mom and I were driving alone to our stands in the state park. The plan was if I shot a deer, I could walk the mile and a half down toward the Lake where Mom would park the car before walking to her stand. Although I was too young for a driver's license, I would be allowed to drive the car home to get Rex who would help me gut the deer and lift it into the trunk.

Randy shoved me with affection and whispered, "Don't forget to load your gun, you retard."

"Don't shoot yourself in the foot, sissy," I replied.

Dad warned us one last time to never shoot at what you can't clearly see; then we slipped out the door.

Mom drove to my spot, patted my arm, and wished me good luck. I got out, quietly closed the door, and watched the taillights disappear down the dirt road. I crossed the darkened ditch with my gun pointing down the trail, took a tentative step into the blackened forest, and stumbled over a tree root. My heart pitched as I caught myself and the gunstock hit my thigh. I double-checked the safety. I knew of hunters who had tripped, discharged the gun, and killed themselves. Ashamed, I stood still until I could breathe properly, and the dark outline of the track reappeared. "Think Indian," I told myself. "Try to creep." I crunchwalked through the dry leaves, pausing between each step to listen for anything ahead, or worse, something following behind.

I paused and something crashed through the underbrush to my left. It seemed to be moving parallel to my path. Trying to cut me off? Bear? Timber wolf? Carl Grovum? My body flushed adrenalin to every cell and I decided, "That's it, I'm getting off the trail to hide."

I flailed through the brush and fallen leaves, ducked under a dark pine with my back against its rough trunk, and prayed that nothing else would want the same hiding place. I wasn't moving until daylight. I switched off the safety, pulled the gun to my shoulder, and pointed in the direction of the noise. It was now completely still. Not a branch moved. A planet glimmered in the eastern sky. My arms began to tremble and ache, and finally I lowered the gun as the air brightened and night gradually lifted. Small sounds emerged. A woodpecker drummed. A chickadee called, "dee, dee, dee." There was a rustling at my feet and a tiny mouse with black, beady eyes ran along a moss-covered log and disappeared. I peered through thickets of birch and bracken. Nothing. I shivered. The cold had penetrated my layers. It was time to move to my stand. Slowly, I emerged and quietly walked up the track.

When I was about forty yards from the deer trail, a young buck cautiously stepped out of the woods. He stopped and looked at me, his ears forward, small horns glinting. He didn't even flag his tail, just curious, trying to fathom what I was as I stood downwind in the dawning light. Slowly, slowly, I brought the gun to my shoulder and found him in the sights. He stood still, presenting his profile for a perfect shot—right behind the front shoulder. One bullet and he would be quickly and painlessly dispatched.

Remembering to aim a little low I pulled the trigger. A resounding crack and the buck leapt from the trail with a graceful bound. As I ran up I could hear him thrashing in the underbrush. The bullet had hit him right above the shoulder breaking his back, but he was still valiantly trying to get away. Raising his neck and looking at me with a terrified eye, he scraped the ground with his front hooves. Shaking, I shot him in the head. Still, he convulsed. Crying and loathing myself, I shot him two more times, until at last he lay quiet. Panting and hot, I dragged him beneath a spruce tree whose boughs touched the ground, and covered the drag marks, hiding him so no one could find him. I turned away thinking I never wanted to do this again.

As I walked along the road to the car, I passed three strangers, men posted at intervals, waiting for their hunting party to drive deer out of the woods so they could pick them off. They looked like models for Cabella's with their shiny new .30-06s, powerful scopes, and fashionable down parkas in blaze orange. The first one I passed glanced at my little .410 with open sights and smirked, "Got your deer already?" My chagrin about shooting the buck passed directly away.

"Yes, I have." I gave him what I hoped was a scathing stare.

"It took four shots, huh?"

He'd heard my volley, and I could see he didn't believe me at all. When I passed the other two I ignored their questions.

I drove home and picked up my little brother and he helped me dress the deer. As he held the hind legs open, I awkwardly split open the buck's belly with a butcher's knife and sawed away at the pelvic bone. When I finally got through, the steaming guts rolled onto our feet. Rex jumped back, gagging at the smell. I looked at us; our boots were bloody, our hands were a mess, and our pants were stained. We tried to clean up with dead grass, but it only stuck to us. Back home we hung the deer from the clothesline post—the first of the season. I admired it swinging there with a mangled head but none of the meat damaged. Dad was going to love this.

At noon Mom came home without having seen a deer, but when she saw my carcass hanging from the post she threw her arms around me and laughed.

The second thing happened that afternoon: we finally moved into the new house. The week before, Grandpa had completed everything. Some painting and staining still remained, but Mom could do that when she had the time. Aunt Beatty Frolander, Mom's sister-in-law, drove out from Warroad for a visit and a look at our new house. She wanted to see what Grandpa had done. I trailed

Mom and Aunt Beatty on the tour. Even on that cold gray afternoon the emp-ty rooms were flooded with light. Mom showed her all the closets with clean shelves ready to be used.

Aunt Beatty asked why we hadn't moved in. "What's the hold-up?" Mom didn't know. She was strangely paralyzed after so many years of waiting. She guessed she was waiting for Dad to initiate the process. "During hunting sea-son?" Aunt Beatty was incredulous. "Vat's vrongk vitch you, you dumb Svede?" she mocked, using her best Swedish accent. "Let's do it now! Today! I'll help."

Suddenly, we were delirious. Mom and I got the tractor hitched to the hay wagon and pulled it up to the steps. We tore down the beds, heaped bedding on top, packed up the kitchen, and loaded our clothing onto the wagon. In just a couple of hours and several loads, the three-room shotgun house was empty.

Mom built a wood fire in the barrel stove in the basement. Aunt Beatty helped me set up the beds while Mom unpacked the kitchen and started sup-per. Warmth and the smell of roast venison and baked potatoes soon spread through the house. When Dad came home with Randy he grinned and said to me, "I see you got a nice little buck. I suppose you're pretty proud of that." I start-ed to tell him how it happened, but he'd already turned to Mom, and kissing her said, "So then, how do you like your one-dollar house?"

That night sleep was strange. Happiness seemed to settle everywhere on this new home. The wood stove crackled nearby, there were footsteps overhead, and the flush of water down the sewer pipes. Then silence. My brothers and sisters were spread out in the basement, no curtain between us yet, surrounded by ce-ment block walls and tiny high windows. Outside, our dogs, Jingles and Duffy, peered down at us through the windows, wondering at these new arrangements until at last they left for warmer places in the haystack by the barn. If I looked up I could still see a bright patch of stars through the darkened window. When I recalled Amy Carmichael's words, "When my spirit was overwhelmed within me, thou knewest my path," I didn't know it would only be three years until God would lead me to a young man who would fall in love with me and together we would lift a little corner of darkness, raise a family, and welcome other wander-ers in search of home.

I was sleeping in a new house and I had shot my first deer. I would never shoot another. I shoved my toes under Roxanne's fuzzy pajamas.

———

Sunday evening in the bathroom. The sink, tub, and toilet are baby blue porcelain. The floor has blue wall-to-wall carpeting. The entire wall above the sink and counter is tiled with mirrors. Miraculously, four people can stand in front of the long counter and put on make-up, curl hair, brush teeth, or closely examine the face without touching another person. The water runs hot and cold. There is a built-in bookshelf right in front of the commode where you can read *Reader's Digest* and *Daily Light* in perfect comfort with a light on, even. I could live in this place. In fact, I try to—making up for years of sitting in a dark and frozen outhouse, and washing my hair in an enamel basin. I enter the bathroom with my two sisters. We lock the door behind us to bathe and groom in languid luxury. I put Roxanne in the tub where she floats in warm water, her long hair streaming out behind her. Jan sits on the commode, her bare toes curling in the soft shag, and I sit on the counter to shave my legs in the sink. Our faces are lit with pleasure as we watch ourselves, and laugh, and pretend we're rich—until our brothers pound on the door and demand we come out, it's our turn, and Dad yells for us to hurry it up in there or we'll be sitting in the outhouse again and do we want our butts kicked?

The $1.00 house.

## Blueberry Pie

Pastry for 9-inch two-crust pie
4 cups fresh blueberries
1-1/2 cups sugar
1/4 cup flour
1 tsp lemon juice
2 tbsp butter

Preheat oven to 425 degrees. Prepare pastry. Mix flour and sugar.
Place berries in pastry-lined pie plate. Sprinkle with lemon juice. Spread
flour and sugar on top, do not stir in. Dot with butter. Cover with top
crust, seal and flute edges. Cut vents in the middle and sprinkle lightly with
sugar. Bake for 10 minutes. Turn oven to 400 degrees and bake another
45 minutes until crust is brown and filling bubbles through the vents. (The
extra sugar makes a sweeter, more runny filling.)

# EPILOGUE

Mom tells me that one day in spring, just eighteen months after we moved into the new house, she and I were driving home from town. It was a cold, gray day; most of the snow had melted, leaving behind a naked, sopping-wet landscape. Just to get from our back door to the car we had to walk on two-by-twelve planking to keep out of the mud. I looked out the car window as we passed fields under water and ditches running full, and commented, "I can't wait to get out of this stupid swamp." I remember lots of things—enough to have written a book—but I don't remember that remark, which proves how insolent memory can be.

I was seventeen when I graduated from high school a few weeks later; by that age my mother had already been pregnant and widowed. I left home immediately for the Twin Cities where I had a work-study job on the St. Paul campus of the University of Minnesota. To my know-nothing ears, just the words—Department of Plant Pathology—sounded exotic, like it would be a place worthy of my intellect and attention. I thought I would never look back.

It only took about three days of standing hour after hour in a hot greenhouse pollinating tray after tray of alfalfa by tripping the tiny little pistils on the tiny little blossoms to begin seeing my family and our farm in a more charitable light. I ached to go home. I missed my mother, the familiar sounds of my brothers quarreling, the horses and dogs, and the long view to the edge of the tree-line where the sun rose and set. Eventually, I got over the acute loneliness, but I didn't know then that I would never return to live, except for brief visits, in this place permanently lodged in my bones.

Many years later, on Valentine's Day, 2009, my stepfather passed away. He was eighty-five years old. Seven years earlier, he had a stroke that stole his speech and movement on the left side of his body. After a lengthy stay in the hospital and rehab, he moved home where my mother continued to care for him until just days before his death. Throughout the remainder of his life she remained steadfast in patience and love. Although he could no longer talk, he understood what was being said. My sister Jan had a special gift for figuring out what he was trying to say. For him it was an extremely frustrating process, but when she hit on the right interpretation, he would nod vigorously and give a lop-sided grin. It was a tender and beautiful thing to witness.

He clearly had ways of communicating emotion that left you no doubt about what he was feeling. Tears came often when he felt sad. He enjoyed rides in the country. He lit up when his children and grandchildren visited. And you could still tell how much he loved my mother.

Before one of my last visits, my brother Dallas told him I was coming and cautioned Dad. He told him, "You'd better be nice to her or I'll make you sorry." (Dallas often helped Mom with his care, not only because he lived next door—Dallas' humor, physical strength, and matter-of-fact ways in caring for Dad was a blessing to everyone.) In his way, Dad promised to be good.

When I arrived and walked into the room his attitude toward me was the same as ever. I spoke to him, but he was cold and withdrawn. When other family members joined us, there was a distinct change in his demeanor. You could tell he was glad to see them and remained alert and listened to the conversation, at times shaking his head in agreement or trying to say something. When it was just my mother and I, he sank into his inner world and refused to come out. Somehow the expression on his face was one of distaste. I wouldn't have known this difference if I hadn't observed it. There was still a power in his presence and I fought against feeling tense and on guard. His life ended without the reconciliation I hoped for.

Wendell Berry, the essayist and poet-farmer, asks the question: "Is life a miracle?" He answers, saying that he believed everything that exists is a divine gift, which places us in a position of extreme danger, solvable only by love for everything that exists, including our enemies.

I have recognized and loved many divine gifts in my landscape. It was easy to accept Norway pine, browsing deer, and falling snow. Poverty and a stepfather who liked me about as well as a broken trailer hitch were more difficult to receive, and yet I sense the danger that awaits one who refuses such gifts. So it was here, in the midst of glory and brokenness, where I found a miracle, or at least, it's pretty near to one: the thread of redemption that ran through my childhood, even through the dark hours after midnight. If I had been fat with well-being and contentment I believe I would have missed the love of God that still tracks through the wilderness leading me toward Home. I am, I was, in the exact place I needed to be.

# ENDNOTES

## FOREWORD and PROLOGUE

1   *Modern Theology,* Volume 29 Issue 2, Special Issue: "Creation 'Ex-Nihilo' and Modern Theology". Guest Editor: Janet Martin Soskice. April 2013, Pages 156-171.

2   Stephen Colbert and Anderson Cooper's conversation about grief on CNN

3   This phrase was not original to this author. Many writers have used this quote that is often attributed to Mark Twain, but there is no reliable proof that he said it according to the website Words and Deeds. https://www.emtwytte.com/2016/04/04/never-let-the-truth-get-in-the-way-of-a-good-story/

4   Kathleen Norris, *Dakota: A Spiritual Biography* (Boston, MA: Houghton Mifflin, 2001), p. 231.

5   W.B. Yeats, "Crazy Jane Talks with the Bishop," from *The Collected Poems of W.B. Yeats: A New Edition,* ed. Richard J. Finneran (New York: Macmillan Publishing Company, 1989).

## COME HOME

1   *All Will be Well* by Julian of Norwich (Ave Maria Press; 2008) page 81.

## N IS FOR NEEDS IMPROVEMENT

1   Ludwig Bemelmans, *Madeline* (New York: Viking Press, 1939).

2   Louisa May Alcott, *Little Women* (SDE Classics, 2008), p. 390.

## SHAG CARPET FOR A BLUE BATH

1   William Shakespeare, *Henry IV,* Part One, Act II, Scene 4.

2   Amy Carmichael, *His Thoughts Said . . . His Father Said . . .* (Fort Washington, PA: Christian Literature Crusade, 1941), p. 9.

The shotgun house as it stood in 2010.

# About the Author

MARGIE HAACK is a writer living in Savage, MN, with her husband Denis, on a half-acre lot next to a wooded park where she tries to attract bumble bees and hummingbirds with marginal success. Nature and place connect her to the spiritual geography that has shaped her. She has a deep love for home and hospitality, art and culture, and an awareness of God's presence in everyday life. It has been her persistent quest to name what is holy, what is funny, and what is suffering in the ordinary and routine. She and her husband delight in three adult children, their spouses, nine grandchildren, and a great-grandson. Between 1983 and 2020 they worked as directors of Ransom Fellowship, a ministry encouraging Christians to learn to be discerning and to live faithfully in the midst of our culture. Besides the *Place* trilogy, Margie's writing has appeared in *Arthouse America, Comment Magazine* and other publications. You can find both Margie and Denis' writing at *Critique-Letters.com.*

# ACKNOWLEDGEMENTS

It was Marsena Adams-Dufresne who first said, "Mom, you should write a book" after hearing about my childhood shenanigans. Thank you for being the first to inspire me.

My deep love and gratitude go to my mother who chose to keep me when I was born rather than give me up for adoption as she could have when the offer came in.

I am grateful for my siblings, for the fun we shared, the affection, and even the fights. I'm glad for them; their experiences with Wally were not the same as mine.

I'm especially grateful to Ransom Fellowship's Board of Directors. At our annual meetings, Ed Hague (now deceased), Steve Garber, Donald Guthrie, Bonnie Liefer and Henry Tazelaar listened patiently to new chapters year after year. They believed in the project from the first and prayed this book would find a publisher even as I doubted.

Thanks to friends who were part of our small group and gave feedback over the years. Special thanks to Sandy Oster and Randy Massot whose comments were pointed and helpful.

Jennifer Disney, who understands and love loves the child I was and the adult I became, prayed for my work with a confidence that helped keep me steady.

Dave and Paula Kaufman blessed us with their cabin on Pike Lake for extended writing retreats. The quiet beauty of the setting allowed me to focus in a way I couldn't always manage in my home office.

Christopher Noel, a manuscript editor, respectfully pointed out deep flaws in the first draft. He tore off my layers of reserve and prompted me to take scary risks in rewriting my story. He helped make this book far more compelling than it ever would have been without his honest critique.

Ruth Defoster, your ferocity about grammar and punctuation spared me shameful public errors—any that remain are not her fault.

Anita Gorder, our dear friend and assistant, freed me from some household management to find more time to write.

Thanks to Andi Ashworth, another precious friend who gave extravagant praise even to untidy early drafts.

I owe everything to Katy Bowser Hutson who pushed and pep-talked, tried the recipes, scolded my doubts, and finally beseeched the world to get this published after I had given up.

Ed Eubanks formerly the editor at Kalos Press became my first publisher. For that I'm very grateful.

Now at the release of this new edition, thanks to Ned and Leslie Bustard of Square Halo Books who have believed in and steadily pursued this project. You are both awesome. It was Ned's vision to release all three books (*The Exact Place, No Place,* and *This Place*) as a trilogy recognizing they were each about *Place* and how it shapes us. As an artist, Ned approached the project with a creative eye for covers and design. I love the results.

The am most indebted to Denis, my life partner, co-worker, and friend for his persistent encouragement of my gift. He steadfastly believed *The Exact Place* would one day be launched. I couldn't have done it without his support.

And finally, thanks to God for never losing track of me in that remote corner of the state.

# A good PLACE to find some great books . . .

**NO PLACE: A DESERT PILGRIMAGE**
**—BOOK TWO OF THE *PLACE* TRILOGY**
"In *No Place,* Margie tells her story of becoming. Weaving through joy and through pain, through periods of confidence and bewilderment, the story's persistent thread is Margie seeking Jesus while befriending others wit compassion. Written with humility, humor, and the unique insight gained from a rare path taken, Margie invites us to join her as she finds her place of service "among the hippies and the stoners, the Jesus freaks and the drop-outs," learns her rhythm of hospitality as an act of Christian faith, and grows into a profound wisdom.
—Nancy Nordenson, author *Finding Livelihood: A Progress of Work and Leisure*

**THIS PLACE: A FEW NOTES FROM HOME**
**—BOOK THREE OF THE *PLACE* TRILOGY**
"Margie Haack tries to accept life as it presents itself rather than bending it toward her preferences. In her trials, joys and blunders, we see ourselves. And this is Margie's humble gift to us."
—Zack Eswine, author of *Sensing Jesus: Life and Ministry as a Human Being*

**GODLY CHARACTER(S): INSIGHTS FOR SPIRITUAL PASSION**
**FROM THE LIVES OF 8 WOMEN IN THE BIBLE**
". . . these 'great eight' propel you towards habits of godliness—putting you in a place to receive grace and fall more deeply in love with your savior—and that in His love you might be re-shaped and re-formed."
—Robert William Alexander, author of *The Gospel-Centered Life at Work*

**SPEAKING CODE: UNRAVELING PAST BONDS**
**TO REDEEM BROKEN CONVERSATIONS**
"*Speaking Code* is a powerful primer on using our words to enhance relationships. I especially appreciate the practical section on overcoming common barriers to effective communication . . . If you've ever longed for an effective tool to help replace hurtful speech or deadly silence with words that give life and heal hearts, *Speaking Code* is a must-read."
—Kimberly Miller, author of *Boundaries for Your Soul: How to Turn Your Overwhelming Thoughts and Feelings into Your Greatest Allies*

**A BOOK FOR HEARTS & MINDS: WHAT YOU SHOULD READ AND WHY**
"Curators of the imagination, stewards of the tradition, priests of print, [Hearts & Minds Bookstore has] always done more than sold books: they have furnished faithful minds and hearts. This book is a lovely testimony to that good work."
—James K.A. Smith, Calvin College, author of *You Are What You Love: The Spiritual Power of Habit*

# SquareHaloBooks.com